MW01484264

CYCLE
in NOVA SCOTIA

ADAM BARNETT

NIMBUS
PUBLISHING
—— NIMBUS.CA ——

Nimbus Publishing Limited
3660 Strawberry Hill Street, Halifax, NS, B3K 5A9
(902) 455-4286 nimbus.ca

Printed and bound in Canada

NB1420

Design: Jenn Embree
Editor: Angela Mombourquette
Proofreader: Paula Sarson

Library and Archives Canada Cataloguing in Publication

Title: Where to cycle in Nova Scotia : a guidebook for exploring the back roads and trails of Nova Scotia / Adam Barnett, of Bicycle Nova Scotia.
Names: Barnett, Adam author.
Description: Includes bibliographical references and index.
Identifiers: Canadiana 20189068655 | ISBN 9781771087247 (softcover)
Subjects: LCSH: Bicycle touring—Nova Scotia—Guidebooks. | LCSH: Bicycle trails—Nova Scotia—Guidebooks. | LCSH: Rural roads—Nova Scotia—Guidebooks. | LCSH: Nova Scotia—Guidebooks. | LCGFT: Guidebooks.
Classification: LCC GV1046.C32 N69 2019 | DDC 796.609716—dc23

Nimbus Publishing acknowledges the financial support for its publishing activities from the Government of Canada, the Canada Council for the Arts, and from the Province of Nova Scotia. We are pleased to work in partnership with the Province of Nova Scotia to develop and promote our creative industries for the benefit of all Nova Scotians.

CONTENTS

Many of the highlighted routes in this book will take cyclists along the spectacular Bay of Fundy, famous for having the world's highest tides. (KIMBERLY SMITH)

Cycling in Nova Scotia often comes with the reward of a gorgeous ocean view. (DOUG BROWN)

FOREWORD

Nova Scotia is full of low-traffic roads and recently improved rail trails that are a joy to explore by bicycle, and our small coastal and rural towns never fail to surprise with hidden gems. This book is meant to highlight some of the best cycling routes around the province, taking you from shore to shore to shore on interesting and challenging rides. The world-renowned Cabot Trail, not for the faint of heart, over-delivers every time; the calming landscape of the Annapolis Valley features farms and wineries; the coastal loops on the Eastern Shore boast some of our best beaches; the route along the South Shore showcases many vibrant and beautiful communities; the Acadian Shore offers a rich cultural landscape; and the Northumberland Strait provides roads that wind through vibrant fishing communities and lead to the warmest ocean swimming in the province.

Over the past decade, the popularity of cycling in Nova Scotia has increased significantly, as proven by the fact that the Gran Fondos reach capacity every year. More and more charity rides continue to pop up, and we see a continued increase in people booking trips to explore our province by bicycle. Slowly, many of our municipal and provincial roads are being improved through the addition of cycling lanes, paved shoulders, and signage. We know that we have a lot of work still to do, and we encourage you to let your local elected officials know that cycling infrastructure is important for our environment, our economy, and our health.

Bike shops can now be found all over the province—another sign of the strength of the growing cycling community. (If you can't find a shop nearby, just ask at a Visitor Information Centre or a local hardware store to see if there is anyone nearby who can facilitate a quick repair.) To help meet the needs of cyclists travelling in the province, Bicycle Nova Scotia has been working together with local businesses to develop a "Bicycle Friendly Business" network that encourages businesses to provide the small extras that show recognition that cyclists are important customers and clients. We encourage you to seek out these businesses on your travels.

Bicycle Nova Scotia has also been working hard to establish the Blue Route, which, once completed, will include approximately 3,000 km of cycling routes across the province. This is a long process, but already its effects are being seen as more municipalities and towns get on board with the concept—recognizing its value for visitors and for citizens who are increasingly demanding more in the way of active transportation.

As the number of cyclists increases on our roads, so does the potential for conflicts with drivers of motor vehicles. Nova Scotia has a one-metre rule, which makes it the law that motorists must leave a minimum of one metre of space between themselves and a cyclist when passing. While this is certainly a step in the right direction, it is important that cyclists use lights and bells to be seen and heard. The routes detailed in this book have been carefully selected for maximum safety; however, given the inherent vulnerability of cyclists, we urge readers and users to know about, and abide by, the rules of the road.

We hope that, no matter what you ride and how you ride—whether you're enjoying a few hours of riding with your children, leisurely riding the rail trails, or tackling multi-day cycling trips—that Nova Scotia provides a positive and enjoyable cycling experience, and that you let us know where we need to improve.

Wishing you the best in cycling,

Susanna Fuller and lola doucet
Co-presidents, Bicycle Nova Scotia

This scenic trail takes cyclists through Tatamagouche on the province's north shore.
(SHERRY HUDSON, PRESENCE PHOTOGRAPHY)

JOIN BICYCLE NOVA SCOTIA

Bicycle Nova Scotia is a not-for-profit organization that is invested in promoting cycling culture, improving infrastructure, and strengthening the cycling community in Nova Scotia. We advocate for and support all types of cycling, and are committed to improving conditions within the province so that cyclists of all ages and abilities can enjoy the thrill, the fun, and the practicality of riding a bike.

Most of the work that takes place within Bicycle Nova Scotia is done by volunteers, whether through the board that oversees operations, or through the many dedicated cyclists and advocates who generously give their time throughout the year.

Bicycle Nova Scotia's Projects and Initiatives

- Professional and amateur cycling competition governance and administration
- Amateur athlete training and development
- Bicycle network planning and design
- Blue Route provincial cycling network planning, development, and marketing
- Advocacy and partnership development
  - Urban and rural infrastructure
  - Policy and legislation
- Bike Friendly Certification
- Cycle-tourism marketing and promotion
- Self-guided touring itineraries
- Recreational cycling events
- Member insurance

As a member, you will be adding your voice to the conversation and contributing to the work that we do. The more people we have involved with the organization, the stronger the cycling community becomes. We hope you can join us!

facebook.com/bicyclenovascotia

twitter.com/bicyclens

instagram.com/bicycle_ns/

BICYCLE NOVA SCOTIA

bicycle.ns.ca

PREFACE

The idea of writing a cycling guidebook for Nova Scotia is not a new one. Back in 1995 Walton Watt took his experiences of touring the province and pulled together a collection of cycling routes to create *Nova Scotia by Bicycle*—the first book put out by Bicycle Nova Scotia. It has been a long time since that book has been in print, but you will still see it around some homes and in used bookstores, which attests to its success. At the time, it was a powerful force in helping to open up the idea of Nova Scotia as a cycling destination.

The routes in the original book were mostly focused on long-distance, self-supported rides, which were very popular at the time. Touring is still going strong today, but much has changed in the cycling world. We are seeing more and more people get involved in all types of cycling as its many benefits in terms of health and active living become clearer. Along with this, we are seeing more options for what kinds of bicycles are available, which is opening up cycling to people who might not have previously been into the sport.

The idea with this guidebook is to look at the province in a new way and to update the routes so they take a more modern approach to cycling. Instead of long, multi-day rides, most of the routes in this book focus on loops that take riders back to where they started. This allows them to plan day trips based on where they want to visit. Many areas will have multiple routes, allowing for different choices based on length and the type of riding desired.

Bicycle Nova Scotia has been receiving more and more questions about where to cycle in Nova Scotia from people who are travelling locally and from those visiting from out of province. In response to this demand, BNS has worked with Tourism Nova Scotia to create the Cycle Nova Scotia map series, which highlights a selection of routes around the province. These have proven so popular, it is clear that the time is finally right for an updated cycling guidebook for Nova Scotia.

It's important to note that this book could not have happened without the help and encouragement of the local cycling community. All of the routes in this book were submitted in some form by local riders who wanted to share their love of the areas they live and ride in. People offered time for conversation, sent maps, provided feedback on the routes, and even went so far as to send along photos from their cycling adventures around the province.

We want to send a massive shout-out to the cyclists, bike shops, bike businesses, and cycling clubs who helped us put these routes together, and also to the citizens and groups who continue to promote active living and advocate for cycling infrastructure in Nova Scotia. The work you do is important, and we thank you for it.

This is a project truly created by the cycling community of Nova Scotia; we hope you enjoy it.

Disclaimer

Cycling on roads and trails comes with an inherent risk of injury or damage. By choosing to ride a bicycle in Nova Scotia, you assume the full responsibility for that risk. As a rider, you need to know and practice the rules of the road and the proper use and maintenance of your bicycle.

Bicycle Nova Scotia assumes no responsibility for any actions taken by an individual as a result of using the rides presented in this book.

Feedback

Part of the vision for this project is to have these routes available online so users can view the maps and/or download the routes to the device of their choice. Visit bicycle. ns.ca to get the most up-to-date information about the routes in this book and to provide real-time feedback about the routes.

Rail trails offer cyclists a chance to experience the province's natural beauty up close. (SWEET RIDE CYCLING)

The topography of Nova Scotia makes for occasional steep and challenging hills. (ADAM BARNETT)

ACKNOWLEDGMENTS

Thank you to our supporters!

This book was a big undertaking and we truly couldn't have done it without our sponsors, so we would like to say a massive "Thank you!" to the people and businesses that have offered their support for the production of this book.

If you get a chance, please support our sponsors, and be sure to let them know how much you appreciate them for helping to make this guidebook happen.

Canada's go-to place for outdoor gear, know-how, and inspiration, MEC is a co-op owned by over 5 million members. A lifetime membership is $5, the same since 1971. Over the years, MEC has invested $41.65 million and counting into community groups and non-profit organizations that support outdoor recreation and conservation.

A significant grant from MEC helped make this book a reality. Thank you, MEC!

Take a DEEP BREATH. Kentville, Nova Scotia, is active, alive, and full of energy and enthusiasm for outdoor activity and exploration. Nothing about Kentville is over-manufactured or overdone; it is natural and real. We like to get out there and experience life, and we welcome you to join us. Stroll through a bird sanctuary, race down nationally recognized mountain bike trails, or have a picnic in a one-hundred-year-old hemlock forest. Kentville has it all, seconds away from a lovely downtown area. It's a breath of fresh air. We enthusiastically invite you to join us and find out for yourself. Plan your visit today; you can start by visiting **Kentville.ca**.

Marcel Morin, cartographer, GIS analyst, graphic designer, and lifelong cyclist has worked in the field of mapping and design for the past twenty-seven years. His company specializes in Indigenous Knowledge and Ecological Values mapping and has published the Summit Series, specialized maps for the mountaineering community.

Since 2013, Lost Art's focus has been on signage, interpretation, and print media. Some notable clients include the Landscape of Grand Pré Inc., the Friends of McNabs Island Society, Parks Canada, the Annapolis Valley Trails Coalition, the Grand Pré Trails Society, the Wine Association of Nova Scotia (WANS), the Annapolis Valley Regional Enterprise Network, and the Hornby Island Community Economic Enhancement Corporation in BC.

INTRODUCTION

The approach with this book has been to create a collection of routes that will be accessible to many different types of cyclists. It's important to clarify that there is no "right" way to ride a bike. It doesn't require particular clothing, fancy gear, or expensive equipment. It isn't about how far you've ridden or how fast you've gone, unless you want it to be. This book was written in appreciation of the simple joys of what it means to ride a bicycle and get outside. It's about that lovely connection with childhood freedom, and that deep satisfaction of travelling a landscape using the power of your own body. It doesn't need to be any more complicated than that.

It is our belief that cycling is the best way to see the world. There is something so perfect about touring an area when you are in the elements and all your senses are engaged—when you can feel the sun on your face, smell the salt in the air, hear the activity from the people and wildlife all around you, and be at that right speed to stop and take in a beautiful view or check out an oddity that grabs your interest. And truly, there is nothing better than a hot meal or a decadent treat after a ride, when you know you deserve it.

We love this province and all it has to offer, and we hope this book encourages you to get out and find some places you may not have otherwise visited. Take your time as you travel around. Visit the shops and say hello to the small business owners who make this province what it is. Enjoy the many restaurants and get to know the local cuisine. Cycle up big hills to take in the even bigger views. Stay out a little longer than usual to watch the sunset, and then a little longer to watch the stars come out. Take in the natural beauty and dynamic culture that will be offered to you in your travels and let them sink in deep.

Nova Scotia is a special spot that can get inside you and not let you go. Don't say we didn't warn you.

Adam Barnett
Bicycle Nova Scotia

PS
Be curious.
Stay open to adventure.
Dress for the weather.
Play in the water.
Keep exploring.

ROUTE HIGHLIGHTS

TOURING NOVA SCOTIA

Culture

Nova Scotia is shaped by the sea. Our people are drawn to the water for both livelihood and recreation, and the saltiness of the ocean is in our blood. There is something unique and quietly intriguing about this province that is hard to put into words. There is a subtle beauty that slowly accumulates as you travel across the dynamic landscape and along the ever-changing coastline.

This is an area that is rich in history and storytelling. There is a rootedness in Nova Scotia that feels solid and purposeful, providing a sense of place and identity you can feel as you visit its many regions. Traditions run deep here and reflect a rich mosaic of the founding cultures of this land. This province is home to the Mi'kmaw people who have been stewards of Mi'kma'ki for over ten thousand years. The area was settled by the French Acadians; it was also deeply shaped by Scottish immigrants (this is "New Scotland" after all) and by numerous settlers of African ancestry, including Black Loyalists, Jamaican Maroons, and refugees from the War of 1812.

All of the founding cultures had a few things in common: love of music, family, tradition, and celebration. These are defining features of Nova Scotia, which can be seen, felt, and heard as you travel the province, stepping into microcosms of culture, tradition, and language. Some cultural features are particularly distinct—the French Shore's Acadian flags and fiddle music, the ceilidhs in the community halls of Cape Breton, or the powwows celebrated in Mi'kmaw communities. But there are also more subtle traditions that come up in the foods people make and the art they are inspired to create. This is most certainly a culture that likes to celebrate; when in doubt, head to the kitchen if you are wondering where the party is—and don't forget your dancing shoes.

Seasonal Businesses

Many small towns in Nova Scotia have seasonal businesses designed to take advantage of the busy summer tourist season. These include restaurants and accommodations, so keep this in mind if you're travelling in the shoulder seasons, before June and after September. Call in advance to ensure that businesses are open.

Accommodations

The availability of accommodations can vary greatly depending on the location and the time of year, and options can be limited, so book in advance whenever possible. Larger centres offer hotels, motels, and bed and breakfasts, in addition to Airbnb options. If you prefer to camp, the province has both provincial and national parks with campgrounds. These parks fill up quickly in the summer, especially on long weekends, so reservations are recommended. Most of the parks are also seasonal, so call in advance. There are also many independent businesses that run campgrounds around the province.

Whichever type of accommodation you choose, ask about storing your bicycle in a locked area, or whether it's okay to bring bikes inside to keep them safe and dry.

Bicycle Nova Scotia has been hard at work expanding a "Bike Friendly Business" network that encourages the hospitality industry to accommodate the needs of cyclists as they travel around the province. To see a map of bicycle-certified businesses in Nova Scotia, go to bikefriendlyns.ca.

Cellular Reception

Cellphone coverage in Nova Scotia depends upon your service provider. In urban areas and relatively populated spots there will most likely be coverage, but you may encounter rural zones where there is no cellphone reception at all. If you use maps on your phone to guide you, it's recommended that you download maps and/or routes in advance.

Food and Drink

This is a subject dear to many cyclists' hearts, as there is nothing quite as rewarding as a good meal, and perhaps a few drinks, after a solid day of riding and exploring.

Nova Scotia's restaurant scene is varied. There are many establishments that incorporate local food and provide fantastic experiences, while at the same time, there are many basic spots that might feed you, but won't necessarily inspire. It is worth your time to do some research if you plan on eating out, especially in more rural areas.

If you are looking for fresh, local food, keep your eyes open for farm markets in towns and cities around the province; farmersmarketsnovascotia.com provides information about what's in season and where markets are located. There are also many self-serve markets along rural roads.

If you're hoping to pick up food supplies on the road, plan ahead. Gas stations and convenience stores provide only basic snacks, and mostly junk food. Many small towns have grocery stores, but even these may have limited options in terms of fresh food.

The coffee culture in Nova Scotia is on the rise, with more local roasters and trained baristas all the time, even in rural areas. That said, quality coffee isn't guaranteed. If you love your coffee, you may want to consider picking up fresh coffee and bringing along a portable coffee-making device.

Nova Scotia has an abundance of excellent wineries, breweries, and distilleries scattered around the province, and many offer tours and tastings. Keep your eyes open for local products when visiting restaurants and bars. With a few exceptions, takeout alcohol is sold only at businesses where it is produced and in provincially regulated liquor stores.

Don't Drink and Cycle!

It's important to note that you should not drink and cycle; it's the law and it's not safe. If you are going to do tastings, be sure to limit your amount, drink lots of water to rehydrate, eat food to slow the absorption of alcohol, and take time before getting back on your bicycle. If you really want to do a proper tasting tour, consider taking one of the many bus tours available.

Cannabis

In 2018, cannabis was legalized in Nova Scotia and across Canada. As with alcohol, it is available only at provincially regulated stores and the legal age to buy and possess cannabis is nineteen. There are a number of regulations you should be aware of. Information can be found at novascotia.ca/cannabis/laws.

Potable Water Access

If you plan to cycle in remote areas, it is important to carry water with you; it will not always be available, and it can be a long way between towns. Potable water is also not always available in provincial parks, so consider this when planning your route (call Nova Scotia Provincial Parks at 1-888-544-3434 to inquire).

Lakes and Beaches

Nova Scotia is surrounded by water, and there are rivers and lakes scattered throughout the province. Lakes usually start to warm up mid-July, getting warmer throughout the summer months. As you travel around the province, you'll encounter a variety of different conditions, with water temperatures ranging from pleasant to frigid.

Halifax has a surprising number of lakes and coastal beaches within city limits—Dartmouth's nickname is actually "The City of Lakes." Many of the swimming spots are within an easy bike ride of the city centre.

The Northumberland Strait offers the warmest ocean swimming in the province. Because of its shallow depths, water temperatures can reach up to 25°C at the height of summer. There are public beaches all along this coast.

The Bay of Fundy has the highest tides in the world, so swimming can be challenging in certain areas. If you plan to go swimming in this region, try to time it with high tide, when the water will be warm from coming up the sun-soaked beach, and you will not need to walk through mud to get to the water.

The South and Eastern Shores have some of the province's most amazing beaches, but the water is often quite brisk, with water temperature changing depending on tides, currents, and time of year. There are usually a few weeks near the end of summer when the water warms up, making for exceptional swimming. Don't be afraid of the cold water, but be ready for it.

If you do plan to visit the beaches around Nova Scotia, be sure to pay attention to signs about wildlife and what you can do to help protect it. The piping plover is an endangered shorebird that nests on some thirty or more beaches around the province. Some beaches are partially closed during the birds' breeding season to help protect the vulnerable eggs.

Wildlife

Nova Scotia has abundant wildlife, but luckily most of it is fairly harmless. The only animals you really need to pay attention to in terms of safety are black bears and coyotes. Incidents involving these animals are rare, but they can happen, and they are more likely if you are cycling in remote areas.

The government of Nova Scotia offers the following tips on what to do if you encounter a bear or a coyote.

Black bear
- Stay calm.
- Speak in a firm, authoritative voice and slowly back away; do not look the bear in the eyes.
- Leave escape routes open for the bear.
- If the bear begins to follow you, drop something (not food) to distract the bear as you move away.
- Do not make threatening gestures or sudden movements unless you are being attacked.
- Never run or climb a tree; bears excel at both activities.

- If a bear attacks you, fight back with anything and everything you can, and make a lot of noise; do not "play dead"; use pepper spray if you have it.

Coyote
- Do not feed or touch the animal.
- Do not photograph the animal from up close.
- Slowly back away while remaining calm; do not turn and run.
- Use a personal alarm device to frighten or threaten the animal.
- Encourage the animal to leave; provide an escape route.
- If animal exhibits aggressive behaviour, become larger and noisier by throwing sticks and rocks.
- Fight back aggressively if the animal attacks.

Hunting Season

If you are heading into the woods, it's important to remember that there is an annual hunting season in Nova Scotia. The dates vary around the province, based on the location and animal, but it's safe to assume that there will be some hunting in September and that deer season will start sometime after mid-October. If you are riding in the woods during this time, be sure to wear bright clothing to increase visibility; hunter's orange is recommended. To find out more, contact Lands and Forestry at **902-424-5935**.

Insects

Insects are the scourge of spring and early summer in Nova Scotia. There are a number of insects that bite and annoy, so be prepared if you are in or near the woods. Insect repellent is definitely a worthwhile thing to have in your kit. Note that insects are worst at dusk and dawn and they are particularly attracted to dark clothing. If you keep moving at 15 kmh, it will help keep bugs away; when taking a rest, look for a bit of breeze.

Ticks are a growing concern in Nova Scotia. Some ticks can carry Lyme disease and reported incidences have been growing. Ticks are usually found in tall grass where they can get onto your clothes and eventually burrow into your skin. If you are venturing into the woods, it's a good idea to do a "tick check" when you return home.

To find out where tick populations are high and how to remove them safely, visit **novascotia.ca/ticksafety**.

Wayfinding and Signage

All of the routes in this book have cue sheets to help you find your way, but don't expect road signs to necessarily always be there. Especially in rural Nova Scotia, signs can be missing or damaged, making it difficult to navigate. Always bring a map when you go riding. If you're using the cue sheets in this book, use an odometer to keep track of distance so you know when to make the next turn.

Potholes and Road Conditions

Rough roads are a fact of life around Nova Scotia and the conditions change on a yearly basis. For cyclists, rough roads are not only uncomfortable—they can be dangerous. Be aware that the spring is the worst time for potholes, as winter road damage might not yet have been repaired. If you're cycling on particularly rough roads, be alert to vehicles and try to ensure that you have room to negotiate any hazards.

If the roads you are riding are in particularly rough shape, contact the province's Transportation and Infrastructure Renewal department to make a report **(1-844-696-7737)**.

It is also worth noting that Nova Scotia has a lot of unpaved roads; these are not always noted on maps, so be aware that you may come across them in rural areas. (This book endeavours to indicate where there are unpaved roads to help with your planning.) Unpaved roads can lead to some amazing places; just make sure you have the right sort of bike and tires to handle the terrain.

Rules of the Road

Cycling on roads means sharing the pavement with motorized vehicles and other cyclists. For safety reasons, it's important to know the rules and to follow them consistently.

Here are the legal rules around cycling in Nova Scotia:
- Every cyclist must wear a helmet.
- Every bicycle must be equipped with a bell or horn.

- From thirty minutes before sunset (dusk, not dark) and up to thirty minutes before sunrise, you must have a front white light and a rear red light and/or a rear red reflector (rear lights are recommended).
- Cyclists must signal their intention to turn and make lane changes.
- Cyclists must ride on the right-hand side of the road, with the flow of traffic, and as near as practical to the road edge (roughly one metre from the road edge depending on the speed of traffic and the width of the road edge).
- Cyclists may take the full lane if they are going through a roundabout, making a left turn, or if they otherwise feel that they need to do so for their safety.
- Cyclists may pass motor vehicles on the right if it is safe to do so.
- Except when passing another cyclist, people cycling on public roads shall ride in single file.
- Bicycles are allowed on all roads in Nova Scotia unless otherwise posted with "No bikes or slow-moving vehicles" signs.
- Cyclists must follow the same laws as motor vehicles, unless the law has specific exemptions.
- Cyclists may not ride on sidewalks or use crosswalks while riding.
- Children (sixteen and under) may cycle on a sidewalk in a public square, park, city, or town.

One Metre Rule

Bill 93 requires drivers to leave at least one metre of space when passing a cyclist; motor vehicles may cross a yellow line, if necessary, to pass a bicycle safely. They must pass only if there is no oncoming traffic; otherwise they must wait until it is safe to pass. The bill also  requires drivers to avoid driving or parking in bike lanes, unless they are avoiding a hazard, a left-turning car, or are under instruction by a police officer.

Bill 93 requires cyclists to ride single file except when passing another cyclist; to ride on the right side of the road except when riding through a roundabout, turning left, or avoiding obstacles; and to use designated bike lanes where they are present and free of obstructions.

Safety Tips

In addition to following the rules of the road, cyclists should follow these other safety guidelines:

- Always wear a helmet; make sure the helmet fits correctly and that the chin strap is comfortably secured.
- Use front and rear lights on your bicycle during the day, as well as at night; get the brightest lights you can.
- Increase your visibility by wearing bright clothing or reflective gear.
- Use a bicycle mirror so you are aware of upcoming traffic.
- Turn off your phone to avoid distractions while cycling.
- Be aware of your surroundings at all times.
- Be predictable and signal your intentions.
- Make sure your bike is in good working order.
- Watch for potential hazards.

Etiquette

Etiquette is not about following rules so much as it's about agreeing to social norms that bring a level of consideration and civility to an activity. Following proper etiquette while riding helps maintain respect in the cycling community and also helps keep people safe.

Trail Etiquette
- Be courteous and respectful.
- Respect private property.
- Pack it in, pack it out.
- Keep right, pass left.
- Give audible warning before passing.
- Avoid wearing earphones.
- Single-up when meeting up with others on the trail for easier passing.

Road Etiquette
- Be predictable; signal your intentions.
- Ring your bell and/or vocalize when you are going to pass.
- Follow the rules of the road.
- Keep space between you and a forward rider.
- Be visible (reflective clothing; bright lights).

Riding in Packs
- Learn the norms of the group you are riding with; ask before you head out.
- Be predictable; hold your line whenever possible; communicate with others.
- Don't overlap wheels; stay behind, beside, or in front of other riders.
- Avoid gaps; ride close together.
- Look after newbies; be a mentor and make people feel welcome.
- Point out hazards; shout out when necessary.
- If you are going to spit or blow your nose while riding, consider the proximity of other riders.

Yielding Etiquette
- Bikers should yield to hikers.
- Bikers should yield to horses: stop; get off your bike; try not to spook the animal; if you are passing, do so slowly and do your best to bring attention to yourself without startling the horse.
- Motorized vehicles should yield to bikers.

In Case of a Vehicle Collision

Incidents happen, and when they do, it's important to follow some basic procedures to focus on your safety and to ensure that you are legally protected.

This section borrows from a collaborative project between the Halifax Cycling Coalition, Bicycle Nova Scotia, and the Dalhousie University Bike Centre.

If you are involved in a collision with a vehicle, the following checklist may be helpful.

At the scene of the crash
- Remain calm; get out of harm's way.
- Call police (**dial 911**) and wait for them to arrive.
- Remind the driver that he or she must remain at the scene of the collision until the police arrive.
- Record the time and location of the accident.
- Record the driver's first name, last name, phone number, and driver's license number; record the driver's insurance company and policy number.
- Record the vehicle make, model and colour, and the licence plate number.
- Get the names and phone numbers of witnesses.
- Get the police report number and the police officer's name.
- Take photos of the vehicle, the driver's licence plate, your bicycle and any damage, the area where the collision occurred, and any injuries.

When you get home

- Get a medical examination right away; visit the hospital to tend to any injuries (remember, concussions can go unnoticed for hours or days).
- Document your account of the event ASAP, and keep it in your records.
- If police were not present, you must file a report online within twenty-four hours; obtain a copy of the police report.
- Contact witnesses and ask them to email their detailed version of the events.
- Consider talking to an attorney before contacting an insurance company.

Follow-up

- Document any injuries and take photos; keep a daily account of how injuries are progressing, noting dates.
- Document and save all evidence (medical statements, receipts, records of lost work time, diary of injuries).
- Fill out the "Incident Report Form" on Bicycle Nova Scotia's website: bicycle.ns.ca/incident-report-form (for data collection only).

Take care of yourself and tend to any injuries. Recover and build up your strength and confidence; do your best not to get discouraged. Only you will know when you are comfortable enough to get back on the saddle and start riding again.

Medical Emergencies

Call 911 if there is an emergency.
Call 811 for non-urgent medical questions.
Cellular coverage is not always available; do your best to be prepared for emergencies.

PREPARING TO RIDE

Cycling Through the Seasons

If you live in Nova Scotia, winter can seem to stretch on and on—until, suddenly, it's summer. Spring does happen in this province, but when it hits and how long it lasts is anyone's guess; it might bring warm days and be a gentle prelude to summer, or it can be raining with flurries until April or May. The moral of the story is: be prepared for all types of weather.

Summers in Nova Scotia are generally warm and comfortable, with nice weather usually beginning in June or July and lasting into the fall. Weather can vary dramatically around the province, especially along the coast or in the highlands of Cape Breton. It is always good practice to check the weather where you plan to be cycling to ensure that you are adequately prepared.

September and early October are the most dependable months for weather, and many cyclists would agree that it is the nicest time of year to be out. In September, you will often find blue skies and sunshine, with warm days and cool evenings. There isn't usually a lot of rain during this month and the bugs are finally gone. October can be a bit more unpredictable, but there are generally warmer days and less rain earlier in the month.

Fall is also when the province is arguably at its most beautiful. We are blessed with many hardwoods in Nova Scotia, making for an incredible show when the trees start to change colour. It is a fleeting display, lasting for only two to three weeks at its peak, and it changes every year. Riding by bicycle is an amazing way to take in the spectacle.

Wintertime in Nova Scotia is cold, wet, and snowy. Temperatures can also vary widely from day to day. The air is damp in this part of the world, and the cold can get deep into your bones. Dress warmly if you plan on cycling during this season; layers can help with adapting to temperature fluctuations when you're riding in the cold.

Fog

No matter the season, if you are going to be doing any sort of coastal riding around Nova Scotia, you will want to pay attention to the potential for fog. Having a fog bank roll in can take a warm, sunny day and quickly turn it cold and damp. It can also mean lower visibility, underscoring the importance of wearing bright clothing.

Some parts of Nova Scotia are more prone to fog than others. The Eastern Shore, in particular, is known for foggy conditions, and fog can be a regular occurrence in the southwestern part of the province around Yarmouth.

The best advice: if you are planning on doing a coastal ride, check the weather beforehand; Environment Canada is probably the most reliable source. If fog is in the forecast, pack your gear accordingly so you can ride in comfort and safety. And if you end up in fog, enjoy it. It's quite beautiful and is truly a part of Nova Scotia's dynamic character.

Wind

A windy day can also significantly alter your ride, especially along the coast. Many of the routes in this book follow the coast and then loop back inland. Where wind is usually significant, the routes have been chosen to position the prevailing winds at your back on the coastal sections. Check the wind forecast in advance to determine whether you should alter your route.

It can definitely get muddy out here. The moral of the story in Nova Scotia is this: be prepared for all types of weather. (KEVIN GALLAGHER)

Packing Considerations

How much you bring along on any trip is open for discussion. Some people like their comforts, while others are the ultimate minimalists. There is no list that will suit every individual, and there is no right way to dress or pack as a cyclist. How you ride and how you prepare for a ride are all part of your particular style.

Some questions to consider:
- What do I need to feel safe? (Bright reflective clothing, daytime lights.)
- Do I get cold easily? Do I tend to overheat? (Layers, layers, layers.)
- How long can I last without food before my energy lags? (How much food to bring? What kind?)
- What do I need to feel comfortable? (Tissues, moisturizer, sunglasses.)
- Has anything changed recently that I need to adapt to? (Injuries, health concerns.)

Next, consider the specifics about the ride you are about to embark on:

- How long is the ride going to be? (Lighting, clothing, comforts, food, water, safety.)
- Will the weather change? (Extra clothes, layers, rain jacket, sunglasses.)
- Will you be out in the dark or near dusk? (Front/rear lights, reflective clothing.)
- How familiar are you with the area? (Download/print out maps, tell people where you are going.)
- What is the condition of your bike? (Special tools, spare parts.)

Depending on your needs on a given day, you may fall into one of the following rider categories.

Minimalist: Jersey with seat bag

This type of rider likes to ride fast and ride light. Assuming there will be amenities along the way to supplement food, basic gear might include:

- Seat bag (tools, spare tube)
- Bike pump (attached to frame) or CO_2 cartridges
- Food (banana, energy bar, gels)
- Phone/GPS Device
- Keys (car/bike lock)
- Wallet (credit card, ID, cash)
- Water bottle(s)

Lover of Comfort: Handlebar bag and/or panniers

This type of rider likes to bring along some extra clothing, or maybe a blanket and some picnic supplies. Here are some things you might bring along if this is you (in addition to the list above):

- Extra water (or other hydration)
- More layers of clothing (comfort, non-cycling clothing)
- Walking shoes/sandals
- Food/snacks
- Book/journal
- Camera

Multi-day Rider: Panniers with lots of gear

There are many ways to pack for a multi-day trip, but inevitably you will need extra clothes, toiletries, and other basic necessities. If you are going to be camping along the way, you will need to bring your camping gear, along with food and a way to cook it. In addition to the items previously mentioned, you'll need:

- Camping gear
- Camp stove and cooking gear
- Extra food
- Extra clothes
- Repair kits and tools

- First aid kit
- Individual comforts
- Toiletries
- Personal electronics

Taking a few minutes to assess the details of your ride will help you plan a safe, comfortable, and enjoyable ride. The goal is to find a balance between what you want and the bare minimum of what you need.

Car Considerations

If you are going to be driving somewhere and riding from where you've parked, consider keeping a few things in your car for when you return:

- Extra water
- Dry clothes and footwear
- Phone charger
- Towel
- Cooler with snacks

- Thermos of tea/coffee/hot chocolate
- Plastic tub (for wet and/or stinky gear)

Planning a Day Ride

If you are planning on using your phone for directions, it's important to consider what will happen if the battery dies or there is no cell reception; don't be too dependent on your phone. Cellular service is not available everywhere in Nova Scotia. Your GPS will still work without a connection, so download any maps or routes before heading out and make sure your phone or device is fully charged.

If you are travelling to a destination such as a B & B, consider printing or writing out contact information and basic details.

If leaving your car behind, be sure to lock your vehicle and hide or remove any valuables.

Before heading out:
- Check the Bicycle Nova Scotia website for any route updates.
- Download map (Google Map of area) or route to your device.
- Check wind and weather; plan and pack accordingly.
- Print out cue sheets, notes, maps, and important details.
- Set up your odometer if using cue sheets.
- Check that your phone/GPS device is charged.
- Check that your front and rear lights are charged.
- Check over your bike to make sure it is running properly.
- Fill your water bottles and pack food.

Pre-ride checklist
The following list offers ideas for what you might want to bring on a ride.

Essentials
- Helmet
- Front/rear lights
- Keys (house, car, bike lock)
- Wallet (credit card, ID, cash)
- Water (water bottles/water bladder)
- Food (power snacks)
- Phone/GPS device
- Wristwatch (safety, emergencies; in case phone dies)
- Small first aid kit

Bike tools and accessories
- Pump (with correct adapter) and/or CO_2 cartridges
- Patch kit and/or spare tube
- Multi-tool
- Tire levers (3)

Optional
- Extra clothing (different layers, depending on the day)
- For cold weather
  - Rain jacket, windbreaker
  - Vest
  - Leg warmers/long underwear
  - Arm warmers
  - Wrist warmers
  - Gloves
  - Earmuffs
  - Bandana/skullcap/Buff
- Maps and/or guidebook
- Camera
- Bike lock
- Sunglasses
- Zipper-lock bags
- Wet wipes (with zipper-lock bag)
- Sunscreen
- Portable charger for phone/devices (with cables)
- Towel and bathing suit
- Shoes/sandals

Planning a Bike Trip with a Child

Riding with children is similar in terms of basic needs, but there are a number of things you can do to ensure children feel safe, secure, and comfortable for the duration of your ride together.

Before heading out
- Choose a route that you and the child will feel comfortable with; get them involved in the planning to keep them interested.
- Go over the rules (staying within sight, stop when told, etc.).
- Make sure their helmet fits and is securely fastened.
- Ensure you have the right clothing for the day (layers, rain jacket).
- Check that the child's saddle height is comfortable.
- Do a quick maintenance check to make sure the bike is safe.

While on the road
- Take a break every hour, or as frequently as necessary; find diversions and places to explore to keep it interesting.
- Pay attention to their energy; have lots of food and drink available.
- Make sure they are warm, dry, and comfortable.
- Plan for ice cream stops.
- The goal is to have fun; don't make it a slog.

Pre-ride Checklist

Essentials
- Helmets
- Front/rear lights
- Food/snacks (easy to access)
- Water/drinks for everyone
- Wallet
- Phone
- Bike repair kit
- Extra clothes for warmth
- Wristwatch (safety, emergencies; in case phone dies)
- Small first aid kit

Optional
- Wet wipes
- Chocolate (for bribes and energy)
- Crayons, games (for breaks)
- Favourite toys
- Toilet/tissue paper

Routes for Kids

The following routes are considered kid-friendly because they are on rail trails, paved shoulders, and/or low-traffic roads. Only you and the child you're riding with can determine what is comfortable for you. If in doubt, stick to rail trails or roads that have protected bike lanes.

Rail Trails
② Shearwater Flyer and Salt Marsh Trail (Halifax Metro)
⑥ Rum Runners Trail (South Shore)
⑫ Mahone Bay–Bridgewater–Lunenburg: Rail trail section (South Shore)
⑲ Brookfield Mines Trail (South Shore)
㉛ Kejimkujik: Fire Tower Trail (Bay of Fundy: Annapolis Valley)
㊵ Harvest Moon Trailway (Bay of Fundy: Annapolis Valley)
㊕ Cobequid Trail (Bay of Fundy: Minas Basin)
㊔ Museum of Industry (Northumberland Shore)
㊤ Celtic Shores Coastal Trail (Cape Breton Island: Beyond the Cabot Trail)
⑩⑤ Musquodoboit Harbour (Eastern Shore)

Paved Shoulders/Quiet Roads
㉟ Annapolis Royal: Fort-to-Fort (Bay of Fundy: Annapolis Valley)
㊸ Caribou Island (Northumberland Shore)
㊆ Margaree Valley (Cape Breton Island: The Cabot Trail)

Nova Scotia has a number of rail trails that offer a leisurely ride away from traffic.
(SANDY WIRTANEN)

Planning an Overnight/Self-Supported Trip

Multi-day cycling trips require a different sort of planning than day rides. It's important to consider what the weather is going to be like, what sort of riding you will be doing, how remote the area is you will be travelling, and where you will be staying. It will also make a big difference if you are making your own food or eating out along the way.

Consider investing in lightweight gear: camping, cooking, clothing. It costs more, but it will lighten your load considerably.

General strategy
- Pack as lightly as possible:
  - Bring only as much food as you need; plan around frequent restocking.
  - If you are camping, measure out food in advance of your trip; put in zipper-lock bags or containers and write the recipe on the outside for quick reference.
  - Put everything you can into small bottles or packages; remove extra packaging.
- Share the load of gear (food, tent) if travelling with other people.
- Invest in merino wool clothing: it's warm and comfortable, it dries quickly, and it doesn't stink.
- Print off important information (accommodations, local contacts) whenever possible, in case your phone dies.

Before heading out
- Check weather forecasts and plan accordingly.
- Consider what tools you'll need to do general repairs.
- Charge headlamp, phone, etc.
- Research the availability of water and food along your route.
- Measure and label all food.
- Download or print out maps and routes.
- Print out phone numbers and any important information.
- Make sure your stove is working and fuel bottles are filled.
- Test spare batteries.
- Fill up bottles (moisturizers, sunscreen, cooking fuel).
- Confirm reservations/details for accommodations.

After your trip
- Reach out to loved ones who might be worried about you.
- Set out sleeping bag, pillow, and tents to dry; store loosely.
- Clean out all bottles; wash gear.

- Review the trip: What worked? What could be improved for next time?
- Start planning for your next trip.

Pre-ride checklist

Most people will be travelling with panniers (back and possibly front), a handlebar bag for quick access to valuables, and a seat bag for quick access to tools.

The following list is extensive and is meant to cover a full range of gear for both local multi-day trips, as well as longer trips abroad. It is not necessary to bring everything, but it should give you a good frame of reference for planning. Of course, if you are travelling from inn to inn and eating out, you will need much less gear than if you are travelling more remotely.

Try to pare down your gear list as much as possible; the more you bring, the more energy you need to move it.

Bike tools and accessories
- Pump (with correct adapter) and/or CO_2 cartridges
- Patch kit and/or spare tubes
- Multi-tool
- Tire levers (3)

Extra tools and accessories
- Pedal wrench
- Zip-ties
- Compression straps/bungees
- Bottle of lubricant
- Duct tape (a few lengths, wrapped around some cardboard)
- Extra cables, replacement spokes, replacement chain links.

Technical Clothing
- Warm long-sleeved base level (merino)
- Long johns
- Padded bike shorts
- Bike jersey
- Waterproof/breathable rain jacket
- Waterproof rain pants

- Biking gloves
- Cold-weather gloves
- Bandana/skull cap/Buff
- Vest
- Puffy jacket
- Leg and arm warmers

Clothing and accessories
- T-shirts
- Quick-dry shorts (for swimming or general use)
- Wool sweater
- Hoodie
- Pants or jeans
- Socks: merino, waterproof
- Underwear
- Belt
- Hat
- Toque/warm hat
- Sunglasses
- Small travel towel
- Wristwatch
- Shoes: hiking, biking, sandals (waterproof), dress-up

Toiletries

- Razor and small shaving cream
- Toothpaste and toothbrush
- Nail clippers
- Wet wipes
- Small sunscreen
- Biodegradable soap
- Lip balm
- Hand lotion
- Sanitary pads/tampons

Electronics

- Bluetooth speaker
- Phone
- Spare batteries
- Portable charger
- Cables for all electronics

Other

- First aid kit
- 1-litre wide-mouth Nalgene bottle (soaking, storing leftovers, water)
- Fox whistle
- 2 lengths nylon cord (for drying clothes, repairs)
- Small backpack (for hikes/jaunts around town)
- Headlamp (charged, with spare batteries and charge cable)
- Bike lock
- Multi-tool knife
- Waterproof map case
- Maps
- Toilet paper (in zipper-lock bag)
- Small towel (for wiping sweat, cleaning grimy hands; attached to outside of gear)
- Thermos
- Books (fiction/local guidebook/ journal)

- Insect repellent
- Water purifier
- Fire starter
- Eye mask and ear plugs (for sleeping)
- Toys/recreation
- Zipper-lock bags (large and small)

Camping

- Tent (with ground sheet)
- Sleeping bag (with silk liner)
- Pillow (inflatable/compressed)
- Sleeping pad (with repair kit)
- Blanket (lightweight, fleece/cotton)
- Small mosquito net
- Candle lantern
- Lightweight tarp (with ropes and attachments)

Cooking

- Cooler (soft, small)
- Bowl (lightweight)
- Spork
- Coffee maker (AeroPress or similar)
- Thermal drinking cup
- Knife
- Small cutting board
- Frying pan
- Spatula
- Medium-sized pot
- Grabber tool
- Stove (multi-fuel, with repair kit)
- Fuel bottle (full)
- Lighter (and/or matches in waterproof bottle with sandpaper)
- Biodegradable dish soap
- Scrubbing sponge (in zipper-lock bag)
- Chamois/dishtowel
- Plastic bags (for garbage)

INTRODUCTION TO ROUTES

The routes in this book have all been mapped out using online mapping tools, providing high levels of detail in terms of length, elevation profiles, and cue sheet information. The challenge has been to take this information and express it in print in a way that is helpful and continues to be both relevant and up-to-date after publication.

All routes have some sort of description attached to them, along with points of interest, and cue sheets to help guide you (see **Understanding Route Notes** on page 31). They have also been mapped out, but not always to a level that can be used to navigate effectively. Readers can use a number of different tools to find out where they need to go and to help them navigate while on the road. In this section, there are some suggestions for other materials and strategies that will help you understand the routes and navigate them successfully.

It's important to note that you should never totally depend on the information provided here; road signs can go missing, unpaved roads may have been paved, an old landmark may have disappeared. The same goes for depending on your phone or device; technology is great, but it doesn't replace human judgement. Stay aware when you are cycling; if something doesn't feel right, stop and check in. When in doubt, ask a local for directions. You might even get invited in for a cup of tea.

How to Use This Guide

The routes in this book are arranged clockwise around the province, starting in Halifax Metro, and are grouped into different regions to help you find rides that work with your travel plans. These regions are based on Tourism Nova Scotia's *Doers & Dreamers Regional Map*, with one exception: the Bay of Fundy has been split up into two different regions—Annapolis Valley and the Minas Basin.

The regions are:
- Halifax Metro
- South Shore
- Yarmouth and Acadian Shores
- Bay of Fundy: Annapolis Valley
- Bay of Fundy: Minas Basin
- Northumberland Shore
- Cape Breton Island: The Cabot Trail
- Cape Breton Island: Beyond the Cabot Trail
- Eastern Shore

Most of the routes have been created as loops so they can be ridden in a day; they range from short and sweet to long and challenging. There are a few exceptions in which rides are several days long, most notably on converted rail trails that are about a hundred kilometres long in one direction. The Cabot Trail and Digby Neck have also been presented as multi-day trips.

All of the routes have a specific direction associated with them. Sometimes this is arbitrary, but very often it is chosen to offer a specific view, to approach a climb from a preferred direction, or to avoid loose gravel roads on a steep descent. All routes can, of course, be reversed based on your preference and travel plans. Read through the **Ride Considerations** and **Side Trips/Variations** in the route notes to help make any decisions in terms of how you might want to customize the route.

Restaurants and accommodations are rarely mentioned in this guidebook, although occasionally a restaurant or a café is considered unique enough to be a **Point of Interest**.

Below are some of the criteria used in choosing the routes in this book.

Roads
- Low traffic roads.
- Loops, starting in, and returning to, a town with amenities.
- Coastal, lake, or river rides.
- Interesting terrain: rolling hills, good views.
- Beautiful areas: farmland, coastal, valleys, harbours, islands, highlands.

Rail trails
- Good wayfinding; enough signs to help guide riders.
- Decent access points to amenities and services.
- Trails that are regularly maintained and have some consistency in surfaces.
- Routes that are not too remote and are usually parallel or close to roads.

> ### *Road and Trail Conditions*
>
> It's important to note that the road and trail conditions described in this book cannot be guaranteed. Route notes will indicate when roads are in either exceptionally good or exceptionally poor shape, but conditions can change. Roads sometimes get upgraded, frost heaves make them worse, and what might have once been dirt might now be paved. Always be prepared for variable road conditions, especially on high-traffic roads or when coming downhill.
>
> Note: If you encounter issues with any route, please go the BNS website, where you can provide updates to help keep routes current for other users.

Understanding Route Notes

Route Name
- A distinctive identifier for each route outlined in this guide.
- (RT) in the route name indicates that any unpaved portions of the route are on rail trails, off of the main road.

Map Number
- Indicates the detailed route map that can be found at the back of this book.

> **Types of Rides**
>
> There are a few different types of rides in this book; most routes will be rideable with a road bike, unless otherwise indicated:
> - Entire route is on paved roads.
> - Some unpaved sections or rail trail.
> - Gravel grinder: mostly unpaved or dirt roads.
> - Rail trails: converted railway trails, usually maintained.

Start Point
- This is the address where you can park your vehicle; it is the starting point for the cue sheet. (Note that parking availability can change; when in doubt, ask someone nearby about the best place to leave your vehicle.)

Summary
- A brief summary of what to expect on the rides, with information regarding challenging hills, unpaved roads, remoteness, beach access, lake or coastal views, and more.

Description
- An overview of the route with some details to be aware of or to look out for.

Ride Considerations
- Things to consider before you head out for the ride. These will include such things as prevailing winds, traffic, road conditions, supplies, and remoteness.

Side Trips/Variations
- These are routes that are in a similar area or that overlap the current route; this will help if you want to do multiple rides in a day or mix and match.
- These may include hikes or other types of trips.
- Options for lengthening or shortening the ride will be listed here.
- If you are using an odometer for your ride, it is advised that you turn it off when taking a side trip and then turn it back on when resuming the main route; this will help keep your cue sheet accurate.

Points of Interest

- Special spots to consider visiting en route, including such things as swimming holes, museums, picnic parks, ice cream, look-offs, local breweries or wineries, and local attractions.
- Most points of interest will have a kilometre marking to show where they are on your route.

Cue Sheets

- These provide turn-by-turn directions for the ride; use your phone, odometer, or GPS device to keep track of your kilometres.
- Note that cue sheets are a rough guide; any sort of side trip or backtracking will change the overall distance; resetting your odometer on every turn and using the "next turn" is the most reliable way to keep on track.
- Road signs will not always be present, especially in the more remote areas; use kilometre distances to help determine the next turn.

How to Read a Cue Sheet

- **Distance** The distance your odometer will read when you arrive at a turn, assuming you haven't taken any side trips.
- **Type** The direction of the turn you will be making at that kilometre marker.
- **Note** A detailed description of the turn.
- **Next** The number of kilometres until your next turn.

Sample Cue Sheet

Dist	Type	Note	Next
0.0	●	Start of route	0.0
0.0	⚑	(Start) Shelburne: 115 King St; head west on NS-3	1.1
1.1	←	L onto Water St (signs for Sandy Point)	0.6
1.7	←	L onto Williams St	0.2
1.9	→	R onto Hammond St/Lighthouse Rte	29.5
31.4	←	L onto Jordan Branch Rd	3.3
34.7	←	L onto King St/NS-3 W	1.0
35.7	●	End of route	0.0

Overview Tables

Each route also includes a table near the top that offers a quick overview of the ride; it includes:

Sample Overview Table

Distance (km)	Duration	Max Grade +	Elevation Gain (m)	Unpaved
118.5 (one way)	5:23/7:54	4.3	755	94% (111 km)

Distance

- The distance of the main route (not including side trips), in kilometres.
- "Return" means the notes and cue sheets are for a back-and-forth trip, which is usually meant to be done in one day.
- "One way" means the route is described as a two-day trip.

Duration

- There are two travel-time estimates for each route. The first number shown is for someone travelling at an average of 22 kmh; this assumes one is keeping a fairly brisk and steady pace. The second is for someone travelling at an average of 15 kmh, most likely taking their time and stopping to enjoy the views. These numbers are a quick reference for how long the route might take, based on how you like to cycle.
- Note that the estimated time does not take into consideration breaks, side trips, or type of terrain; look at all of these factors when estimating your total travel time.
- To personalize your travel times, note how long a ride in this book actually takes you, then compare that to suggested ride times and adjust accordingly for your next trip.

Max Grade +

- This is the steepest slope (in degrees) you will be climbing on the route.

Elevation Gain (m)

- This is the sum total elevation of all climbs on the ride.

Definitions

Access point An area where cyclists can get on or off a trail.

Challenging hill This is based on the route profile; it is subjective and may be interpreted differently by different riders.

Gravel grinder A route that has a lot of unpaved roads; it is often ridden on a bike with wider tires.

Kid-friendly A designation chosen because it is on some combination of rail trail, paved shoulder, bike lane, or low-traffic road.

OHVs Off-Highway Vehicles; these include four-wheelers, motorbikes, snowmobiles, and other similar motorized vehicles.

Peak hours Hours when vehicle traffic will be heaviest due to commuters; traffic is generally heaviest in both urban and rural areas between 7 am and 9 am and 3 pm and 6 pm.

Rail trail An off-road path made from a converted railway bed; many rail trails are shared-use, meaning you may encounter OHVs, pedestrians, and horses.

Remote area An area with few accessible resources and possibly lacking cellular phone reception.

Steep descent A particularly steep hill on which cyclists need to pay extra attention to ride safely.

Unpaved Road Gravel road, dirt road, or rail trail.

Unpaved

- Indicates, in both percentages and kilometres, how much of the ride is on unpaved roads and/or rail trails; numbers may not be exact, but give a fairly accurate representation.
- Note that these sections are not necessarily contiguous.

Using Printed Maps

We highly recommend that you pick up a *Nova Scotia/Prince Edward Island Mapbook* (**backroadmapbooks.com**) for high-level detail of the roads in the province. You might not want to take it cycling, but it will help you with planning and understanding routes. It will also provide more information in terms of alternate routes.

A *Doers & Dreamers Companion Map* (available from Tourism Nova Scotia) will help provide a greater context for routes and how they might fit into your overall travel plans, but it does not show road names, except within Halifax and Dartmouth.

Check with both provincial and local visitor information centres wherever you are travelling; they often have maps specific to each area with rail trails and other cycling routes mapped out.

Downloading Maps and Routes

There are many online mapping tools available that can help enhance your trip and keep you on track.

Bicycle Nova Scotia
- All of the routes are available on the Bicycle Nova Scotia website in a number of different formats so you can download them to your GPS device or phone; routes are regularly updated based on user experience.
- Cue sheets are available on the website; print these out in advance if you are not going to bring this book with you or to make them easier to use.

Online maps
- Google Maps is the gold standard for online maps; it was used for most of the planning in this book.
- Google maps can be downloaded to your phone using a Wi-Fi connection; they will include the detail you would expect when using Google Maps, including street names.
- We highly recommend that you download maps if you are going to be riding remotely, as road signs and cellular service will not always be available.

Mountain Biking

Nova Scotia has some incredible mountain biking, on rides that range from fast, well-groomed, single-track trails to abandoned forest roads in the backcountry. For this book, it was decided to not cover mountain bike trails in order to stay focused on road and rail trail riding around the province. Mountain bike trails are constantly being added and adapted and it would require another book to fully explore the breadth of mountain biking around the province.

The local bike shop is the best place to find trails and get status updates. There are also a few valuable resources online that will give you everything you need to start exploring Nova Scotia by mountain bike. We recommend the following:

Trail Forks
· This is the most comprehensive site for mountain biking in Nova Scotia, and for trails all over the world. Most trail networks that are used on a regular basis are listed here, and because it is a wiki-style site, the information is updated regularly. **(trailforks.com/region/nova-scotia)**

East Coast Mountain Biking
· This is a forum created specifically for the Maritimes by a community of passionate mountain bikers who share ideas, talk about trail advocacy, and also organize weekly rides. The forum welcomes new members and inquiries of all kinds. **(ecmtb.net)**

Helpful Links

- Nova Scotia Backroad Mapbook backroadmapbooks.com/backroad-mapbooks/atlantic-canada-backroad-maps/nova-scotia-backroad-mapbook
- Nova Scotia transportation options novascotia.com/about-nova-scotia/getting-around
- Halifax Stanfield International Airport transportation options halifaxstanfield.ca/transportation
- Provincial ferries information novascotia.ca/tran/hottopics/ferries.asp
- Highway safety and maintenance information; highway webcams novascotia.ca/tran
- Nova Scotia tourism general information novascotia.com
- Nova Scotia tourism cycling information novascotia.com/see-do/outdoor-activities/cycling
- Halifax tourism information discoverhalifaxns.com
- Bicycle Nova Scotia bicycle.ns.ca
- Cycle Nova Scotia cyclenovascotia.ca
- Weather (Environment Canada) weather.gc.ca/forecast/canada/index_e.html?id=NS

Long-Distance Rides: Tip-to-Tip

This province is well suited to long-distance touring by bicycle. Most of the province has secondary highways that are relatively low-traffic, connecting small towns and communities. Many of these routes follow the coast or alongside rivers, making for some exceptional rides.

Although the province is well connected, the routes are not necessarily designated for cycling. The roads in Nova Scotia are still mostly focused on motor vehicles, although this is starting to change, thanks to continued pressure from many hard-working advocates and organizations.

Long-distance touring routes are not covered in this book, but we've included some resources you can find online to help you put together a cross-province ride that suits your needs.

- *Nova Scotia by Bicycle* (1995): This is the original book put out by Bicycle Nova Scotia. It was mostly focused on multi-day rides and has some excellent suggestions for getting around the province. You can view a PDF of the book on the Bicycle Nova Scotia website: **bicycle.ns.ca**.
- The Blue Route is a working vision of creating a 3,000 km cycling network around the province, and is the official home for updates and changes to our connected cycling infrastructure. Visit the website to view the map, and keep up to date on new developments: **blueroute.ca**.
- Randonneurs Nova Scotia: This cycling club does long-distance rides all around Nova Scotia: **randonneurs.ns.ca**.
- Bike Across Canada: This Facebook page has an incredible amount of information about cycling across Canada, including routes that connect Nova Scotia from tip to tip: **facebook.com/groups/bikeacrosscanada**.
- The Great Trail: This is the longest recreational trail in the world, covering Canada from coast to coast to coast. If you are interested in staying off the roads and exploring rail trails and other off-road methods, this is a good place to look: **thegreattrail.ca/explore-the-map**.

ROUTES BY REGION

(BICYCLE NOVA SCOTIA)

CYCLING ROUTES OF HALIFAX METRO

Route	Route Name	Distance (km)	Duration	Max Grade +	Elevation Gain (m)	Unpaved	Map
1	Halifax Peninsula	15.0	0:40/1:00	5.4	149	—	1
2	Shearwater Flyer and Salt Marsh Trail (RT)	37.3	1:41/2:29	1.9	146	100% (37 km)	1
3	Cow Bay	31.7	1:26/2:06	4.6	230	—	1
4	Sambro Loop and City Swim Spots	48.9	2:13/3:16	7.0	521	—	1

Halifax Metro Regional Overview

Halifax is the essence of a Maritime city, with its busy harbour, fog-laden streets, and many bars and restaurants. Over the years it has become known for its arts and culture, and more recently, for its food culture, which continues to grow and mature. It's also historically known for the Halifax Explosion, a maritime disaster that took place on December 6, 1917, which at the time was the largest human-made explosion in history.

Although the streets are sometime steep, the city itself is fairly small, making it easy to explore by bicycle. There are significant landmarks to visit, such as the Public Gardens, Citadel Hill, the Commons, and the historic waterfront. Then there are the commercial districts such as the Hydrostone, located in the ever-popular North End, and the dense collection of bars and restaurants downtown around Argyle Street. Along with the many beautiful buildings that reflect the history of the city, Halifax also boasts internationally renowned modern architecture, such as the Central Library. Opened in 2014, this building has garnered attention from around the world, and has become a destination with its inviting open concept and edgy, yet whimsical, design.

Across the harbour is Dartmouth, otherwise known as "The City of Lakes." This area has become a strong competitor with Halifax for the best side of the harbour on which to live and play. Dartmouth easily holds its own with its growing commercial district, community projects, and its many parks, lakes, and multi-use trails. Take the ferry across the harbour and explore both sides of this amazing urban environment.

Although Halifax and Dartmouth are modern cities, cyclists are never far away from the water or wilderness parks. Cycle around Halifax and then head out to Crystal Crescent Beach, passing accessible lakes for a swim along the way. Or head over to Shubie Park in Dartmouth before hitting Lawrencetown Beach via the ❷ **Shearwater Flyer and Salt Marsh Trail**. There are many nice cycling routes out of the city, quickly taking you to quiet areas where you can tap into nature.

Additional Notes
- Halifax Metro is Nova Scotia's largest urban centre. A lot of work has been done to improve bike lanes and to make the streets safer for cyclists, but there is still a lot left to be done. Stay alert when riding in the city centre and in surrounding areas
- Halifax has an excellent map that shows all the bike lanes, multi-use paths, and preferred bike routes around the city; find it at **halifax.ca/transportation/cycling-walking**.

Halifax Area Bike Shops

- The Bike Pedaler (Dartmouth) 902-406-7773
- Cyclesmith (Halifax) 902-425-1756
- Giant Bicycle Halifax (Halifax) 902-407-2462
- Halifax Cycles (Halifax) 902-407-4222
- Ideal Bikes (Halifax) 902-444-7487
- Long Alley Bicycles (Halifax) 902-404-9849
- MEC (Halifax) 902-421-2667
- Sportwheels Sports Excellence (Sackville) 902-865-9033
- Trailside Bike Shop (Brookfield) 902-298-5785

Halifax Area Emergency Services

- Halifax Infirmary (QEII Halifax)
- IWK Health Centre (Halifax; Children's)
- Cobequid Community Health Centre (Lower Sackville)
- Dartmouth General Hospital (Dartmouth)

 **Halifax Peninsula**

MAP 1

Start Point

Halifax: Halifax Ferry Terminal, next to 5075 George St.

Summary

Hilly; busy roads; some bikes lanes; local food/drink; cultural experiences; shopping; museums.

Distance (km)	Duration	Max Grade +	Elevation Gain (m)	Unpaved
15.0	0:40/1:00	5.4	149	—

Description

This ride takes you on a tour of the Halifax Peninsula, guiding you through commercial districts, parks, historic sites, and water frontage. It is just a taste of what Halifax has to offer, but it will introduce you to some of the highlights while orienting you to the city. The route starts on the waterfront where you are separate from the traffic and free to explore the wharves and shops. Visit the Seaport Farmers' Market before heading toward Point Pleasant Park where you can go for a stroll along the many walking paths or bike through the park on designated trails. Afterward, head north toward the Hydrostone district and explore the dynamic and popular North End. Finally, take a tour of the Halifax Citadel for a 360-degree view of the city before heading back to the waterfront where you started.

Ride Considerations

- This route is a mix of downtown commercial and residential, with some multi-use paths and protected bike lanes. Stay alert to traffic at all times; try to avoid doing this tour during peak hours.
- There is a $2.50 fee for a one-way trip on the ferry to Dartmouth; bicycles are allowed at no additional cost.
- Bring a bike lock with you and secure your bicycle whenever you leave it unattended.
- If you plan to take the bridge between Halifax and Dartmouth, be aware that only the Macdonald Bridge allows bicycles; there are separate lanes for cyclists and pedestrians.

Side Trips/Variations

- Take a ferry tour over to Dartmouth to create a nice little water loop on multi-use paths. Take your bike on the ferry to Alderney Landing (where there is a farmers' market and art gallery), then head east on the Trans-Canada Trail and follow this all the way to the Woodside Ferry, riding along the water the entire way. Take the ferry from Woodside back to Halifax to complete the loop. (To explore Dartmouth, head downtown from the Alderney Landing terminal before continuing on the tour.)

Points of Interest

- **Halifax Waterfront (Start/Stop)** This is the first kilometre of the ride, with shops to visit and wharves to wander around.
- **Bishop's Landing (0.9 km)** A dense collection of shops and restaurants on the waterfront.
- **Halifax Seaport Farmers' Market (1.4 km)** This market is open seven days a week, but has limited vendors most days; visit on the weekend for the liveliest experience. The historic Brewery Farmers' Market is nearby, at 1496 Lower Water St. (open on Saturday mornings only).
- **Point Pleasant Park (3.6 km)** This is a popular green space on the Halifax Harbour with many walking trails; cyclists are allowed to ride on designated trails seven days a week.
- **Quinpool Road (7.5 km)** This is a busy street, but one that is full of shops and restaurants.
- **The Hydrostone (10.2 km)** Built after the Halifax Explosion in 1917, the Hydrostone is a National Historic Site of Canada; the commercial district is full of nice shops and restaurants and has plenty of green space.
- **Agricola Street (10.5 km)** Keep your eyes out for shops, breweries, restaurants, and all sorts of interesting businesses along this route.
- **The Halifax Commons (11.9 km)** This is a large green space right in the middle of the city; it is a popular spot for all sorts of sports and recreation.
- **Halifax Citadel (12.5 km)** Originally built in 1749 to protect the city of Halifax from invaders, the Citadel is now a historic site where you can visit and learn about the city's military history. It also has one of the most impressive views of the city.
- **Argyle Street (14.6 km)** This commercial street has traffic-calming devices to make the area more enjoyable for walking and biking. This is where the action takes place in the evenings at the many bars and restaurants.

Halifax Peninsula Cue Sheet

Dist	Type	Note	Next
0.0	●	Start of route	0.0
0.0	⚑	(Start) Halifax Ferry Terminal, next to 5075 George St; head south, following the waterfront	1.4
1.4	↑	Continue onto Marginal Rd	0.1
1.5	↑	Continue onto Terminal Rd	0.1
1.6	←	L onto Hollis St	0.0
1.6	→	R onto South St	0.1
1.7	←	L onto Barrington St	0.4
2.2	→	Slight R onto Inglis St	0.3
2.4	←	L onto S Bland St	0.2
2.6	→	S Bland St turns R and becomes Atlantic St	0.3
2.9	←	L onto Young Ave	0.7
3.6	→	R onto Point Pleasant Dr	0.2
3.8	→	R onto Tower Rd	0.9
4.8	←	L onto Inglis St	0.9
5.7	→	R onto Beaufort Ave	0.6
6.3	↑	Continue onto Oxford St	2.2
8.5	→	R onto Almon St	1.3
9.8	←	L onto Gottingen St	0.4

Dist	Type	Note	Next
10.2	←	L onto Young St	0.3
10.5	←	L onto Agricola St	1.4
11.9	↑	At the roundabout, get the 2nd exit onto North Park St	0.4
12.3	↑	At the roundabout, get the 3rd exit onto Cogswell St	0.1
12.4	→	R onto Rainnie Dr	0.0
12.4	→	Slight R towards Citadel Hill	0.0
12.5	←	L uphill to Citadel Hill	0.1
12.6	↗	Slight R to go around Citadel Hill; afterwards, come back down the way you came	1.3
13.9	→	R toward Rainnie Dr	0.0
13.9	→	R onto Rainnie Dr	0.3
14.3	→	R onto Gottingen St	0.2
14.4	↑	Continue onto Duke St	0.3
14.8	→	R onto Hollis St	0.1
14.9	←	L onto George St	0.0
14.9	←	L onto overpass	0.1
15.0	●	End of route	0.0

MAP 1

2 Shearwater Flyer and Salt Marsh Trail

Start Point
Shearwater: parking lot, intersection of Swordfish Dr. and Boundary Rd.

Summary
Easy terrain; rail trail; wildlife; beach access, kid-friendly.

Distance (km)	Duration	Max Grade +	Elevation Gain (m)	Unpaved
37.3 (return)	1:41/2:29	1.9	146	100% (37.3 km)

Description
This route takes you along the hugely popular Shearwater Flyer and Salt Marsh Trail. Because it follows along an old rail bed, the whole ride is an easy grade, and most of the trail is in good condition, making for an ideal ride. The trail will take you through beautiful salt marshes teeming with wildlife; at one point on the ride, you will be out on a spit of land with water directly on either side of you. This is a well-marked trail that also has amenities and interpretive signage. Don't forget to bring your swimwear for when you get to Lawrencetown Beach, which is the turnaround point for this ride.

Ride Considerations
- There are very few amenities on the trail after Cole Harbour; there is a convenience store (with ice cream) in Lawrencetown that can be accessed by getting off the trail and heading east on Conrad Road (15.8 km), then heading south on Route 207.
- This is a shared trail with walkers and other cyclists; OHVs are allowed only on the Shearwater Flyer (the first 8.6 km, up to Bissett Road).
- Although this is a maintained rail trail, there can be variable trail surfaces; be prepared for sections that are soft or in rough condition. Contact the Cole Harbour Parks and Trails Association to report any issues on the trail (902-435-3952).
- This is a rail trail, so be sure to have the appropriate tires for hard-packed gravel.
- Visit the Cole Harbour Parks and Trails Association online for maps and more information: chpta.org.

Side Trips/Variations

- Carry on past Lawrencetown Beach to ⑩⑥Three Fathom Harbour, taking Causeway Road to Fisherman's Beach and to a working wharf (16 km return).
- Make it a shorter ride by starting in Cole Harbour where the trail starts off of Bissett Road; there is parking just west of where the trail starts. This makes for a 15.2 km return trip.

Points of Interest

- **Lawrencetown Beach (18.6 km)** This beach is well known for its surf, attracting all sorts of adventurers looking to catch the next perfect wave. The beach is beautiful and there are lots of amenities, including showers to wash off sweat or salt water. This is the turnaround point for the ride.

Shearwater Flyer and Salt Marsh Trail Cue Sheet

Dist	Type	Note	Next
0.0	●	Start of route	0.0
0.0	⚑	(Start) Shearwater: parking lot, intersection of Swordfish Dr and Boundary Rd; head south on Swordfish Dr	0.1
0.1	←	L at Provider Rd and onto the rail trail	2.9
3.0	↑	Continue on Shearwater Flyer Trail	15.1
18.1	←	Trail turns slightly L onto Lawrencetown Rd/Marine Dr/NS-207 E	0.0
18.1	→	R into parking lot	0.5
18.6	↷	Lawrencetown Beach; turnaround point	0.5
19.2	←	Slight L onto Lawrencetown Rd/Marine Dr/NS-207 W	0.0
19.2	→	Slight R onto Salt MarshTrail	18.0
37.2	→	R onto Swordfish Dr	0.1
37.3	●	End of route	0.0

The Salt Marsh Trail follows along an old railbed, so the whole ride is an easy grade. (GEORGE LONG)

 **Cow Bay**

MAP 1

Start Point

Eastern Passage: parking lot 200 m south of Caldwell Rd./Hines Rd.

Summary

Some busy residential roads; beach access; rail trail option.

Distance (km)	Duration	Max Grade +	Elevation Gain (m)	Unpaved
31.7	1:26/2:06	4.6	230	—

Description

This is a fun, fairly quick ride, found just outside of the city centre. Bring along your swimwear as this route passes by Rainbow Haven Provincial Park, a popular and often busy white sand beach. The ride will also take you to Cow Bay, where you can strike a pose beside the famous 3.6 m concrete moose, while looking out to the sea where surfers are often seeking out the next set of breaks. Finish off the ride on the east side of Halifax Harbour, where you can see the city from across the water, with Lawlor Island and McNabs Island in the foreground.

Ride Considerations

• A few sections of this ride go through high-density residential areas; stay alert to cars turning into and pulling out of driveways.
• Bissett Road can get busy in the summer, with a lot of traffic going to and from Rainbow Haven Beach; use care on this section of road, especially on weekends and on hot, sunny days.

Side Trips/Variations

• You can make this route shorter and avoid some of the residential sections by taking the ❷ Shearwater Flyer rail trail for the first and final parts of your trip. To access, get on the trail 100 m north of the parking lot. Head east on the rail trail until you meet with Bissett Road (5 km) where you will connect with the route. Follow the loop until you get back onto Hines Road in Shearwater, where you can then get back onto the rail trail to finish the ride. This makes for a 29.9 km loop.
• You can also take the ❷ Salt Marsh Trail to Lawrencetown Beach and back, adding 20.6 km to your ride; get on the rail trail where it intersects with Bissett Road (11 km), just north of Rainbow Haven Beach.

Points of Interest

- **Rainbow Haven Provincial Park (13.4 km)** This is a very popular beach due to its white sand and proximity to downtown Halifax.
- **Fisherman's Cove (26.1 km)** Visit a restored two hundred-year-old fishing village, where you can wander the boardwalk and check out the variety of shops—and maybe grab an ice cream.

Cow Bay Cue Sheet

Dist	Type	Note	Next
0.0	◉	Start of route	0.0
0.0	⚑	(Start) Eastern Passage: parking lot 200 m south of Caldwell Rd/Hines Rd; head north on Caldwell Rd	0.2
0.2	→	R to stay on Caldwell Rd (signs for Cole Harbour)	5.1
5.4	→	R onto Deerbrooke Dr	0.6
6.0	→	R onto Colby Dr	1.6
7.6	→	R onto path	0.1
7.6	→	R, then slight L, continuing on trail	0.3
7.9	←	L onto Brookview Dr	0.4
8.3	→	R onto Patrick Ln	0.2
8.5	→	R onto Bissett Rd/NS-322 N	4.8
13.4	→	R onto Cow Bay Rd/NS-322 N	1.2
14.6	↑	Continue straight on Cow Bay Rd	4.8
19.4	←	L onto Cow Bay Rd/NS-322 N	1.7
21.1	←	L onto Samuel Danial Dr	0.3
21.4	→	R onto Melrose Crescent	0.8
22.2	←	L onto a pathway toward Shamrock Ct	0.2
22.4	←	L onto Shamrock Ct	0.0
22.4	→	R onto Thorncrest Ct	0.1
22.5	←	L onto Caldwell Rd	1.1
23.6	→	R onto Shore Rd	2.7
26.3	←	L onto Cow Bay Rd/Marine Dr/NS-322 N	2.3
28.6	→	R onto Hines Rd	2.9
31.5	→	R onto Caldwell Rd (signs for Cow Bay)	0.2
31.7	◉	End of route	0.0

 Sambro Loop and City Swim Spots   MAP 1

Start Point

Halifax: Chocolate Lake Recreation Centre, 14 Purcells Cove Rd.

Summary

Challenging hills; busy roads; some paved shoulders; beach access; swim spots.

Distance (km)	Duration	Max Grade +	Elevation Gain (m)	Unpaved
48.9	2:13/3:16	7.0	521	—

Description

This is considered by many to be one of the classic routes out of Halifax. Within minutes you will be hugging the Halifax Harbour and the Atlantic Ocean on your way to Williams Lake, a relatively quiet swim spot loved by the locals. If fresh water isn't your thing, you can wait until you get to Crystal Crescent Beach, where the water will be chillier but there will also be white sand beaches where you can soak up the warmth of the sun. This is a great area to have a picnic, explore the beaches, and do some rock-hopping. The rest of the ride is inland, with a number of good climbs to take you back to where you began. Finish the day off with a swim at Chocolate Lake, then head into the city for a well-deserved post-ride treat.

Ride Considerations

- These roads can get busy, especially during commuting times; try to avoid travelling during peak hours.
- A good portion of this route has paved shoulders, starting just south of Herring Cove (13.1 km) and ending south of Spryfield (42.4 km).

Points of Interest

- **Williams Lake (3 km)** On a nice day you will most likely see cars parked on the west side of the road where you can access Williams Lake (there is no sign); it's a quick walk down to the water from there.
- **Crystal Crescent Beach (28.1 km)** This is a spectacular beach worth spending some time at. You will go down an unpaved road to get there, but once you do, you will be treated to white sand beaches and glistening ocean views. There is also excellent rock-hopping here, where you can explore the coastline by foot. Access it by getting onto Route 349, turning onto East Pennant Road, then heading east on Sambro Creek Road and down Crystal Crescent Beach Road.
- **Chocolate Lake (Start/Stop)** This is a local favourite and a great way to finish off the ride with one more swim to complete the day.

Sambro Loop and City Swim Spots Cue Sheet

Dist	Type	Note	Next
0.0	◉	Start of route	0.0
0.0	⚑	(Start) Halifax: Chocolate Lake Recreation Centre, 14 Purcells Cove Rd	0.0
0.0	←	L onto Purcells Cove Rd/NS-253 S	12.0
12.0	←	L onto Ketch Harbour Rd/NS-349 S	15.8
27.8	→	Slight R onto Old Sambro Rd/NS-306	17.1
44.9	↑	Continue onto Sussex St	0.6
45.5	←	L onto Herring Cove Rd/NS-349 N	3.3
48.8	→	R onto Purcells Cove Rd/NS-253 S	0.0
48.8	↑	Use crosswalk	0.0
48.9	←	L onto Chocolate Lake Rd	0.0
48.9	◉	End of route	0.0

CYCLING ROUTES OF THE SOUTH SHORE

Route	Route Name	Distance (km)	Duration	Max Grade +	Elevation Gain (m)	Unpaved	Map
5	Peggys Cove	81.9	3:43/5:28	6.6	722	—	1
6	Rum Runners Trail (RT)	118.3	5:23/7:54	4.3	755	94% (111 km)	2
7	Aspotogan Peninsula	50.1	2:16/3:20	6.5	425	—	3
8	Seaside and Rail Trail (RT)	28.7	1:18/1:54	5.8	231	35% (10 km)	4
9	Second Peninsula	18.9	0:52/1:16	7.5	211	—	3
10	Blue Rocks (RT)	19.2	0:53/1:18	4.3	136	20% (4 km)	3
11	Hirtles Beach	47.5	2:09/3:10	7.1	386	—	4
12	Mahone Bay–Bridgewater–Lunenburg (RT)	64.4	2:55/4:17	5.2	455	22% (14 km)	3
13	Bridgewater–Petit Rivière–LaHave	50.8	2:18/3:23	6.7	391	—	5
14	Rissers–Liverpool	54.7	2:29/3:38	8.2	382	—	5
15	Liverpool–Carters Beach	46.7	2:07/3:06	6.7	388	—	5
16	Western Head	15.4	0:42/1:01	4.6	99	—	5
17	Molega Lake	78.8	3:36/5:17	4.6	543	—	6
18	Caledonia–Westfield	20.9	0:57/1:24	3.4	153	48% (10 km)	6
19	Brookfield Mines Trail (RT)	36.5	1:39/2:26	1.4	153	100% (36.5 km)	6
20	Jordan Bay	35.7	1:39/2:25	4.3	254	—	7
21	Crow Neck	51.5	2:18/3:23	2.3	212	20% (10 km)	7
22	Cape Sable Island	40.7	1:51/2:42	2.9	181	—	7

South Shore Regional Overview

When you live in Nova Scotia, you always feel a bit of envy when someone says they are heading down to the South Shore for the weekend. The words conjure up images of sun-drenched beaches, historic towns, long, slow days, and delicious meals eaten while overlooking the ocean. This is just a taste of what the area is about, but it reflects some of the well-known qualities that the South Shore has to offer.

The journey starts as you head west down the coast from Halifax, coming to Peggys Cove, easily one of Nova Scotia's most recognizable landmarks. The lighthouse was built in 1915 and is located in a picturesque fishing community where colourful houses perch on the rocks looking out toward the unforgiving Atlantic Ocean. Be aware that this is a very busy attraction, so if crowds are not your thing, it's a good idea to get there early, or instead visit one of the many other lighthouses in the region.

One of the great cycling developments in the province has been the creation of the Rum Runners Trail, an old railway bed that has been turned into a multi-use trail, connecting small towns between the city of Halifax and Lunenburg. There is wayfinding along the trail and access points to visit the many beautiful towns you will pass along the way. The trail parallels the main road, providing options for both paved roads and trail riding as you journey down the coast.

Hubbards is well known to many cyclists because of the ❼ Aspotogan Peninsula, a favourite ride for many people coming from the city. This community is home to the Shore Club, the oldest surviving dance hall in Nova Scotia, where you can also experience a traditional lobster dinner. Nearby is Chester, known for its deep-rooted sailing tradition and as the home of Chester Race Week, North America's largest annual keelboat race held annually in August.

Mahone Bay is a beautiful town filled with vibrantly coloured homes, nestled into a bay where sailboats abound. This is where you'll find the iconic three churches lining the water's edge, letting you know you've arrived. Take a stroll around the bustling town and visit the local bike shop before heading down to Lunenburg, a UNESCO World Heritage Site and home to *Bluenose II*. This is a stunning town that deserves to be explored, both by foot and by bicycle. There are many good cycling routes between here and Mahone Bay that can keep you busy for days.

Although there are great beaches up to this point, heading farther down the coast will only raise the bar higher. There are large white sand beaches all along this coast, ranging from popular ones with amenities to quiet, off-the-beaten-path gems that you can have all to yourself. Visit Rissers Beach to get a sense of what a summer vacation is like in Nova Scotia, then head down to Cherry Hill to see surfers looking to catch the next wave, and finally out to Carters Beach where you will find deceptively "tropical" turquoise waters.

On the way down the coast, stop in Bridgewater, the largest town in the area and the one with the most amenities. Visit the Black Loyalist Heritage Centre in Birchtown, Shelburne, which showcases the eighteenth-century history of "the world's largest free African population outside of Africa." Head down toward Yarmouth to explore secluded beaches, ride quiet roads, and spend some time at the many lighthouses along the way. Keep your eyes open for the protected piping plover on the beaches in this area.

The South Shore offers many potential adventures. Be sure to bring along your beach gear and a hunger for the many delicacies you will find along the way. The cycling down here is excellent and provides consistently stunning views, along with many opportunities to visit secluded beaches and beautiful towns.

Additional Notes

- Trunk 3 is the main route through the South Shore other than the highway; this can be a busy road, so try to avoid it during peak hours.
- Watch yourself around popular beach spots like Rissers Beach; sometimes traffic can get congested, especially on weekends and holidays.
- This part of the province is well known for fog, which can come in quickly, especially in the area toward Yarmouth. Check the weather before you go and bring adequate layers for warmth.

South Shore Bike Shops

- Lunenburg Bike Shop (Lunenburg) 902-521-6115
- Spin Your Wheels (Bridgewater) 902-530-7746
- Sweet Ride Cycling (Mahone Bay) 902-531-3026
- Train Station Bike and Bean (Upper Tantallon) 902-820-3400

South Shore Emergency Services

- South Shore Regional Hospital (Bridgewater)
- Fisherman's Memorial Hospital (Lunenburg)
- Queens General Hospital (Liverpool)
- Roseway Hospital (Shelburne)

The Rum Runners Trail was created through the joint effort of the many small communities the trail runs through. (BRIANNE STEINMAN)

5 Peggys Cove

Start Point
Halifax: 1311 Prospect Rd.

Summary
Very busy roads, especially in summer; variable road conditions; soft shoulders; lighthouse; shoreline walks.

Distance (km)	Duration	Max Grade +	Elevation Gain (m)	Unpaved
81.9	3:43/5:28	6.6	722	—

SOUTH SHORE

Description
Peggys Cove is the main attraction for this ride. The lighthouse here is iconic and is what many people envision when they think of Nova Scotia. The first part of the ride takes you inland and is fairly straightforward. Once you get to Whites Lake, the road starts to follow the coast, providing some wonderful views and fun little hills. Follow the twisty (and often very busy) roads toward Peggys Cove where you can walk on the rocks, grab some lunch, and explore a beautiful fishing community. The next part of the ride follows the eastern side of St. Margarets Bay, where afterward you can choose to finish the route along Trunk 3 or take the Rum Runners Trail for the final portion of your trip.

Ride Considerations
- This is a very busy road with tight, twisty corners for most of the ride. This road can be filled with tourists coming to Peggys Cove, and in the summer numerous tour buses may pass you; it is a not a ride for the faint of heart. Make sure you are comfortable with heavy traffic and large vehicles passing you, and with soft or gravel shoulders. If you are okay with these, you will be treated to a beautiful ride.
- Some of the roads in this area can be pretty rough and will have small shoulders, adding to the challenge of riding with heavy traffic.

Side Trips/Variations
- You can finish the last 20 km of this ride on the ❻ Rum Runners Trail to get back to where you started. Get onto Sonnys Road, directly across from the intersection of Peggys Cove Road and Trunk 3 (St. Margarets Bay Road); there is a parking lot here with access to the trail. Head east for 18.8 km, then turn south onto Lakeside Park Drive (just past the Coca-Cola plant); head east on Trunk 3 and finally south on Route 333 back to your start point.

Where to Cycle in Nova Scotia **51**

Points of Interest

- **Polly Cove (33.4 km)** This is a lesser-known hiking area east of Peggys Cove with multiple trails to choose from, where rock-hopping opportunities are plentiful and you can enjoy a quieter perspective of this incredible shoreline. Look for parking spaces on the road and trails heading off to your left.
- **Peggys Cove (35.7 km)** The main event for this ride. If you have seen photos of Nova Scotia, you've probably seen the iconic lighthouse at Peggys Cove. This is a beautiful community with colourful houses and fishing vessels. It does get busy in the summertime, so be extra cautious around the main entrance.

Peggys Cove Cue Sheet

Dist	Type	Note	Next
0.0	◉	Start of route	0.0
0.0	⚑	(Start) Halifax: 1311 Prospect Rd; head south on Prospect Rd/NS-333 W	35.7
35.7	*i*	Peggys Cove turnoff	25.2
60.9	→	R onto NS-3 E (signs for Bedford/Halifax/NS-103/NS-213)	20.8
81.7	→	R onto Lighthouse Rte/Prospect Rd/NS-333 W	0.2
81.9	◉	End of route	0.0

---

⑥ Rum Runners Trail (RT)

MAP 2

Start Point

Halifax: 3601 Joseph Howe Dr. or Lunenburg: 10 Dufferin St.

Summary

Rail trail; mostly flat; good access points; wayfinding; coastal views; beach access; kid-friendly.

Distance (km)	Duration	Max Grade +	Elevation Gain (m)	Unpaved
118.3 (one way)	5:23/7:54	4.3	755	94% (111 km)

Description

The Rum Runners Trail has changed the way people travel by bicycle on the South Shore for the better. The road down the coast is a lovely drive with its vistas, but the traffic and lack of paved shoulders have made it difficult to relax and fully enjoy the ride by bicycle. The trail provides the chance to ride away from traffic, while being only a quick side trip away from the water and from towns at any point along the way. The Rum Runners Trail was created through the joint effort of the many small communities this trail runs through; these communities have helped build and maintain their own sections over the years. With the trail complete, it is now possible to cycle from the city of Halifax to Lunenburg, all on converted rail trail, separate from the road.

The ride starts from Halifax by heading west on the Chain of Lakes Trail, a paved section of trail that makes for a fast and smooth ride. (This is the only paved section on the trail; you can expect to see a fair number of other users this close to the city, especially on weekends.) After Bayers Lake, the trail has a hard-packed crusher dust surface, which is what you can expect for the remainder of the ride.

Continue on to Upper Tantallon where you can stop for lunch and a tune-up at the Train Station Bike and Bean before heading toward Hubbards, home to some very popular beaches and the classic ❼ Aspotogan Peninsula cycling loop. The next town along the way is Chester, a bustling community known for its sailing traditions; soon after that, you will pass through Gold River and Martins Point before reaching Mahone Bay, where you will find an exquisitely charming coastal town with lots of options for food and drink. The last stretch of the ride takes you into Lunenburg, a UNESCO World Heritage Site, considered the best surviving example of a planned British Settlement in North America, dating back to 1753. This is a beautiful town, full of restaurants and shops, and with many other cycling routes close by.

Ride Considerations

- Read **Preparing to Ride: Packing Considerations** to learn more about packing and preparing for a long trip.
- The distance indicated here is for a one-way trip.
- This route can be done from either direction; the cue sheets for this route description start in Halifax.
- Some sections of the trail can be fairly remote and cellphone reception can't be guaranteed; ensure that you are adequately prepared.
- You always have the option to ride the parallel roads; just be aware that they can be busy and should be avoided during peak hours.
- There is signage along the route indicating the many access points where you can get onto the trail or get off for amenities; visit the trail's website for more details.
- This is a shared trail with OHVs, pedestrians, and horses; read **Road Safety: Etiquette** to learn more about how to share the trail with others.
- This is a rail trail, so be sure to have the appropriate tires for hard-packed gravel.

- To get to the start point of the Rum Runners Trail from downtown Halifax, visit the Halifax Regional Municipality's website, where they have a detailed map showing cycling paths and preferred routes to get around the city by bicycle. As an alternative to cycling or driving to the trail, taxi and public transit bus services are available within the municipality.
- Although this is a maintained rail trail, there can be variable trail surfaces; be prepared for sections that are soft or in rough condition. Contact the Rum Runners Trail association about any trail issues that should be taken care of: **902-275-3490**, or **1-800-565-2224**.

Side Trips/Variations

- **5** Peggys Cove
- **7** Aspotogan Peninsula
- **8** Seaside and Rail Trail
- **9** Second Peninsula
- **10** Blue Rocks
- **11** Hirtles Beach

Rum Runners Trail Interactive Map

Visit the official Rum Runners website to get the most up-to-date information about the trail, and for an excellent interactive map, which offers a comprehensive look at amenities available on the trail, including look-offs, picnic parks, and washrooms: rumrunnerstrail.ca

Points of Interest

- **Train Station Bike and Bean**
  (26.8 km) Good turnaround point for a solid back-and-forth from Halifax with lunch in the middle; there is a bike shop, and rentals are available here.
- **Cleveland Beach Provincial Park (44.6 km)** This is a nice white sand beach accessible just off the trail; access via a driveway near 8877 St. Margarets Bay Rd.
- **Queensland Beach, Hubbards (47.4 km)** A very popular white sand beach that is often busy on nice days due to its proximity to Halifax; access via Queensland Lane.
- **Gold River Bridge (88.1 km)** This is a lovely trestle bridge that takes you over Gold River.
- **Saltbox Brewery, Mahone Bay (107.9 km)** Local beer and nice vibes.

Suggested Itinerary (Rail and Road)
Kilometres provided are daily riding distances
- **Day 1** Halifax to Hubbards. Stop at the Bike and Bean for lunch or a snack and finish the day at Queensland Beach. Grab some dinner in town and check to see if there is any live music happening at the Shore Club (50.1 km).
- **Day 2** Cycle the **7** Aspotogan Peninsula, visiting Bayswater Beach, and carrying on to Chester (52.9 km) or Mahone Bay (85.9 km).
- **Day 3** Chester to Lunenburg (41.6 km) or Mahone Bay to Lunenburg (12.1 km); add side trips of **9** Second Peninsula and/or **10** Blue Rocks.
- **Day 4** Ride the trail back toward Halifax; make a full day of it or stop and stay overnight. Alternatively, take the daily bus service back to the city.

Towns en Route (Accommodation and/or Amenities)

- Upper Tantallon (26 km)
- Hubbards (50 km)
- Chester (76 km)
- Mahone Bay (106 km)
- Lunenburg (118 km)

Shuttles/Luggage/Getting Around

- Some cycling shops and businesses will shuttle cyclists and/or their luggage for a fee; it is best to call around to see if this option is available. If they are unable to help, they should know the most up-to-date information about this sort of service.
- Maritime Bus provides daily back-and-forth bus rides between Lunenburg and Halifax. For more information, call Maritime Bus: 1-800-575-1807.

Bike Shops/Repairs/Rentals between Halifax and Lunenburg

- Train Station Bike and Bean (Upper Tantallon) 902-820-3400
- Freewheeling Adventures (Hubbards) 902-857-3600
- Pedal and Sea (Black Point) 877-777-5699
- Sweet Ride Cycling (Mahone Bay) 902-531-3026
- Lunenburg Bike Shop (Lunenburg) 902-521-6115
- For bike shops in Halifax, see Cycling Routes of Halifax Metro: Regional Overview: Halifax Area Bike Shops (page 39).

SOUTH SHORE

Rum Runners Trail (RT) Cue Sheet

Dist	Type	Note	Next
0.0	⚲	Start of route	0.0
0.0	⚑	(Start) Halifax: 3601 Joseph Howe Dr; exit parking lot and cross the road	0.1
0.1	←	L on paved trail	7.3
7.4	↑	Continue onto Beechville Lakeside Timberlea Trail (unpaved trail)	3.9
11.3	→	R onto NS-3 W	0.0
11.3	←	L onto Beechville Lakeside Timberlea Trail	6.9
18.2	→	R to stay on Beechville Lakeside Timberlea Trail	2.2
20.4	↑	Continue onto NS-3 W	0.0
20.4	→	Slight R onto St. Margarets Bay Trail	15.7
36.1	←	Slight L to stay on St. Margarets Bay Trail	16.2
52.3	↑	Continue onto Aspotogan Trail	11.8

Dist	Type	Note	Next
64.1	↑	Continue onto Chester Connection Trail	13.1
77.2	→	Slight R to stay on Chester Connection Trail	0.1
77.3	←	Slight L onto Chester Connection Trail/Lighthouse Rte	11.8
89.1	→	Slight R to stay on Chester Connection Trail	5.3
94.4	←	Keep L to stay on Chester Connection Trail	1.9
96.3	←	Slight L to stay on Chester Connection Trail	1.2
97.5	↑	Continue onto Dynamite Trail	9.8
107.3	←	Sharp L onto Bay to Bay Trail	10.3
117.6	→	Slight R to stay on Bay to Bay Trail	0.7
118.3	⚲	End of route	0.0

7 Aspotogan Peninsula

MAP 3

Start Point
Hubbards: carpool parking lot, where Mill Lake 1 Road intersects with Trunk 3.

Summary
Small, challenging hills; rail trail option; coastal views; beach access.

Distance (km)	Duration	Max Grade +	Elevation Gain (m)	Unpaved
50.1	2:16/3:20	6.5	425	—

Description
Ask any Halifax cyclist where they like to ride outside of the city and there is a good chance they will mention the Aspotogan Peninsula. It's an easy drive from Halifax and provides the opportunity to ride nearly 40 km of beautiful coastline. Not only that, it is also filled with fun, punchy hills, twisty roads, fishing villages, and many gorgeous views. For the first part of the ride, you will be following alongside St. Margarets Bay on your way to Bayswater Beach, where you can stop for a swim and a rest. Next, you will head to Blandford; you'll have views of Little Tancook Island and Big Tancook Island to the east, and a view of Chester across the water. Ride along Route 329 to East River where you can decide to stay on the road using Trunk 3, or get on the ❻ Rum Runners Trail for the last leg of your ride.

  This is a classic ride and a beautiful introduction to the South Shore.

Ride Considerations
- There are many twisty roads along this route and not a lot of shoulder; be cautious in traffic, especially during peak hours or on summer weekends. Drivers in the area are generally used to cyclists, thanks to public awareness campaigns over the years led by local community groups.
- The last section of this route is on Trunk 3, which can be busy; try to avoid this road during peak hours.

Side Trips/Variations
- You can finish this ride on the ❻ Rum Runners Trail to avoid Trunk 3. Access the trail in East River (40.9 km) and head east; when you intersect with Trunk 3, head briefly west and back to your vehicle. If you take the rail trail option, be sure you have tires suitable for crusher-dust trails.
- **Queensland Beach** This is a very popular white sand beach that is often busy on nice days due to its proximity to Halifax. To get there, head east out of Hubbards on Trunk 3 (10 km return).

Points of Interest

- **Castle in Southwest Cove (15 km)** Head down Southwest Cove Road until you get to the cove, where you will see a small castle that looks like it came straight out of a fairy tale.
- **Bayswater Beach Provincial Park (21.5 km)** A very pretty white sand beach with all the basic amenities.

Aspotogan Peninsula Cue Sheet

Dist	Type	Note	Next
0.0	◉	Start of route	0.0
0.0	⚑	(Start) Hubbards: carpool parking lot, where Mill Lake 1 Rd intersects with NS-3	0.0
0.0	←	L onto NS-3 E (signs for NS-329/Hubbards)	0.8
0.9	→	R onto NS-329 W (signs for Bayswater/New Harbour/Mill Cove/Fox Point/Blandford)	40.2
41.1	→	R onto NS-3 E	9.0
50.1	←	L onto Mill Lake 1 Rd	0.0
50.1	◉	End of route	0.0

Seaside and Rail Trail (RT)

MAP 4

Start Point
Mahone Bay: public parking lot, across from 33 Edgewater St.

Summary
Some rough roads; rail trail; coastal route; beach access.

Distance (km)	Duration	Max Grade +	Elevation Gain (m)	Unpaved
28.7	1:18/1:54	5.8	231	35% (10 km)

Description
This ride gives you a taste of both road and trail. Start off by riding the ❻ **Rum Runners Trail** from Mahone Bay down to Lunenburg; be sure to bring some walking shoes so you can take your time to explore this beautiful and historic city. Afterward, ride the back streets toward Garden Lots where you will turn around, taking Route 332 back toward Mahone Bay. This is a lovely stretch of coastal route that provides some nice options for side trips. Finish off the ride in Mahone Bay, where you can visit the local bike shop, get something to eat, and stroll around in a beautiful South Shore town.

Ride Considerations
- Although this is a maintained rail trail, there can be variable trail surfaces; be prepared for sections that are soft or in rough condition.
- A small section of the route is on Trunk 3, which can get busy; try to avoid this road during peak hours.

Side Trips/Variations

- **Blue Rocks (13.4 km)** This is a sweet little ride (11 km return) on back roads to a quiet fishing village. Access it by following Blue Rocks Road east instead of turning back on Route 332. See ⑩ **Blue Rocks** for more details.
- **Second Peninsula (19.2 km)** This is a twisty road, following along protected coves, past a picnic park, and out to a nice beach (14.3 km return). See ⑨ **Second Peninsula** for more details.

Points of Interest

- **Lunenburg (10.9 km)** A UNESCO World Heritage Site, a beautiful town, and home of the famous *Bluenose II*. Plan to spend some time exploring here.
- **Small Beach (24 km)** This is a small, unmarked beach just before Maders Cove.

Seaside and Rail Trail (RT) Cue Sheet

Dist	Type	Note	Next
0.0	●	Start of route	0.0
0.0	⚑	(Start) Mahone Bay: public parking lot, across from 33 Edgewater St; head toward town on Edgewater St	0.2
0.2	↖	Stay L at the monument	0.0
0.2	←	L onto Lighthouse Rte/Main St/NS-3 W	0.0
0.2	→	R onto Clairmont St	0.3
0.5	↑	Continue onto Kinburn St	0.1
0.7	←	L onto Hawthorn Rd	0.3
0.9	←	L onto Bay to Bay Trail	9.2
10.1	→	Slight R to stay on Bay to Bay Trail	0.7
10.8	←	L onto NS-3 W	0.1
10.9	↑	Continue onto Lincoln St	0.1
11.0	→	R onto Linden Ave	0.2
11.2	→	R onto Bluenose Dr	0.6
11.8	→	R onto Montague St	0.1
11.9	←	L onto Kempt St	0.1
11.9	→	R onto Pelham St	0.5
12.4	↑	Continue onto Blue Rocks Rd	1.0
13.4	←	L onto NS-332 N	3.8
17.2	→	Slight R onto NS-3 E (signs for Mahone Bay)	1.0
18.2	→	R onto Second Peninsula Rd	1.0
19.2	↑	Continue onto Princes Inlet Rd	1.6
20.8	→	Slight R onto Hermans Island Rd	1.4
22.2	←	L onto Maders Cove Rd	0.2
22.5	→	R to stay on Maders Cove Rd	1.7
24.2	←	L to stay on Maders Cove Rd	1.1
25.3	→	R onto NS-3 E	3.2
28.5	→	R onto Edgewater St/NS-3 E (signs for Chester)	0.2
28.7	●	End of route	0.0

SOUTH SHORE

9 Second Peninsula

MAP 3

Start Point
Lunenburg: 4 Dufferin St.

Summary
Easy ride; some rough roads; beach access.

Distance (km)	Duration	Max Grade +	Elevation Gain (m)	Unpaved
18.9 (return)	0:52/1:16	7.5	211	—

Description
The Second Peninsula is a gem of a ride and it is only a short jaunt from Lunenburg. After getting out of town, this route takes you down fun, twisty roads, following alongside Martin Cove on your way to Backman Beach. Bring your swim gear and a picnic, as this is a lovely spot to spend some time on a nice day. This is the turnaround point, so you can then enjoy the ride in reverse on your way back to the town of Lunenburg.

Ride Considerations
- A small section of the route is on Trunk 3, which can get very busy; try to avoid riding here during peak hours.
- Second Peninsula Road heading out to Backman Beach can be very rough at times; be alert to traffic in order to safely avoid hazards.

Side Trips/Variations
- Combine with a trip to ⑩ **Blue Rocks** for a total of approximately 38.2 km; access it by getting on Route 332 and heading east before coming back to town, following paved shoulders to Blue Rocks Road.

Points of Interest
- **Second Peninsula Provincial Park (6.2 km)** Sheltered picnic area with beach access and some basic amenities.
- **Backman Beach (9.5 km)** A nice little swimming beach located in Sandy Cove. This is a popular spot for locals on a hot summer day; there are no amenities here, so come prepared.

SOUTH SHORE

Second Peninsula Cue Sheet

Dist	Type	Note	Next
0.0	◉	Start of route	0.0
0.0	⚑	(Start) Lunenburg: 4 Dufferin St; head north on Dufferin St/NS-3	1.2
1.2	←	L to stay on NS-3 E	0.2
1.4	→	Slight R to stay on NS-3 E (signs for Mahone Bay)	1.0
2.4	→	R onto Second Peninsula Rd	1.0
3.4	→	R to stay on Second Peninsula Rd	6.1
9.5	↶	Backman Beach; turnaround point	6.1
15.6	←	L to stay on Second Peninsula Rd	1.0
16.6	←	L onto NS-3 W	1.0
17.6	←	L to stay on NS-3 W (signs for Blue Rocks/Lunenburg)	0.1
17.7	→	R to stay on NS-3 W (signs for Lunenburg)	1.2
18.9	◉	End of route	0.0

⑩ Blue Rocks (RT)

MAP 3

Start Point
Lunenburg: 4 Dufferin St.

Summary
Easy ride; rail trail and road; coastal route; fishing village.

Distance (km)	Duration	Max Grade +	Elevation Gain (m)	Unpaved
19.2 (return)	0:53/1:18	4.3	136	20% (4 km)

Description
This ride takes you out of town on the rail trail and then quickly puts you onto back roads heading toward Blue Rocks. At about 3.5 km, you will come around the corner to a startlingly beautiful view of the ocean. The rest of the ride follows the shore, winding along bays, passing by beautiful homes, fishing boats, and small communities. The Point General (see page 61) is the perfect stop before heading back toward Lunenburg, following along Herring Rock Road, and then back onto Blue Rocks Road, returning the way you came.

Ride Considerations

- At 4 km, the trail will intersect with Blue Rocks Road (you will see a sign with directions to Battery Point Road and Mahone Bay); this is where you will get onto the road segment.

Side Trips/Variations

- If you want to avoid the rail trail, head north on Trunk 3 out of town, then head east on Route 332 along paved shoulders toward Blue Rocks.
- Take a side trip out to Heckmans Island if you want to add more distance to the ride (up to 10 km); the road is mostly inland so doesn't provide many views. Access Heckmans Island Road at 6.2 km.

Points of Interest

- **The Point General (9.8 km)** This café and general store is the treasure at the end of the rainbow. Grab an ice cream or a coffee and sit on the rocks or walk on the rocky shore; buy some local crafts before you head back to town.

Blue Rocks (RT) Cue Sheet

Dist	Type	Note	Next
0.0	●	Start of route	0.0
0.0	▶	(Start) Lunenburg: 4 Dufferin St; head north on Dufferin St/NS-3	0.0
0.0	→	R onto Bay to Bay Trail	0.7
0.7	→	Slight R to stay on Bay to Bay Trail	0.8
1.5	←	Slight L to stay on Bay to Bay Trail	2.4
3.9	←	Slight L onto Blue Rocks Rd	4.7
8.6	→	R toward the water at the entrance to Darbys Head Road	0.3
8.9	←	L onto The Point Rd	0.8
9.7	↰	The Point General; turnaround point	0.8
10.5	↑	Continue onto Herring Rock Rd	0.4
10.9	←	L onto Blue Rocks Rd	4.4
15.3	→	Slight R onto Bay to Bay Trail	3.2
18.5	←	Slight L to stay on Bay to Bay Trail	0.7
19.2	←	L onto NS-3 W	0.0
19.2	●	End of route	0.0

The Blue Rocks route offers riders a startlingly beautiful view of the ocean. (ALEX MOORE)

Hirtles Beach

MAP 4

Start Point
Lunenburg: 53 Falkland St.

Summary
Some challenging hills; coastal ride; beach access.

Distance (km)	Duration	Max Grade +	Elevation Gain (m)	Unpaved
47.5	2:09/3:10	7.1	386	—

Description
This route takes you on some hilly terrain and along some incredible coastal roads. Take Masons Beach Road out of town; pass the Lunenburg Academy while tackling two steep hills in quick succession, providing you with an exceptional view of Lunenburg from across the water. In Rose Bay you will head toward Hirtles Beach, riding on good pavement and passing many beautiful, modern-styled beach homes. After exploring the shoreline, get back onto Route 332 to follow the LaHave River north, before heading inland back toward Lunenburg on a fairly direct route.

Ride Considerations
- There is often a breeze coming off the ocean and it can get cool quickly, especially if fog rolls in; it's good to have a few layers handy, even on a nice summer day.
- Some of the pavement along this route is in bad shape; be especially careful on the steep descents near the beginning of the ride.

Side Trips/Variations
- **The Ovens (13.0 km)** This side trip (9 km return) takes you to some unique caves that make blowhole music as the waves crash into them; you can also pan for gold here. There is a fee to explore the caves. Restaurant on-site.
- **Gaffe Point** When you're at Hirtles Beach, there is an option for a nice looped hike that takes you out to Gaff Point (7 km return); access it by going west along the beach, where you will come across the trail.
- **LaHave Bakery** There is an excellent diversion that takes you to this famous South Shore bakery. Soon after crossing the bridge west of Riverport (32.0 km), take the ferry across the river (free of charge with your bike); the bakery is 200 m south once you get to the other side. After filling up with treats, catch the ferry back to continue on the main route.
- You can make this route into a longer ride by connecting with **⑫ Mahone Bay–Bridgewater–Lunenburg.**

- Make it a shorter trip by skipping the ride down to Hirtles Beach (cuts 11.4 km).

Points of Interest
- **Hirtles Beach (21.1 km)** Take your time and explore this beautiful, rugged beach. You will sometimes see surfers here, as there can often be a good break. There are bathrooms at the parking lot and picnic tables near the water.

Hirtles Beach Cue Sheet

Dist	Type	Note	Next
0.0	●	Start of route	0.0
0.0	▶	(Start) Lunenburg: 53 Falkland St; head west on Falkland St	0.1
0.1	←	Falkland St turns slightly L and becomes Tannery Rd	0.7
0.8	→	R onto Masons Beach Rd	3.8
4.6	←	L onto Old Lunenburg Rd	0.2
4.8	←	L onto NS-332 W	10.4
15.2	←	L onto Kingsburg Rd	4.3
19.5	→	R onto Hirtles Beach Rd	1.6
21.1	↰	Hirtles Beach; turnaround point	1.5
22.6	←	L onto Kingsburg Rd	4.3
26.9	←	L onto NS-332 W	9.9
36.8	→	R onto Grimm Rd (signs for Grimm Road/Crouse Settlement/First South)	7.3
44.1	←	L onto NS-332 E	1.3
45.4	→	R onto NS-3 E (signs for Lunenburg)	1.9
47.3	↑	Continue onto Victoria Road	0.2
47.5	←	L onto Falkland St	0.0
47.5	●	End of route	0.0

SOUTH SHORE

⑫ Mahone Bay–Bridgewater– Lunenburg (RT)

MAP 3

Start Point
Mahone Bay: public parking lot, across from 33 Edgewater St.

Summary
Challenging ride; some busy sections; variable road conditions; rail trail; coastal views.

Distance (km)	Duration	Max Grade +	Elevation Gain (m)	Unpaved
64.4	2:55/4:17	5.2	455	22% (14 km)

Description
This is a great ride that connects the towns of Mahone Bay, Bridgewater, and Lunenburg. It takes the Adventure Trail out of Mahone Bay to avoid Route 325, which can often be heavy with traffic, and brings you all the way into Bridgewater. The rest of the ride is on pavement and starts out heading south along the east side of the LaHave River. This is a lovely section of road with ever-widening views as it passes by the LaHave ferry on the way to Riverport and then Rose Bay. From here, the ride follows the coast up to Masons Beach and then along the western edge of Lunenburg toward Second Peninsula. The rest of the trip is cycling along twisty roads, making your way along the coast, and coming into Mahone Bay from the south.

Take your time on this one and explore the towns you will be visiting; all of them have their own charms and are worth spending some time in. Consider making this into a multi-day trip by adding on some of the side trips and staying overnight along the way.

Ride Considerations
- The section through Bridgewater is a commercial district, so be alert to potential traffic coming off the rail trail; try to avoid this section during peak hours.
- This ride can also be started in Lunenburg or Bridgewater, or can be reversed.
- There is an option to take Route 325 across from Mahone Bay to Bridgewater, but this is not recommended due to high traffic volumes, especially during peak hours.

Side Trips/Variations

- **LaHave Bakery (34.8 km)** Take the ferry across the river (free of charge with your bike); the bakery is 200 m south once you get to the other side. After filling up with treats, catch the ferry back to continue on the main route.
- **Hirtles Beach (39.8 km)** Nice paved roads down to a beautiful beach (add 11.4 km). See ⑪ **Hirtles Beach** for more details.
- **The Ovens (41.9 km)** Visit the musical caves and pan for gold (add 9 km).
- **Blue Rocks (53.1 km)** This is an easy and beautiful ride to an active fishing village. See ⑩ **Blue Rocks** for more details.
- **Second Peninsula (54.0 km)** This is a fun diversion to Backman Beach, a local hangout and swim spot (14.3 km return). See ⑨ **Second Peninsula** for more details.

Mahone Bay–Bridgewater–Lunenburg (RT) Cue Sheet

Dist	Type	Note	Next
0.0	○	Start of route	0.0
0.0	⚑	(Start) Mahone Bay: public parking lot, across from 33 Edgewater St; head toward town on Edgewater St	0.1
0.1	→	Keep R to continue on Edgewater St//NS-325 N, follow signs for Bridgewater	0.1
0.2	→	R onto Main St/NS-325 N	0.9
1.1	→	R onto Bay to Bay Trail	0.3
1.4	↑	Continue onto Adventure Trail	2.0
3.4	→	Slight R to stay on Adventure Trail	14.5
17.9	←	L onto Glen Allan Dr	0.3
18.2	←	L onto NS-3 E	4.5
22.7	→	R onto NS-332 E	30.4
53.1	←	L onto NS-3 E	0.9
54.0	→	R onto Second Peninsula Rd	1.0
55.0	↑	Continue onto Princes Inlet Rd	1.6
56.6	→	Slight R onto Hermans Island Rd	1.4
58.0	←	L onto Maders Cove Rd	0.3
58.3	→	R to stay on Maders Cove Rd	1.7
60.0	←	L to stay on Maders Cove Rd	1.1
61.1	→	R onto NS-3 E	3.2
64.3	→	R onto Edgewater St/NS-3 E (signs for Chester)	0.1
64.4	○	End of route	0.0

SOUTH SHORE

⑬ Bridgewater–Petite Rivière– LaHave

MAP 5

Start Point

Bridgewater: Pijinuiskaq Park, 480 King St.

Summary

Challenging ride; some busy roads; river/coastal views; beach access; local food/drink.

Distance (km)	Duration	Max Grade +	Elevation Gain (m)	Unpaved
50.8	2:18/3:23	6.7	391	—

Description

This is a fantastic ride that covers some beautiful terrain and has lots of great stops along the way. Plan to take your time for this one in order to appreciate all the offerings of the area. The first 2.4 km coming out of town is a steady uphill taking you to Jubilee Junction where there is a busy section before roads get quieter. There are lots of nice punchy roads along the way from this point on, and the roads are generally in good condition.

Your first stop on the tour will be the Petite Rivière Vineyards in Crousetown, in an area that is said to be one of the earliest grape growing territories in North America. Stop off for a glass, take a tour, and pack a bottle for later. The ride after the winery is twisty and flows along the lazy Petite Rivière River, with a fantastic rolling descent to Petite Rivière Bridge where you will find the local general store.

The ride to LaHave has some beautiful houses and nice ocean views. Stop off at Rissers Beach for a swim and some time on the sand before checking out Crescent Beach, another local favourite. There is no way the ride can be considered complete without stopping at the renowned and much-loved LaHave Bakery. Fuel up on tasty food and coffee before finishing the final stretch that takes you up the LaHave River and back into Bridgewater.

Ride Considerations

- Getting out of Bridgewater can be busy; stay alert to traffic.
- The ride along Route 331 can be busy, especially around Rissers Beach, where there are a lot of cars accessing the beach and campgrounds. Try to avoid this stretch during checkout time (between 11 A.M. and 1 P.M.).

SOUTH SHORE

Points of Interest

- **Petite Rivière Vineyards (17.6 km)** Take the time to stroll around the vineyards and sample some local wines.
- **Rissers Beach (23.2 km)** This is a popular campground during the summer vacation months, so expect the beach to be a bit busier than some others along the South Shore. There is also a long boardwalk just west of the beach where you can stroll over marshlands.
- **Crescent Beach (24.4 km)** This is a large and fairly popular beach with a nice ride that takes you out to LaHave Island (12.4 km return).
- **LaHave Bakery (33.6 km)** This bakery is pretty much legendary and is known around the province for its bread, sweet treats, and comfy vibe. Lunch is available here as well.

Bridgewater–Petite Rivière–LaHave Cue Sheet

Dist	Type	Note	Next
0.0	○	Start of route	0.0
0.0	⚑	(Start) Bridgewater: Pijinuiskaq Park, 480 King St; head south on King St/NS-3	0.1
0.1	→	R onto Dufferin St/NS-3 W	0.2
0.3	←	L onto Alexandra Ave	0.9
1.2	→	R onto Jubilee Rd	1.5
2.7	←	L onto NS-3 W	0.2
2.9	←	L onto Conquerall Mills Rd	6.7
9.6	→	R onto Conquerall Rd	0.2
9.8	←	L onto Crousetown Rd	6.4
16.2	←	L onto Italy Cross Rd	3.1
19.3	↑	Continue onto Petite Riviere Rd	2.3
21.6	←	L onto NS-331 (signs for Bridgewater)	29.2
50.8	○	End of route	0.0

14 Rissers–Liverpool

Start Point
Petite Rivière Bridge: Rissers Beach, 5366 Rte. 331.

Summary
Some rough roads; local food/drink; beach access.

Distance (km)	Duration	Max Grade +	Elevation Gain (m)	Unpaved
54.7 (one way)	2:29/3:38	8.2	382	—

Description
Leaving Rissers Beach, there will be one steep hill at Petite Rivière Bridge before the route heads inland until Broad Cove, where you will get back beside the water. Stop off at Cherry Hill Beach before heading west, where you will soon cross Highway 103 to enter the quiet back roads of Mill Village. Take your time on this section as you follow along the lazy Medway River on a beautiful tree-lined road. You will be crossing Highway 103 a second time before heading toward Port Medway, where you can make a small diversion to visit the Port Grocer. The final part of the ride takes you along some beautiful curvy roads toward Beach Meadows where you can stop at another fantastic, and lesser known, beach. Finish the trip in Liverpool and explore this lovely South Shore town.

Ride Considerations
- This route crosses Highway 103 twice; be aware that cars will be travelling at highway speeds.

Side Trips/Variations
- This trip is designed to be one-way with an overnight in Liverpool, but it can be done as a back-and-forth to make a one-day ride of 110 km.
- Head east from Rissers Beach (your start point) for 1 km to visit Crescent Beach, a large and fairly popular beach with a nice ride that takes you out to LaHave Island (12.4 km return trip).

Points of Interest
- **Cherry Hill Beach (13.6 km)** This is an impressive rocky beach that is off the beaten path; you will often see surfers here looking for the next wave. Access via Henry Conrad Road.
- **The Port Grocer (34.6 km)** This is a great little restaurant and general store that serves up excellent food, local hospitality, and lots of live music; access it by following Port Medway Road for 2 km.

- **Beach Meadows (46.1 km)** One of Nova Scotia's hidden gems; check out Coffin Island in the distance while exploring a white sand beach. Access via the Beach Meadows Crossing Road.

Rissers–Liverpool Cue Sheet

Dist	Type	Note	Next
0.0	○	Start of route	0.0
0.0	⚑	(Start) Petite Rivière Bridge: Rissers Beach, 5366 NS-331; head west on NS-331 W	17.1
17.1	→	Slight R onto Old Voglers Cove Rd	0.6
17.7	→	Slight R onto NS-331 W	10.1
27.8	↑	Continue onto Old Hwy 3	0.6
28.4	←	L onto Port Medway Rd	1.0
29.4	↑	Cross the road and continue straight	1.1
30.5	←	L to stay on Lighthouse Rte/Port Medway Rd	4.1
34.6	→	R onto Eastern Shore Rd	5.2
39.7	→	R to stay on Eastern Shore Rd	5.5
45.2	←	Slight L onto Brooklyn Shore Rd	5.8
51.0	→	R to stay on Brooklyn Shore Rd	0.7
51.7	←	L onto NS-3 W	3.0
54.7	○	End of route	0.0

15 Liverpool–Carters Beach

MAP 5

Start Point
Liverpool: 162 Old Bridge St.

Summary
Easy ride; coastal views; beach access; bunnies.

Distance (km)	Duration	Max Grade +	Elevation Gain (m)	Unpaved
46.7 (return)	2:07/3:06	6.7	388	—

Description
This route takes you to three incredible beaches along the South Shore. Bring your beach gear and plan to spend time at each of these unique areas, but don't expect the water to be warm—it is known for being fairly brisk in these parts.

SOUTH SHORE

Ride Considerations
- The road can get busy between White Point and Summerville during the summer months with cottage-goers and people visiting the beach.
- Trunk 3 can be a busy road; try to avoid it during peak hours.

Points of Interest
- **White Point Beach Resort (9.1 km)** White Point is a summer tradition for so many Nova Scotian families; visit the beach, try some surfing, have some lunch, and look for the wild bunnies that roam the grounds.
- **Summerville Beach (15.0 km)** This is an incredible white sand beach, considered one of the best on the South Shore.

Liverpool–Carters Beach Cue Sheet

Dist	Type	Note	Next
0.0	⦿	Start of route	0.0
0.0	⚑	(Start) Liverpool: 162 Old Bridge St; head south on Old Bridge St	0.0
0.1	→	R onto Waterloo St	0.4
0.5	↑	Continue onto Lighthouse Rte/White Point Rd/NS-3 W	17.8
18.3	↑	Continue straight onto Lighthouse Rte	1.8
20.1	←	Slight L onto Central Port Mouton Rd	2.5
22.5	↑	Continue straight onto Carters Beach Rd	0.9
23.4	↶	Carters Beach; turnaround point	0.8
24.2	↑	Merge onto Central Port Mouton Rd	2.5
26.7	→	Slight R onto Lighthouse Rte	19.6
46.3	→	Slight R onto Waterloo St	0.4
46.7	←	L onto Old Bridge St	0.0
46.7	⦿	End of route	0.0

- **Carters Beach (23.4 km)** This beach has started to become more popular over the years with its spectacular white sand and clear, cold, turquoise waters. There are no services available here.

16 Western Head (15.4 km, Map 5)

This is an easy loop that leaves from Liverpool and takes you to a working lighthouse on the tip of Western Head. Follow along the Shore Road through quiet residential areas, taking in the ocean views along the way. You might even see some surfers as you round the point, when the conditions are right.

The Western Head Lighthouse was built in 1962 and is 19.2 m tall; it is positioned to mark passage along the western approach to Liverpool Bay.

⑰ Molega Lake

MAP 6

Start Point
South Brookfield: intersection of Trunk 8 and Rte. 208.

Summary
Challenging hills; remote area; some rough roads.

Distance (km)	Duration	Max Grade +	Elevation Gain (m)	Unpaved
78.8	3:36/5:17	4.6	543	—

Description
This ride is a scenic paved loop through north Queens County that circles around Molega Lake from a distance. Stock up on food and water for this one, as it covers a lot of ground in a fairly remote area.

Ride Considerations
- There is a Wilson's gas station in Greenfield with some basic supplies at 29.7 km.
- Caledonia has amenities and is 5 km to the west from where the ride starts and stops.

Side Trips/Variations
- You can finish off the ride on a rail trail that takes you over multiple trestle bridges, providing good swimming and picnic opportunities. Access the ⑲ **Brookfield Mines Trail** in Colpton at 63.5 km. Head west on the trail for 13.5 km until it intersects with Route 208, then head south for 1 km back to your start point.

Points of Interest
- **Camerons Brook Park (4.5 km)** This picnic park has some walking trails and places to sit and relax by the water.

Molega Lake Cue Sheet

Dist	Type	Note	Next
0.0	◉	Start of route	0.0
0.0	⚑	(Start) South Brookfield: intersection of NS-8 and NS-208	0.0
0.0	➡	R onto NS-8	21.4
21.4	⬅	L onto Middlefield Rd	0.9
22.3	⬅	L onto NS-210 E	22.7
45.0	⬅	L onto Knox Rd	4.7
49.7	⬅	L onto NS-325 N	11.6
61.3	⬅	L onto NS-208 W (signs for NS-8/Kejimkujik/Caledonia)	17.5
78.8	◉	End of route	0.0

SOUTH SHORE

18 Caledonia–Westfield

MAP 6

Start Point
Caledonia: parking lot, 25 Co op Store Rd.

Summary
Some challenging hills; remote area; unpaved/rough roads.

Distance (km)	Duration	Max Grade +	Elevation Gain (m)	Unpaved
20.9	0:57/1:24	3.4	153	48% (10 km)

Description
This is a pleasant loop along the backcountry roads of the Caledonia area by way of paved and unpaved gravel roads. Start and finish your ride in the town of Caledonia where there is a restaurant, grocery store, pharmacy, liquor store, and gas station.

Ride Considerations
- This is a remote area; ensure that you have adequate supplies (Caledonia has basic amenities).
- The route is mostly on unpaved and gravel roads, so mountain or cross bikes are best.

Side Trips/Variations
- Combine this ride with 19 Brookfield Mines Trail to make a route totalling 57.5 km; the parking spot is the same for both routes.

Caledonia–Westfield Cue Sheet

Dist	Type	Note	Next
0.0	📍	Start of route	0.0
0.0	▥	(Start) Caledonia: parking lot, 25 Co-op Store Rd; head west on NS-8	0.9
0.9	←	L onto Hibernia Rd	0.2
1.1	→	R onto W Caledonia Rd	4.7
5.8	→	R onto Harmony Rd	4.2
10.0	←	L onto Old Harmony Rd	0.8
10.8	←	L onto NS-8 N	0.2
11.0	→	R onto Old Westfield Rd	5.8
16.8	→	R onto Westfield Rd	4.0
20.8	→	R onto NS-8 N	0.1
20.9	📍	End of route	0.0

⑲ Brookfield Mines Trail (RT)

MAP 6

Start Point
Caledonia: parking lot, 25 Co op Store Rd.

Summary
Easy ride; remote; rail trail; swim spot, kid-friendly.

Distance (km)	Duration	Max Grade +	Elevation Gain (m)	Unpaved
36.5 (return)	1:39/2:26	1.4	153	100% (36.5 km)

Description
This route follows an excellent section of multi-use rail trail between Caledonia and Colpton. There are several nice train bridges to cross along the way: one over the Medway River, and one over Pleasant River. This trail passes through forest, wetlands, and conservation areas that are home to beavers, deer, bear, endangered Blanding's turtles, and many varieties of birds.

Ride Considerations
- This is a remote area; ensure that you have adequate supplies. Caledonia has amenities, but there are no services in Colpton.
- Be aware that the trail will cross many backcountry roads; stay alert to traffic.

Side Trips/Variations
- Combine this ride with ⑱ **Caledonia/Westfield** to make a route totalling 57.5 km; the parking spot is the same for both routes.

Points of Interest
- **Medway River Train Bridge (3.5 km)** A refurbished train bridge and the longest on the Brookfield Mines trail section; it is a good stopping place for picnics, fishing, and swimming.
- **Trailside Bike Shop (11.2 km)** A small bike shop located on an off-grid homestead; it is "open sometimes" and available to help with minor bicycle repairs (902-298-5785).
- **Pleasant River Train Bridge (14.8 km)** Another train bridge with similar attributes.

Note
This ride has no cue sheet because there are no turns. Start by heading east on the trail; the turnaround point is when the trail intersects with Route 208 in Colpton (18.3 km).

SOUTH SHORE

20 Jordan Bay

Start Point
Shelburne: 115 King St.

Summary
Easy ride; coastal views; lighthouse.

Distance (km)	Duration	Max Grade +	Elevation Gain (m)	Unpaved
35.7	1:39/2:25	4.3	254	—

Description
After leaving from Shelburne, visit the Sandy Point Recreation Area to take some photos of the lighthouse and to do some rock-hopping on the beach. As you round the southern point of the peninsula, you will see McNutts Island in the distance, which you can visit by arranging a boat tour in advance. Follow along the water up to Jordan Branch where you will then head west back to your starting point along Trunk 3.

Ride Considerations
• Trunk 3 can be a busy road; try to avoid it during peak hours.

Points of Interest
• **Sandy Point Lighthouse (9.8 km)** This lighthouse is accessible by walking on the sand during low tide; check the tide schedule in advance if you are looking to do the visit by foot.

Jordan Bay Cue Sheet

Dist	Type	Note	Next
0.0	●	Start of route	0.0
0.0	⚑	(Start) Shelburne: 115 King St; head west on NS-3	1.1
1.1	←	L onto Water St (signs for Sandy Point)	0.6
1.7	←	L onto Williams St	0.2
1.9	→	R onto Hammond St/Lighthouse Rte	29.5
31.4	←	L onto Jordan Branch Rd	3.3
34.7	←	L onto King St/NS-3 W	1.0
35.7	●	End of route	0.0

Crow Neck (RT)

MAP 7

Start Point

Barrington: intersection of Forest View Dr. and Lighthouse Route.

Summary

Coastal ride; good roads; beach access; lighthouse.

Distance (km)	Duration	Max Grade +	Elevation Gain (m)	Unpaved
51.5	2:18/3:23	2.3	212	20% (10 km)

Description

This route visits two beautiful beaches and a lighthouse; expect to see many islands, bays, and inlets along the way. In general, the road is curvy, quiet, and in good condition.

Ride Considerations

- On the north side of the route, Lyle Road turns into 10 km of multi-use trail to finish the ride; ensure you have adequate tires.

Points of Interest

- **Sand Hills Beach (4.6 km)** This is a nice white sand beach with mud flats that heat up at low tide, warming the incoming water.
- **Baccaro Point Lighthouse (19.5 km)** The road to the lighthouse is gravel for the last 200 m.
- **Crow Neck Beach (21.5 km)** This is a beautiful and isolated beach; it is also home to the protected piping plovers, so some sections of beach might be closed, depending on when you visit.

Crow Neck (RT) Cue Sheet

Dist	Type	Note	Next
0.0	●	Start of route	0.0
0.0	⚑	(Start) Barrington: intersection of Forest View Dr and Lighthouse Rte	0.0
0.0	←	L onto NS-3 E	0.2
0.2	→	R onto Villagedale Rd/NS-309 N	11.1
11.3	→	R onto Lighthouse Rte/Port Latour Rd	0.8
12.1	→	R to stay on Lighthouse Rte/Port Latour Rd	2.9
15.1	→	R onto Baccaro Rd	3.6
18.6	→	R onto Lighthouse Rd	0.2
18.9	→	R to stay on Lighthouse Rd	0.6
19.5	↩	Baccaro Point Lighthouse; turnaround point	0.6
20.1	←	L to stay on Lighthouse Rd	0.2
20.3	→	R onto Baccaro Rd	5.5
25.8	←	L to stay on Lighthouse Rte/Port Latour Rd	15.5
41.3	←	L onto Shelburne County Rail Trail	10.2
51.5	←	L onto Forest View Dr	0.0
51.5	●	End of route	0.0

SOUTH SHORE

22 Cape Sable Island

MAP 7

Start Point
Barrington Passage: 43 Rte. 330.

Summary
Easy ride; good pavement; beach access; birding area; quiet roads.

Distance (km)	Duration	Max Grade +	Elevation Gain (m)	Unpaved
40.7	1:51/2:42	2.9	181	—

Description
This route is all about the beaches, back roads, and working wharfs. Be sure to explore the many side roads that lead toward the water whenever possible; there are many treasures to be found, especially on the southwest side of the island. Along the way, you will come across islands and inlets, with a view that changes constantly. This is also considered one of the best birding areas in Nova Scotia. Enjoy the smooth paved roads and the feel of the sea-spray coming from the waves as they crash on shore. This area feels remote and a little wild, and is absolutely beautiful.

Ride Considerations
- This area is quite exposed, and it can be fairly windy; it's advised that you bring a windbreaker and maybe an extra layer.
- The start of this ride takes you through a commercial area very briefly; the roads will become quiet after you cross the causeway.
- Most beaches here are part of the Cape Sable Important Bird Area; read the signs and follow the instructions at all beaches to ensure that you are not causing damage to nesting areas.

Points of Interest
- **South Side Beach (16.8 km)** This is a beautiful, expansive, endless-feeling beach; it is accessed at the end of Daniels Head Road, where there is also a working wharf just past the beach area.
- **The Hawk (20.5 km)** This is the most southerly peninsula in the province and is a visual treat with its unique landscape. Visit The Hawk Beach off New Road, a white beach that is actually a 1,500-year-old drowned forest, full of petrified tree stumps. From here you can see the Cape Sable Lighthouse—the tallest in Nova Scotia, at 30.7 m.
- **Clarks Harbour (27.2 km)** This is a large, active fishing village that seems to come out of nowhere; you will find lots of amenities here.

SOUTH SHORE

Cape Sable Island Cue Sheet

Dist	Type	Note	Next
0.0	📍	Start of route	0.0
0.0	🚩	(Start) Barrington Passage: 43 NS-330; head south across the causeway	1.2
1.2	←	L onto Stoney Island Rd (signs for Clam Point)	7.5
8.7	→	R to stay on Stoney Island Rd	2.6
11.3	←	L onto NS-330 S (signs for Clark's Harbour)	0.1
11.4	←	L onto Centreville South Side Rd	4.1
15.5	←	L onto Daniels Head Rd	1.3
16.8	↶	South Side Beach; turnaround point	1.3
18.1	←	L onto Centreville South Side Rd	1.9
20.0	←	L onto Hawk Point Rd	2.4
22.4	↶	Turnaround point	2.5
24.9	←	L onto Centreville South Side Rd/NS-330 N	0.9
25.8	↑	Continue onto Main St/NS-330 N	14.9
40.7	📍	End of route	0.0

SOUTH SHORE

Cyclists will enjoy the smooth paved roads of Cape Sable Island. (BRIANNE STEINMAN)

CYCLING ROUTES
OF YARMOUTH
AND ACADIAN SHORES

Route	Route Name	Distance (km)	Duration	Max Grade +	Elevation Gain (m)	Unpaved	Map
23	Pinkneys Point–Morris Island	87.0	3:57/5:48	4.8	484	—	8
24	Cape Forchu	24.6	1:07/1:38	6.0	193	—	8
25	Port Maitland	52.4	2:23/3:30	5.1	303	—	8
26	Mavillette Beach	27.2	1:14/1:48	5.3	119	—	9
27	Church Point–Meteghan	50.8	2:18/3:23	3.4	165	—	9
28	Weymouth–New Tusket	66.4	3:03/4:28	3.8	421	—	9

Yarmouth and Acadian Shores
Regional Overview

Back in the nineteenth century, the Yarmouth area was a major shipbuilding centre and was also the second largest port of registry in Canada. It was a booming marine town in its day, as evidenced by the many Victorian homes built by successful sea captains. These days, it carries on its marine tradition as home to the largest fishing fleet in Atlantic Canada, and boasts the world's largest lobster fishing grounds.

Touring the area by bicycle presents opportunities to experience the coastline and visit the many working marinas and fishing communities along the way. Take a tour to the Cape Forchu Lighthouse, which has been helping guide ships on this coast for 175 years. Then head up the coast to Port Maitland and on to Mavillette Beach, a particularly lovely area with its long expanses of white sand beach. You are now entering the land of the Acadians, French colonists who were expelled from Nova Scotia between 1755 and 1763 by the British. You will see and hear evidence of Acadian culture throughout your tour of this area.

As you pass through the Municipality of Clare, you will see working marinas and a number of small towns. In Church Point, visit the Église Sainte-Marie Church Museum, the largest wooden church in North America, with a steeple rising 56.4 m above the ground. Be sure to visit an Acadian restaurant while in the area and try the rappie pie, a traditional Acadian dish.

This area has become known for the incredible success of the Gran Fondo Baie Sainte-Marie, a long-distance bike race that brings together riders of all abilities. Started in 2015, this event has grown to be the largest cycling event east of Quebec.

It is a fun and competitive race that showcases the hospitality and unique culture of the area.

Additional Notes
- The rides between Yarmouth and Weymouth are along the coast, which is known for strong and steady winds. Before riding a route in this area, check wind strength and direction. If you're riding against the wind, try to go inland where it is less intense; it's best to have the wind at your back when riding along the coast.
- This area can be a bit cooler than other areas, especially with the wind. It is a good idea to bring a windbreaker or some sort of layering.

Yarmouth and Acadian Shores Bike Shops

- Manser's Bike Shop (Yarmouth) 902-742-0494
- Vélo Baie Sainte-Marie (Saulnierville) 902-769-0221

Yarmouth and Acadian Shores Emergency Services

- Yarmouth Regional Hospital (Yarmouth)

23 Pinkneys Point–Morris Island

MAP 8

Start Point
Arcadia: 23 Last Rd.

Summary
Coastal views; remote.

Distance (km)	Duration	Max Grade +	Elevation Gain (m)	Unpaved
87.0 (return)	3:57/5:48	4.8	484	—

Description
This ride takes you cycling down twisty roads along thin fingers of land, with water on both sides most of the time. Keep going to the end of Pinkneys Point where you will come across a working marina, which is your first turnaround point. Morris Island is reached by a number of causeways, taking you out to the end of the point, where you will see Hog Island to the south.

Ride Considerations
- This area is quite exposed and it can be fairly windy; it's advised that you bring a windbreaker and maybe an extra layer.
- This area can also feel fairly remote; ensure that you have adequate supplies.
- A section of the route toward Morris Island is on Trunk 3, which can be busy; try to avoid this road during peak hours.

Side Trips/Variations
The two legs of this route are both return trips and can be done separately, starting from the same location, to reduce the overall distance:
- Pinkneys Point: 30.8 km return
- Morris Island: 56.2 km return

Pinkneys Point–Morris Island Cue Sheet

Dist	Type	Note	Next
0.0	📍	Start of route	0.0
0.0	🚩	(Start) Arcadia: 23 Last Rd; head east on NS-3	0.1
0.1	→	R onto NS-334 S (signs for Wedgeport)	1.1
1.2	→	R onto Melbourne Rd (signs for Comeaus Hill)	14.2
15.4	↩	Pinkneys Point; turnaround point	14.1
29.5	←	L onto NS-334 N (signs for Arcadia/Yarmouth/NS-3)	1.2
30.7	→	R onto NS-3 E (signs for Shelburne)	9.8
40.5	↑	Continue onto NS-308 S (signs for Amiraults Hill/Sluice Point)	6.5
47.0	←	L onto Chemin des Bouleaux	1.7
48.6	←	Slight L onto NS-308 S	10.1
58.7	↩	Morris Island; turnaround point	10.3
69.0	→	Slight R onto Chemin des Bouleaux	1.7
70.7	→	R onto NS-308 N	7.1
77.8	↑	Continue onto NS-3 W (slight left)	9.2
87.0	📍	End of route	0.0

Cape Forchu

MAP 8

Start Point
Yarmouth: Yarmouth Ferry Terminal, 58 Water St.

Summary
Easy ride; some busy roads; coastal views; lighthouse; beach access.

Distance (km)	Duration	Max Grade +	Elevation Gain (m)	Unpaved
24.6 (return)	1:07/1:38	6.0	193	—

Description
This is a great little ride out of Yarmouth that takes you to a lighthouse museum. Once you get out of town, you will be riding through Yarmouth Bar, which gives you a sense of how exposed to the sea this area really is. You will then continue through a fishing village and past a working wharf loaded with lobster traps, then pass a beautiful white sand beach just before you get to Cape Forchu. Take some time to visit the museum and take in the views; explore the walking trails before heading back the way you came.

Ride Considerations
- This area is quite exposed and it can be fairly windy; it's advised that you bring a windbreaker and maybe an extra layer.

Side Trips/Variations
- Combine this trip with 25 **Port Maitland** by continuing north in Overton, after visiting the lighthouse, making for a route totalling 67.1 km.

Points of Interest
- **Lost to the Sea Memorial (7.9 km)** This is a monument to an area that has lost more than its fair share of people to the sea. There is a nice sitting area here, with a great view toward Yarmouth on the other side of the water.
- **White Sand Beach (11.1 km)** There are two coves here, making for some nice sheltered beach walks.
- **Cape Forchu Lightstation Museum (12.2 km)** This museum is filled with exhibits about the lighthouse, which was built in 1840. You will find some nice walking trails and amazing views here; there are facilities available.

YARMOUTH AND ACADIAN SHORES

Cape Forchu Cue Sheet

Dist	Type	Note	Next
0.0	📍	Start of route	0.0
0.0	🚩	(Start) Yarmouth: Yarmouth Ferry Terminal, 58 Water St; head north on Water St	1.9
1.9	➡	R onto Cann St	0.1
2.0	⬅	L onto Evangeline Trail/Main St/NS-1 E	0.2
2.2	⬅	L onto Vancouver St/NS-304 S (signs for Hospital/Sandford/Yarmouth Light)	0.7
2.9	⬅	L onto Grove Rd/NS-304 S (signs for Overton/Pembroke/Yarmouth Bar)	4.0

6.9	➡	R onto Yarmouth Bar Rd/NS-304 S	5.4
12.3	↩	Cape Forchu Lighthouse; turnaround point	0.1
12.4	⬅	L toward NS-304 N	7.2
19.6	➡	R onto Grove Road/NS-304 N	2.1
21.7	➡	R onto Vancouver St/NS-304 N	0.7
22.4	➡	R onto Evangeline Trail/Main St/NS-1 W	0.2
22.6	➡	R onto Cann St	0.1
22.7	⬅	L onto Water St	1.9
24.6	📍	End of route	0.0

25 Port Maitland

MAP 8

Start Point
Yarmouth: Yarmouth Ferry Terminal, 58 Water St.

Summary
Moderate ride; some busy roads; coastal views; beach access.

Distance (km)	Duration	Max Grade +	Elevation Gain (m)	Unpaved
52.4	2:23/3:30	5.1	303	—

Description
This route will take you through rolling countryside on your way to the beautiful Port Maitland Beach Provincial Park on quiet, rural roads. After the beach, the ride brings you via an inland route back to Yarmouth to complete the loop.

Ride Considerations
- The route connects with Route 340 and Trunk 1 coming into Yarmouth, both of which can be busy roads; try to avoid them during peak times.
- Some basic supplies are available in Port Maitland.

Side Trips/Variations
- Combine this trip with ㉔ Cape Forchu by continuing south in Overton, making for a route totalling 67.1 km.

Points of Interest

- **Pembroke Beach (7.3 km)** This is a quiet, unassuming beach not far from Yarmouth; access it by turning down Helen Lucy Road.
- **Port Maitland Beach Provincial Park (23.9 km)** A large and beautiful crescent beach; perfect for a picnic and beachcombing.

Port Maitland Cue Sheet

Dist	Type	Note	Next
0.0	⚲	Start of route	0.0
0.0	⚑	(Start) Yarmouth: Yarmouth Ferry Terminal, 58 Water St; head north on Water St	1.9
1.9	→	R onto Cann St	0.1
2.0	←	L onto Evangeline Trail/Main St/NS-1 E	0.2
2.2	←	L onto Vancouver St/NS-304 S (signs for Hospital/Sandford/Yarmouth Light)	0.7
2.9	←	L onto Grove Rd/NS-304 S (signs for Overton/Pembroke/Yarmouth Bar)	2.1
5.0	→	R onto Overton Rd	1.2
6.2	←	L onto Pembroke Rd/Shore Rd	6.0
12.2	←	L onto Main Shore Rd	5.2
17.4	→	R onto Lake Darling Rd	2.3
19.7	←	L onto NS-1 E (signs for Halifax)	3.3
23.0	←	L onto Main Shore Rd	0.6
23.7	→	R onto Spider Rd	0.3
23.9	↷	Port Maitland Provincial Park; turnaround point	0.3
24.2	←	L onto Main Shore Rd	0.6
24.8	→	R onto NS-1 W	0.9
25.8	←	L onto Richmond Rd (signs for Richmond Road/Lake George)	6.7
32.5	↑	Continue straight onto Lake George Rd	8.6
41.1	→	Slight R onto NS-340 S	4.4
45.5	←	L onto Evangeline Trail/NS-1 W (signs for Yarmouth)	4.9
50.4	→	R onto Cann St	0.1
50.5	←	L onto Water St	1.9
52.4	⚲	End of route	0.0

㉖ Mavillette Beach

MAP 9

Start Point
Meteghan: 8226 Trunk 1.

Summary
Easy ride; often windy; lighthouse; beach access.

Distance (km)	Duration	Max Grade +	Elevation Gain (m)	Unpaved
27.2 (return)	1:14/1:48	5.3	119	—

Description
Most of this ride is slightly inland from the coast, so you will not be riding along the water, but when you get to Mavillette you will be treated to a beautiful area with long stretches of white sand beach. The houses here are a mix of old and new, many of them with weathered cedar shingles. Cruise along the roads, taking in the views, and take your time strolling along Mavillette and Cape St. Marys Beaches. The route back is the way you came.

Ride Considerations
- This area gets very windy, usually coming from the southwest; be prepared for cooler temperatures and slower riding in one direction.
- Trunk 1 is the main road through the area; try to avoid it during peak hours.

Side Trips/Variations
- Combine this trip with ㉗ **Church Point–Meteghan** to add another 50.8 km to your ride.

Points of Interest
- **Smugglers Cove Provincial Park (2.6 km)** Take a hike down into a gorgeous cove where smugglers used to hide their rum from the authorities during prohibition.

Mavillette Beach Cue Sheet

Dist	Type	Note	Next
0.0	📍	Start of route	0.0
0.0	🚩	(Start) Meteghan: 8226 NS-1; head south on NS-1 W	12.6
12.6	→	R onto John Doucette Rd	2.3
14.9	→	R onto Cape St Marys Rd	1.5
16.4	←	L onto Evangeline Trail/NS-1 E (signs for Meteghan)	10.7
27.2	📍	End of route	0.0

- **Mavillette Beach (14.9 km)** This is a stunning 1.5 km white sand beach; you will sometimes see surfers here because it is one of the few beaches in this corner of the province that gets a decent surf break.
- **Cape Saint Mary Lighthouse Park (14.9 km)** This is a short diversion after Mavillette Beach; access it by following Cape St. Marys Road to its end and hiking up the hill.

27 Church Point–Meteghan

MAP 9

Start Point
Church Point: Church Point Social Club, 1838 Trunk 1.

Summary
Some challenging hills; often windy; coastal views.

Distance (km)	Duration	Max Grade +	Elevation Gain (m)	Unpaved
50.8	2:18/3:23	3.4	165	—

Description
This route combines coastal and inland roads for a nice mix of riding. The route starts on the inland portion directly upon leaving Church Point, coming back to the coast just south of Meteghan. The rest of the ride is directly along the coast, with great views of the water all the way back to your starting point.

Ride Considerations • Check wind direction and strength before starting this ride, as winds can be strong along the coast. The wind is much less intense on the inland portion, so it can be preferable to ride this section against the wind.
• Trunk 1 is the main road through the area; try to avoid it during peak hours.

Side Trips/Variations
• Visit Mavillette Beach to add another 27.2 km to your ride; see 26 Mavillette Beach for more details.
• Combine this route with 28 Weymouth–New Tusket to make your own version of the Grand Fondo.

Points of Interest
• Église Sainte-Marie Church Museum Stop in and visit the largest wooden church in North America, with a steeple rising 56.4 m above the ground. This is very near the start/finish point for this ride.

Church Point–Meteghan Cue Sheet

Dist	Type	Note	Next
0.0	◉	Start of route	0.0
0.0	⚑	(Start) Church Point: Church Point Social Club, 1838 NS-1; head south on Patrice Rd	6.7
6.7	→	R onto Second Division Rd	5.1
11.8	←	L onto Saulnierville Rd	2.7
14.5	→	R onto Bangor Rd	3.7
18.2	→	R onto Maza Rd	0.4
18.6	←	L onto Bangor Rd	1.2
19.8	←	L onto Placide Comeau Rd	1.4
21.2	→	R onto 2 Division Rd	6.8
28.0	→	R onto Meteghan Conn	3.1
31.1	→	R onto NS-1 E	19.7
50.8	→	R onto Patrice Rd	0.0
50.8	◉	End of route	0.0

Start Point

Belliveaus Cove: Joseph and Marie Dugas Municipal Park, 3255 Trunk 1.

Summary

Some challenging hills; often windy; coastal views.

Distance (km)	Duration	Max Grade +	Elevation Gain (m)	Unpaved
66.4	3:03/4:28	3.8	421	—

Description

This is one of three rides that have been adapted from the Gran Fondo Baie Sainte-Marie (the largest cycling event east of Quebec); it combines coastal and inland roads for a nice mix of riding. Leaving Belliveaus Cove, you start by heading north to New Edinburgh and cycling around the peninsula. Very soon after, you will head inland for most of the ride until you reach Church Point, when you hit the coast once again. Finish the ride with the wind at your back, returning to where you started.

Ride Considerations

- Check wind direction and strength before starting this ride, as winds can be strong along the coast. The wind is much less intense on the inland portion, so it can be preferable to ride this section against the wind.
- Trunk 1 is the main road through the area; try to avoid it during peak hours.

Side Trips/Variations

- Combine this route with **27 Church Point–Meteghan** to make your own version of the Grand Fondo.

Weymouth–New Tusket Cue Sheet

Dist	Type	Note	Next
0.0	♀	Start of route	0.0
0.0	⚑	(Start) Belliveaus Cove: Joseph and Marie Dugas Municipal Park, 3255 NS-1; head north on NS-1 E	3.2
3.2	←	L onto Riverside Rd	8.8
12.0	→	R onto Evangeline Trail/NS-1 W (signs for NS-101/Saint Bernard)	1.1
13.1	←	L onto Petit Paradis Rd	0.8
13.9	←	L onto Townshipline Rd	3.5
17.4	↑	Continue onto NS-340 S	21.9
39.3	→	R onto Patrice Rd	7.9
47.1	→	R to stay on Patrice Rd	12.2
59.3	→	R onto Evangeline Trail/NS-1 E (signs for Weymouth/Digby)	7.1
66.4	♀	End of route	0.0

YARMOUTH AND ACADIAN SHORES

CYCLING ROUTES OF BAY OF FUNDY: ANNAPOLIS VALLEY

Route	Route Name	Distance (km)	Duration	Max Grade +	Elevation Gain (m)	Unpaved	Map
29	Digby Neck	72.4	3:17/4:49	8.1	586	—	10
30	Digby Lighthouse	18.0	0:49/1:12	5.3	258	—	10
31	Kejimkujik: Fire Tower Trail	35.8	1:37/2:23	6.0	326	100% (36 km)	6
32	Kejimkujik: Jakes Landing–New Grafton	17.6	0:48/1:10	3.8	117	—	6
33	Bear River	21.0	0:57/1:24	6.6	247	—	11
34	Annapolis Royal–Milford	58.8	2:40/3:55	8.1	635	—	11
35	Annapolis Royal: Fort-to-Fort	52.1	2:22/3:28	3.4	347	—	11
36	Annapolis Royal–Bridgetown Loop	47.2	2:08/3:08	5.2	423	—	12
37	Annapolis Royal: North Mountain	62.0	2:49/4:08	10.1	824	—	12
38	Bridgetown: North Mountain	49.2	2:14/3:16	7.3	576	—	12
39	Middleton: North Mountain	50.8	2:18/3:23	8.2	610	—	12
40	Harvest Moon Trailway (RT)	110.0	5:00/7:20	2.7	395	98% (108 km)	13
41	Berwick–Harbourville	33.6	1:31/2:14	9.6	456	—	14
42	Canning–Scots Bay	49.1	1:59/2:55	11.5	555	6% (3 km)	15
43	Starrs Point Loop	48.0	2:10/3:12	5.5	326	—	15
44	Variation: Starrs Point Loop Extension	79.9	3:38/5:20	8.6	749	—	15
45	Wolfville Wine Tour (RT)	29.4	1:20/1:57	9.5	362	17% (5 km)	17
46	Wolfville Area: Winery, Brewery, and Distillery Tour (RT)	76.0	3:27/5:04	10.1	755	11% (8 km)	16
47	Gaspereau Valley	43.5	1:58/2:54	8.8	629	62% (27 km)	17
48	Bishopville–Sunken Lake	73.0	3:19/4:52	6.8	777	38% (28 km)	16

ANNAPOLIS VALLEY

Bay of Fundy: Annapolis Valley Regional Overview

The North and South Mountains run parallel to the Bay of Fundy from Digby to Wolfville, creating a fertile valley with a unique microclimate that results in mild temperatures, which, combined with glacial sedimentary soils, make this excellent farming country. The Annapolis Valley is known for its farm markets, apple orchards, and vineyards.

On the southwest side of the Valley you will find Digby Neck, a long spit of land that is the western extension of the North Mountain; it is interrupted briefly by a deep channel called the Digby Gut. This area is known for its exceptional whale watching, especially around Brier Island. Inland from Digby is Bear River, a small village built partly on stilts over the tidal Bear River, and home to many galleries that feature local artists. This area is known as "Little Switzerland" because of the steep hills coming into town from every direction.

Nearby is Annapolis Royal, a town rich in history and bustling with charm. This is where you will find the local farmers' market, as well as the revered Annapolis Royal Historic Gardens. When you are here, you can access the ⓭ **Harvest Moon Trailway**, which will take you all the way to Grand Pré via a converted railway bed. This trail opened in 2017 with a lot of excitement; it allows cyclists to finally tour the Annapolis Valley without riding on busy roads. The trail runs along the valley floor, passing through or beside many small towns that can be easily accessed.

> ### Annapolis Valley Bike Shops
>
> - Banks Bikes (Wolfville) 902-542-2596
> - Oakhaven Bike Barn (Belleisle) 902-665-5044
> - Valley Stove and Cycle (Kentville) 902-542-7280

> ### Annapolis Valley Emergency Services
>
> - Digby General Hospital (Digby)
> - Annapolis Community Health Centre (Annapolis Royal)
> - Soldiers' Memorial Hospital (Middleton)
> - Valley Regional Hospital (Kentville)

Travelling along the top of North Mountain provides the opportunity to experience the Bay of Fundy, home to the world's highest tides. The Bay of Fundy's unique shape creates a situation where the tide is amplified up to 16 m, making for a dramatic shoreline that is constantly in flux. The tides change, on average, every six hours and thirteen minutes, allowing you the opportunity to see either of the extremes at least once a day. Along the North Mountain you will also see some beautiful fishing communities, including Halls Harbour, famous for big lobster feasts at a local restaurant. On the eastern extreme of the mountain is Cape Split, one of the most popular hikes in Nova Scotia. Cape Split is said to be home to Glooscap, a legendary figure in Mi'kmaw and other Indigenous cultures.

On the eastern end of the Valley is the town of Kentville, where you can visit Miners March, a protected wetland area, and the Gorge, one of the premiere mountain biking trail networks in the province. Just a little farther along is Wolfville, home to Acadia University, and the hub of the region's burgeoning wine industry. Wolfville is a dynamic town known for its local food and drink, and home to the Devour! festival, the largest food film festival in the world.

East of Wolfville is historic Grand Pré, a designated UNESCO World Heritage Site, and the area where the Acadians were forcefully deported from Nova Scotia—a tragic event that happened more than 250 years ago. The Gaspereau Valley lies just over the hill, and here you will find numerous wineries nestled together, all within close proximity, creating a cycling experience that's unlike any other ride in the province.

Additional Notes

- The Wharf Rat motorcycle rally happens annually in the Digby area at the end of August. It is wise to avoid cycling trips to this area during the event because of the increased traffic.

The variety of cycling routes in the Annapolis Valley means that there is something for all types of riders. (WE'RE OUTSIDE)

A group of cyclists enjoy a ride along the grassy dykeland in Nova Scotia's Annapolis Valley. (WE'RE OUTSIDE)

ANNAPOLIS VALLEY

29 Digby Neck

MAP 10

Start Point
Digby: Digby Area Recreation, 27 Shreve St.

Summary
Some challenging hills; coastal views; beach access; swimming spot; side trips.

Distance (km)	Duration	Max Grade +	Elevation Gain (m)	Unpaved
72.4 (one way)	3:17/4:49	8.1	586	—

Description
This is a special trip that most people will make into an overnight, as it is a fairly long haul from Digby to Brier Island. Part of its charm is that you have to take two small ferries to get to Brier Island, which allows for moments to pause and take in the surrounding beauty of this unique area. Although the cycling route is surrounded by water, you'll have fewer ocean views than expected. To get the best views, be sure to take the suggested side trips out to the coves and attractions. All of the side trips are either on or very close to the main road, so they will not add significant distance to your trip.

Brier Island is the westernmost part of Nova Scotia and the southernmost end of the North Mountain Ridge that makes up one half of the Annapolis Valley. It is also the childhood home of Joshua Slocum, the first person to circumnavigate the world alone in a sailboat. He set forth on his historic journey from Sambro Island, near Halifax, on July 3, 1895, and returned nearly three years later after having travelled more than 74,000 km. There is a monument to Slocum in the town of Westport. Enjoy walking and cycling around the town; it is a little piece of paradise at what is truly the end of the line.

Ride Considerations
- Getting to and from Brier Island requires taking two ferries. Call in advance to find out schedules and plan this into the timing of your day; there is no fee for walking on with your bicycles. (Petit Passage to Tiverton Ferry: **902-839-2302**; Freeport to Westport Ferry: **902-839-2882**.)
- There will usually be a headwind going down the Neck, so be prepared for this.
- If you are planning on doing an overnight, book your accommodation in Brier Island well in advance, as there are not a lot of options.
- Time your trip to avoid the Wharf Rat Rally, a massive motorcycle gathering that takes place in Digby, usually around the end of August or in early September.

ANNAPOLIS VALLEY

- Bring along some hiking shoes and swimwear if you are considering any of the many side trips and destinations along this route.

Side Trips/Variations
- This ride can be shortened into a more manageable day ride by parking at the Digby Neck Consolidated School in Sandy Cove (80 km return). There is also a café in the school, open Tuesday through Saturday during the summer months, and every Saturday during the school year.
- Some people have turned this into a round trip by staying overnight on Brier Island and then getting a boat over to Meteghan to finish the ride on the other side of St. Marys Bay. Call the local boat tour companies to see if this can be arranged. Availability and cost will vary depending on schedules and how many people want to get across.
- We highly recommend that you sign up for a whale-watching tour while you're in the area; Brier Island is considered to be one of the best places to see whales in Nova Scotia.

Points of Interest
- **Gullivers Cove (14.0 km)** This is a beautiful spot that has an 800 m hike to some very impressive views out along Digby Neck and Gullivers Cove; access the cove by following Gullivers Cove Road.
- **Lake Midway Provincial Park (26 km)** A great spot for a freshwater swim and for a pit stop.
- **Sandy Cove Beach (31.9 km)** This is a stunning beach, just a few minutes off your route. To access, follow Bay Road to Champlain Road.
- **Balancing Rock (52.2 km)** This is one of the highlights of the route, and one of Digby Neck's most popular attractions. Hike down to a narrow column of basalt that is balanced on its tip, seemingly defying the laws of physics. Access via a groomed 2.5 km trail directly off the road.
- **Brier Island Lighthouse (Finish)** This is officially the end of the line. The first lighthouse was built here in 1809. The lighthouse has since been torn down, rebuilt, burnt down, and then rebuilt again numerous times.

Digby Neck Cue Sheet

Dist	Type	Note	Next
0.0	◉	Start of route	0.0
0.0	⚑	(Start) Digby: Digby Area Recreation, 27 Shreve St; head east on Shreve St	0.1
0.1	←	L onto Victoria St/NS-303 N	0.4
0.5	←	L onto NS-217 W (signs for Digby Neck/Brier Island/Long Island)	47.0
47.5	↑	Ride the ferry from East Ferry to Tiverton	0.8
48.3	←	L onto NS-217 W	17.5
65.8	←	L onto ferry ramp	0.1
65.9	↑	Ride the ferry from Freeport to Westport	1.5
67.4	↑	Continue straight onto ferry wharf	0.1
67.5	←	L onto Water St	0.6
68.1	→	R onto Wellington St	0.7
68.8	←	Wellington St turns slightly L and becomes Lighthouse Rd	3.6
72.4	◉	End of route	0.0

Digby Lighthouse
(18 km, Map 10)

There is a quick and easy trip out of Digby to visit the Point Prim Lighthouse where you can take in fantastic views of New Brunswick across the Bay of Fundy, and of Victoria Beach across the Digby Gut. There are some nice hiking trails here and it is a great place for rock-hopping and walking the shore.

Access the lighthouse by following Lighthouse Road out of Digby. You can return the way you came, or choose to take a scenic ride on the partly unpaved Shore Road, following the water.

31 Kejimkujik: Fire Tower Trail

MAP 6

Start Point
Kejimkujik National Park: Grafton Lake parking lot.

Summary
Challenging hills; unpaved/rough roads; remote; some lake views; kid-friendly.

Distance (km)	Duration	Max Grade +	Elevation Gain (m)	Unpaved
35.8 (return)	1:37/2:23	6.0	326	100% (36 km)

Description
This ride starts at the Grafton Lake parking lot in Kejimkujik and follows dirt roads to Eel Weir Bridge, the original site of a Mi'kmaw fishing weir. Up to this point, the trail is on an old service road, but then turns rougher and starts to weave through a unique old growth forest of sugar maple and yellow birch toward an abandoned fire tower. There will be a final steep climb to the high point of land where the tower sits—and your destination awaits.

Ride Considerations
- This is a remote area; ensure that you have adequate supplies.
- The route is on dirt roads and trail and is best for mountain or cross bikes.
- Facilities at Kejimkujik are open from mid-May (the Victoria Day long weekend) until the last weekend of October; roads remain open outside these dates, but they are not maintained in the winter.

- The fee for day-use in the park is approximately $6 per person, with different rates for youth and seniors.

Side Trips/Variations
- To shorten this ride, park at Eel Weir Bridge and head out from there; this makes a 19.6 km return trip. (The road going to Eel Weir closes after Thanksgiving and re-opens in April when conditions allow. Access is still available for riding by parking in the Grafton Lake area and cycling from there.)
- Make this ride longer by adding **32 Kejimkujik: Jakes Landing–New Grafton**. Connect by continuing north past the parking lot to Jakes Landing, where the route begins.

Kejimkujik National Park

Visit the official Kejimkujik National Park website for the most up-to-date information: pc.gc.ca/en/pn-np/ns/kejimkujik.

Kejimkujik: Fire Tower Trail Cue Sheet

Dist	Type	Note	Next
0.0	📍	Start of route	0.0
0.0	🏁	(Start) Kejimkujik National Park: Grafton Lake parking lot	0.1
0.1	←	L onto Eel Weir Rd	17.9
18.0	↩	Fire Tower; turnaround point	9.9
27.9	↑	Continue onto Eel Weir Rd	7.9
35.8	→	R onto Kejimkujik Main Parkway	0.0

Points of Interest
- **Eel Weir Bridge (7.9 km)** A good place for a picnic or swim before or after heading up to see the fire tower.
- **Fire Tower (17.9 km)** Visit an old, out of service National Park fire tower. This is a great place to stop and have a picnic; check out the tower and ranger cabin before heading back the way you came.

 ## Kejimkujik: Jakes Landing–New Grafton (17.6 km, Map 6)

While in the park, take a short ride on a fairly flat (and sometimes rough) mix of pavement, gravel roads, and trail to the farming community of New Grafton. Start by taking the unpaved road through the woods, opposite the entrance to Jakes Landing; this will take you to New Grafton.

Head west on Grafton Road for 1.8 km before turning right, staying on Grafton Road until you reach Trunk 8. Turn left onto the main road, then quickly left again to get back into the park on Kejimkujik Main Parkway; follow this road back to Jakes Landing.

33 Bear River

MAP 11

Start Point
Bear River: 1277 River Rd.

Summary
Challenging hills; steep descent; river and coastal views; local food/drink.

Distance (km)	Duration	Max Grade +	Elevation Gain (m)	Unpaved
21.0	0:57/1:24	6.6	247	—

Description

Bear River is a special spot. It's one of those places that is home to a creative crowd, with numerous art galleries displaying works by many talented local residents. Maybe its appeal has something to do with the mighty tidal river here (some homes and businesses are built on stilts to accommodate the rising waters), or maybe it's because it's surrounded by hills on all sides, creating a sense that it truly is its own little world.

The ride out of town leaves on one of the less intense hills, following the Bear River toward the Bay of Fundy on a lazy sort of road with lots of water views. After crossing the highway overpass, you will enter Smiths Cove, a mixed residential area (and home to Lazy Bear Brewing, open Thursday evenings), and continue heading toward Digby. This stretch of road passes by cottage country and provides some nice views of the Digby Gut and the Bay of Fundy. After turning inland, you'll encounter a stretch of road that is fairly nondescript, but as you see signs for Bear River you will crest one more hill and be treated to a beautiful expanse of farmland.

The final stretch of the ride is a very steep descent (11.4% grade) coming into Bear River, along a very twisty road. Pay close attention to "steep grade" signs and brake accordingly, as there is a blind corner and an odd intersection as you come into town. Finish off the ride with a hot drink at Sissiboo Coffee Roaster, and check out the local artists' shops in the area.

Bear River Cue Sheet

Dist	Type	Note	Next
0.0	●	Start of route	0.0
0.0	⚑	(Start) Bear River: 1277 River Rd; head toward town on River Rd	0.1
0.1	↑	Continue onto Lansdowne Rd	0.0
0.1	←	L onto River Rd	3.8
3.9	→	Slight R to stay on River Rd	2.5
6.4	↑	Continue onto NS-1 W	5.2
11.6	↑	Continue onto Back Rd	2.9
14.5	←	L onto Lansdowne Rd	6.4
20.9	→	R onto River Rd	0.1
21.0	●	End of route	0.0

Ride Considerations
- There is no cell service in the town of Bear River.
- The last part of this ride has a very steep hill as you come into town; take it slow; there are sharp corners and you enter the town quickly.

Side Trips/Variations
- Combine this ride with **34 Annapolis Royal–Milford** to make an epic 95.3 km ride. Follow Lansdowne Road east out of town, which turns into Clementsvale Road, which will connect you with the other ride when you reach the intersection of Clementsport Road.
- Combine this trip with **30 Digby Lighthouse**, adding another 27 km to your ride. Take the rail trail to get into Digby: access it in Smith Cove via Back Road North (10.8 km); get onto the trail at the end of the cul-de-sac and head west.

---

34 Annapolis Royal–Milford   MAP 11

Start Point
Annapolis Royal: 38 Prince Albert Rd.

Summary
Undulating hills; some rough roads; beach/lake access.

Distance (km)	Duration	Max Grade +	Elevation Gain (m)	Unpaved
58.8	2:40/3:55	8.1	635	—

Description
This is a great ride that leaves Annapolis Royal by following along the Annapolis Basin before heading inland, to continue along the West Moose River on a slow, gradual climb. After passing Clementsvale, you will be heading inland down to Raven Haven, a popular swim spot that feels like an old-school summer camp with its lifeguards and canteen. Getting on Trunk 8, you will head north along twisty roads with lots of lakes, marshlands, and some old cemeteries. Take some time to stop for a swim, or walk along the river in Mickey Hill Picnic Park before finishing with a nice 9 km descent back to Annapolis Royal.

ANNAPOLIS VALLEY

Ride Considerations

- The ride starts on Trunk 1 out of Annapolis Royal, which can be a busy road; try to avoid it during peak hours.
- Raven Haven is a seasonal facility; if you are riding in the shoulder seasons, it is advised to call first if you are expecting to use the canteen or other amenities.

Side Trips/Variations

- Combine this ride with ❸❸ Bear River to make a 95.3 km ride. Head west on Clementsvale Road (19.6 km); this will take you into Bear River along fast, undulating hills.

Points of Interest

- **Raven Haven (33.7 km)** A very popular, and often busy, swim spot; in peak season, there is a canteen to get refreshments.
- **Mickey Hill Picnic Park (48.2 km)** This is a quiet park where you can sit by the stream and relax, or walk along the trails through a hardwood forest to a beautiful swim spot on a lake. The sign for the park is not obvious, so keep your eyes peeled.

Annapolis Royal–Milford Cue Sheet

Dist	Type	Note	Next
0.0	◉	Start of route	0.0
0.0	⚑	(Start) Annapolis Royal: 38 Prince Albert Rd; head west on NS-1 W	12.8
12.8	←	L onto Clementsport Rd	6.7
19.5	←	L onto Clementsvale Rd	2.9
22.4	→	R onto Virginia Rd	13.3
35.7	←	L onto NS-8 N	23.0
58.7	←	L onto Evangeline Trail/NS-1 W (signs for Digby)	0.1
58.8	◉	End of route	0.0

(35) Annapolis Royal: Fort-to-Fort

Start Point
Annapolis Royal: Fort Anne National Historic Site, 323 St. George St.

Easy ride; quiet road; paved shoulders; historic sites; kid-friendly.

Distance (km)	Duration	Max Grade +	Elevation Gain (m)	Unpaved
25.0 or 52.1 (both return)	2:22/3:28	3.4	347	—

Description
This is a relaxing route that takes you from one historic military fort to another. Start your ride in the picturesque town of Annapolis Royal at the Fort Anne National Historic Site, historically one of the most contested pieces of land in North America. Cycle through town, heading to Granville Ferry, where you will follow Granville Road along the westerly edge of North Mountain, which shelters you from the wind off the Bay of Fundy. The road along here was paved with shoulders in 2018, making for a comfortable ride.

Upon arrival, take some time to explore the Port-Royal National Historic Site, one of the first European Settlements in North America, which features a reconstruction of the settlement's early seventeenth-century buildings. At this point, you can turn around, making this a 25 km ride, or you can carry on toward Victoria Beach, where you will find a working wharf that has a fantastic view of the Digby Gut and the ferry that travels back and forth from Saint John, NB. After the wharf, there are a couple of kilometres of punchy hills along a very tight, narrow, and twisty road; this can be fun if you have some extra energy and are craving a bit of burn. Ride this until you hit the gravel road and then turn around. You will be taking the same road back to Annapolis Royal, where you can then finish the day visiting shops, checking out the historic gardens, and grabbing a meal at one of the many eateries.

Ride Considerations
- This area is prone to fog, which can roll in unexpectedly.
- This is a fairly quiet road and there are new paved shoulders from Granville Ferry to Port Royal.
- If you are reading a map, it will look like you can do a loop up the mountain after Victoria Beach, but this is not a viable route: the road turns to dirt and is overgrown, making it impassable.
- To avoid cycling through downtown Annapolis Royal, start the ride in Granville Ferry (236 Prince Albert Road).

ANNAPOLIS VALLEY

Side Trips/Variations

- The route from fort to fort is 25 km (return); this is the best section if you are travelling with children or want to ride a shorter distance.

Points of Interest

- **Fort Anne National Historic Site (Start/Stop)** Walk around the fort and learn about why it was such an important part of this area's history.
- **Tidal Power Project (1.4 km)** Stop and visit an interpretive centre of the only tidal power plant in North America.

Annapolis Royal: Fort-to-Fort Cue Sheet

Dist	Type	Note	Next
0.0	◉	Start of route	0.0
0.0	⚑	(Start) Annapolis Royal: Fort Anne National Historic Site, 323 St George St; head west on St George St	0.1
0.1	→	R onto St Anthony St	0.9
1.0	←	L onto NS-1 E	1.2
2.2	←	L onto Granville Rd	23.9
26.1	↷	Turnaround point	23.9
50.0	→	R onto NS-1 W (signs for Annapolis Royal)	1.2
51.2	→	R onto St Anthony St	0.8
52.0	←	L onto St George St	0.1
52.1	◉	End of route	0.0

- **Port-Royal National Historic Site (12.2 km)** This is a living history museum featuring a reconstruction of the seventeenth-century settlement.

---

36 Annapolis Royal–Bridgetown Loop

MAP 12

Start Point
Annapolis Royal: 236 Prince Albert Rd.

Summary
Some busy roads; rolling hills; rail trail option.

Distance (km)	Duration	Max Grade +	Elevation Gain (m)	Unpaved
47.2	2:08/3:08	5.2	423	—

Description
This is an excellent loop that starts out fairly flat, with good pavement all the way to Bridgetown. The ride is along on Trunk 1, a wide road that follows along the Annapolis River, providing some excellent views. The way back on Route 201 follows the other side of the river and is full of rolling hills with some steep, short sections mixed with longer, steadier grades.

Ride Considerations

- Trunk 1 can be a busy road; try to avoid it during peak hours.
- Route 201 is generally a quiet road, but it can get busy during peak hours.
- There are limited food options between Annapolis Royal and Bridgetown (25 km) and only a few options in Bridgetown itself.

Side Trips/Variations

- There is an option to get on the ④ Harvest Moon Trailway on the south side of the Annapolis River in Bridgetown; access via the parking lot at the End of the Line Pub.
- Another variation of this ride is to do the ㉟ Annapolis Royal: North Mountain loop for a longer, more challenging ride.
- This ride can be started in Bridgetown instead of Annapolis Royal.

Annapolis Royal–Bridgetown Loop Cue Sheet

Dist	Type	Note	Next
0.0	◉	Start of route	0.0
0.0	⚑	(Start) Annapolis Royal: 236 Prince Albert Rd	0.0
0.0	➡	R onto NS-1 E	22.1
22.1	➡	R onto Queen St	0.6
22.7	↑	Continue onto South St	0.7
23.4	➡	Slight R to stay on South St (signs for NS-201 W/Annapolis Royal)	0.1
23.5	➡	R onto NS-201 W	20.9
44.4	➡	R onto St George St/NS-8 N (Annapolis Royal)	1.4
45.8	➡	R onto Evangeline Trail/NS-1 E	1.3
47.1	➡	R into parking lot	0.1
47.2	◉	End of route	0.0

㉟ Annapolis Royal: North Mountain

MAP 12

Start Point
Annapolis Royal: 236 Prince Albert Rd.

Summary
Challenging hills; variable road conditions; steep descent; coastal views; lighthouse.

Distance (km)	Duration	Max Grade +	Elevation Gain (m)	Unpaved
62.0	2:49/4:08	10.1	824	—

Description

This is a great ride if you are looking for a little challenge. As you leave Annapolis Royal, you quickly start climbing the North Mountain toward the Bay of Fundy. Once at the top, you will be treated to quality roads with very low traffic and excellent views. Enjoy the dreamy ride along the coast, stopping in to visit the Hampton Lighthouse before your descent down the mountain. Ride through

ANNAPOLIS VALLEY

Bridgetown and across the river to Route 201, where you will be treated to small rolling hills all the way back to Annapolis Royal.

Ride Considerations

- There are no amenities along Shore Road on the top of the North Mountain.
- Hampton Mountain Road is steep (10% grade) and has some very fast, sharp corners; ride down with caution and be on the lookout for hazards.
- If you want take a different route down the mountain, be aware that Youngs Mountain Road is gravel, and so is the lower half of Phinney Mountain Road. It is advised to avoid these, especially on the descent.

Annapolis Royal: North Mountain Cue Sheet

Dist	Type	Note	Next
0.0	📍	Start of route	0.0
0.0	🏁	(Start) Annapolis Royal: 236 Prince Albert Rd	0.0
0.0	→	R onto NS-1 E	2.2
2.2	←	L onto Parker Mountain Rd	6.1
8.3	→	R onto Shore Rd W	19.4
27.7	→	R onto Hampton Mountain Rd	9.4
37.1	→	R onto NS-1 W	0.1
37.2	←	L onto Queen St	0.5
37.7	↑	Continue onto South St	0.8
38.5	→	R onto NS-201 W	20.9
59.4	→	R onto St George St/NS-8 (signs for Annapolis Royal)	1.4
60.8	→	R onto Evangeline Trail/NS-1 E (signs for Bridgetown/Halifax)	1.1
61.9	→	R into parking lot	0.1
62.0	📍	End of route	0.0

Side Trips/Variations

- Combine this trip with ㊳ Bridgetown: North Mountain loop for a total of 92.2 km.
- You have the option to get on the ㊵ Harvest Moon Trailway in Bridgetown. Access from the parking lot at the End of the Line Pub; this will take you back to Annapolis Royal along a rail trail.
- This ride can be started in Bridgetown instead of Annapolis Royal.

Points of Interest

- **Hampton Lighthouse (26.8 km)** Access via Hampton Wharf Road, just before you turn to come down the mountain.
- **Valley View Park (32.4 km)** This a nice park, just before the steepest section coming down the mountain. It's worth taking a short hike to the look-off area where there are a couple of benches; the view is spectacular.

Visit the scenic Hampton Lighthouse before you continue down the North Mountain.
(DEB RYAN)

ANNAPOLIS VALLEY

(38) Bridgetown: North Mountain

MAP 12

Start Point
Bridgetown: Jubilee Park, 224 Evangeline Trail/Trunk 1.

Summary
Challenging hills; variable road conditions; steep descent; coastal views; lighthouse.

Distance (km)	Duration	Max Grade +	Elevation Gain (m)	Unpaved
49.2	2:14/3:16	7.3	576	—

Description
This first part of this route follows along the base of the North Mountain and is a beautiful section of road with undulating hills that pass by old farmland, providing expansive views toward the valley floor. Heading north, you will have a quick, challenging climb up Mt. Hanley Road to the top of the North Mountain, where you will be treated to a quality road with low traffic and occasional views of the water. The final leg of the journey is the steep descent down Hampton Mountain Road. Finish off back in Bridgetown where you started.

Ride Considerations
- There are no amenities along Shore Road on the top of the North Mountain.
- Hampton Mountain Road is steep (10% grade) and has some very fast, sharp corners; ride down with caution and be on the lookout for hazards.
- Choose to do this route in reverse if you are looking for a more challenging climb, or if you want to avoid coming down the steeper of the two roads.

Side Trips/Variations
- Combine this trip with **❸❼ Annapolis Royal: North Mountain** loop for a total of 92.2 km.
- Combine this trip with **❸❾ Middleton: North Mountain** loop for a total of 90 km.

Points of Interest
- **Hampton Lighthouse (39.4 km)** Access via Hampton Wharf Road, where you turn to come down the mountain.
- **Valley View Park (44.2 km)** This a nice park just before the steepest section coming down the mountain. It's worth taking a short hike to the look-off area where there are a couple of benches; the view is spectacular.

ANNAPOLIS VALLEY

Bridgetown: North Mountain Cue Sheet

Dist	Type	Note	Next
0.0	◉	Start of route	0.0
0.0	⚑	(Start) Bridgetown: Jubilee Park, 224 Evangeline Trail/NS-1; exit parking lot	0.1
0.1	→	R onto NS-1 E	0.3
0.4	←	L onto Church St	2.8
3.2	→	R onto Clarence Rd	15.1
18.3	←	L onto Mt Hanley Rd	4.7
23.0	←	L onto Brown Rd	3.3
26.3	→	R onto Outram Rd	0.4
26.7	←	L onto Shore Rd E	3.1

29.8	→	R onto to stay on Shore Rd E	1.6
31.4	→	R onto Port Lorne Rd	0.1
31.5	←	L onto Shore Rd E	1.2
32.7	←	L onto Brinton Rd	0.5
33.2	→	R onto Shore Rd E/St Croix Cove Rd	6.2
39.4	←	L onto Hampton Mountain Rd	9.4
48.8	→	R onto NS-1 W	0.3
49.1	←	L into parking lot	0.1
49.2	◉	End of route	0.0

 39 ## Middleton: North Mountain

MAP 12

Start Point
Middleton: 7 School St.

Summary
Challenging hills; variable road conditions; steep descent; coastal views; lighthouse.

Distance (km)	Duration	Max Grade +	Elevation Gain (m)	Unpaved
50.8	2:18/3:23	8.2	610	—

Description
This is a great ride if you are looking for some challenging hills; it also offers nice coastal riding that includes two lighthouses. After coming out of Middleton, you will have a solid 2 km climb to get up onto the North Mountain. The first section of riding is along the water, with some excellent views. After visiting the Port George Lighthouse, you will be heading inland for 7 km before coming into the community of Margaretsville, where you have one more lighthouse before your final descent down the mountain toward the valley floor. Finish the ride on Route 221, passing beautiful old farms along undulating hills.

Ride Considerations

- There are no amenities along the Shore Road on the top of the North Mountain.
- Stronach Mountain Road is fairly steep and has variable road conditions; ride with caution and be on the lookout for hazards.
- Route 221 has some poor pavement; stay alert to traffic in order to avoid rough sections.

Side Trips/Variations

- Combine this trip with **39 Bridgetown: North Mountain** loop for a total of 90.0 km.

Points of Interest

- **Port George Lighthouse (17.4 km)** There is a picnic park nearby with washroom facilities and an excellent view of the Bay of Fundy.
- **Margaretsville Lighthouse (28.3 km)** Access via Gordon Road/Lighthouse Road; there is also a nice cove here to explore.

Middleton: North Mountain Cue Sheet

Dist	Type	Note	Next
0.0	◉	Start of route	0.0
0.0	⚑	(Start) Middleton: 7 School St; head north on School St	0.4
0.4	←	L onto Marshall St	0.5
0.9	→	R onto Victoria St	0.3
1.2	←	L onto Veterans Ln	0.6
1.8	→	R onto Brooklyn Rd	5.9
7.7	→	R onto Mt Hanley Rd	6.3
14.0	→	R onto Shore Rd E	3.7
17.7	↑	Continue onto Shore Rd E	2.8
20.5	↑	Continue onto Delusion Rd	3.2
23.7	←	L onto NS-362 S (signs for Margaretville)	8.2
31.9	→	Slight R onto Stronach Mountain Rd	7.5
39.4	→	R onto Spa Springs Rd/NS-221 W	6.2
45.6	↑	Continue straight onto NS-362 S	1.9
47.5	←	L onto Gates Mountain Rd/NS-362 S	2.0
49.5	→	R onto Bentley Dr	0.2
49.7	←	L onto School St	1.1
50.8	◉	End of route	0.0

ANNAPOLIS VALLEY

(40) Harvest Moon Trailway (RT)

MAP 13

Start Point
Grand Pré: South of Grand Pré Historic Site, 2205 Grand Pré Rd. or Annapolis Royal: 151 Victoria St.

Summary
Rail trail; mostly flat; good access points; wayfinding; coastal/river views; beach access; kid-friendly.

Distance (km)	Duration	Max Grade +	Elevation Gain (m)	Unpaved
110.0 (one way)	5:00/7:20	2.7	395	98% (108 km)

Description
The Harvest Moon Trailway officially opened in 2017, creating one continuous ride on a converted railbed all the way from Grand Pré to Annapolis Royal, 110 km away. This was the third such "Destination Trail" to open in Nova Scotia, following the success of the Celtic Shores Coastal Trail in southwest Cape Breton and the Rum Runners Trail, connecting Halifax to Lunenburg. It is a beautiful route that weaves through historic farmland and vibrant small towns, and follows along both the Cornwallis and Annapolis Rivers. This is a fabulous way to experience the Annapolis Valley, while staying off the roads on a relatively flat and regularly maintained rail trail.

Start your ride in Grand Pré, home to the Acadian people who, in the 1600s, built the dykes that created so much of the arable land in this region; this is also the site of the Acadian Deportation that took place between 1755 and 1763. The trail quickly takes you into Wolfville, a bustling university town, and the epicentre of the growing wine industry, and then on to Kentville. The section through Kentville is the only part of the Harvest Moon Trailway that is on roads; there is signage, but be alert to traffic as you come through this section. Also, the section between Grand Pré and Kentville is the only section that prohibits OHVs and other motorized vehicles; once you hit Coldbrook, the trail is multi-use.

From Coldbrook, make your way down the Valley to Berwick, the apple capital of Nova Scotia, then on to Greenwood and Middleton. Lawrencetown is next, and is the home of the Annapolis Valley Exhibition, a large agricultural fair and competition that takes place every summer. In Bridgetown, you will find the End of the Line Pub conveniently positioned directly on the trail, located in an old railway station. The last leg of the journey takes you along the Annapolis River into Annapolis Royal, a beautiful town full of history, with a multitude of attractions to explore.

The Harvest Moon Trail is on an old rail trail, making for a relaxing route where you can take your time and watch for wildlife. (MARIE BROWN)

Ride Considerations

- **Read Preparing to Ride: Packing Considerations** to learn more about packing and preparing for a long trip.
- This route can be done from either direction; the cue sheets for this route description are starting from Grand Pré.

Harvest Moon Trailway

Visit the official Harvest Moon Trailway website for maps, more details, and the most up-to-date information: **harvestmoontrailway.ca.**

- Some sections of the trail can be fairly remote and cellphone reception can't be guaranteed; ensure that you are adequately prepared.
- You always have the option to ride the parallel roads; just be aware that they can be busy and should be avoided during peak hours.
- There is signage along the route indicating the many access points where you can get onto the trail or get off for amenities; visit the trail's website for more details.
- Most of the route is a shared trail with OHV riders, pedestrians, and horses; read **Road Safety: Etiquette** to learn how to share the trail.
- No OHVs or motorized vehicles are permitted on the first 21 km between Grand Pré and Kentville.
- This is a rail trail, so be sure to have the appropriate tires for hard-packed gravel.
- Getting through Kentville can be a challenge; the trail runs through town on a combination of one-way and two-way streets. Follow the signs, and remember that you'll be coming back through town another way when coming from the west.

- Although this is a maintained rail trail, there can be variable trail surfaces; be prepared for sections that are soft or in rough condition. Contact Harvest Moon Trailway about any trail issues that need to be taken care of.

Side Trips/Variations
- Take a small side trip out to Port Williams when the trail intersects with Route 358 in Greenwich (7.7 km) to visit restaurants, orchards, wineries, breweries, distilleries, and shops. See ㊸ Starrs Point Loop and ㊻ Wolfville Area: Winery, Brewery, and Distillery Tour for more details.

The Harvest Moon Trailway officially opened in 2017, creating one continuous ride on a converted railbed all the way from Grand Pré to Annapolis Royal. (ADAM BARNETT)

- In Middleton or Bridgetown, get off the trail and take Route 201 along the south side of the Annapolis River, or take Brooklyn Street/Clarence Road to ride along the base of the North Mountain. Both of these routes are fairly quiet, with nice rolling hills; both will take you to Annapolis Royal.
- ㊹ Berwick–Harbourville
- ㊲ Annapolis Royal: North Mountain

Points of Interest
- **Grand Pré Historic Site (Start point)** This is an impressive historic site where you can learn about the Grand Pré area and its history as an Acadian settlement from 1682 to 1755.
- **Miners Marsh, Kentville (15.6 km)** There are biking paths around this protected wetland just on the edge of Kentville. It's a beautiful and relaxing area to spend some time and watch for wildlife. Access off Leverett Avenue and follow signs to Miners Marsh.
- **Middleton Railway Museum, Middleton (66 km)** This museum is located in an old CP Rail station and features photos and artifacts from the railway over the last one hundred years.
- **Fort Anne National Historic Site, Annapolis Royal (Finish)** At one point, this was one of the most contested pieces of land in North America. Tour around the fort to learn about days gone by and to visit the impressive grounds.

Towns en Route (Accommodation and/or Amenities)
- Wolfville (4 km)
- Kentville (16 km)
- Berwick (36 km)
- Kingston/Greenwood (54 km)
- Middleton (65 km)
- Bridgetown (88 km)
- Annapolis Royal (110 km)

Shuttles/Luggage/Getting around
- Call the local bike shops for the most up-to-date information on what is available in terms of shuttle services in the area.
- Kings County Transit runs a bus service from Grand Pré to Annapolis Royal. The cost is less than $4; it's an economical way to get back to your starting point, but it does include many stops along the way. Visit **kbus.ca** for bus schedules and information.

Bike Shops/Repairs/Rentals between Grand Pré and Annapolis Royal

- Banks Bikes (Wolfville) 902-542-2596
- Valley Stove and Cycle (Kentville) 902-542-7280
- Oakhaven Bike Barn (Between Annapolis and Bridgetown) 902-665-5044
- In 2018, public libraries in Berwick, Wolfville, and Annapolis Royal had bicycles available for loan with the use of a library card. Check valleylibrary.ca for current information.

Harvest Moon Trailway (RT) Cue Sheet

Dist	Type	Note	Next
0.0	○	Start of route	0.2
0.2	⚑	(Start) Grand Pré: South of Grand Pré Historic Site, 2205 Grand Pré Rd; head west on trail	4.3
4.5	↑	Continue straight onto Harvest Moon Trailway	9.9
14.4	↑	Continue straight onto Kentville Rail Trail	1.3
15.7	↑	Continue onto Justice Way	0.1
15.8	↑	Continue onto Station Ln	0.3
16.1	→	R onto Evangeline Trail/Webster St/NS-1 W	0.2
16.3	→	Slight R at River St; the trail continues west from here with no more significant turns	93.7
110.0	○	End of route	0.0

41 Berwick–Harbourville

MAP 14

Start Point
Berwick: 210 Commercial St.

Summary
Challenging climb; some rough roads; steep descent; coastal views.

Distance (km)	Duration	Max Grade +	Elevation Gain (m)	Unpaved
33.6	1:31/2:14	9.6	456	—

Description
This is a lovely ride up and back down the North Mountain that includes some challenging climbs, lovely coastal views, and a fast descent. The ride starts with a nearly 5 km climb out of Berwick to the top of the mountain; you will then be treated to a 7 km descent that includes a stunning view as you come upon the Bay of Fundy. Harbourville is beautiful, with twisty roads, picturesque wharves, and fishing boats; take some time to explore the area before continuing along Long Point Road, where you will find an expansive and rocky beach on the corner, just before heading inland. There is a long, steady uphill for 6 km before your final descent down a steep and curvy road, followed by a quick jaunt along Route 221 before heading back into Berwick.

Ride Considerations
• Long Point Road in Harbourville is in rough shape along the coast, and for the first part of the ride down the mountain; the pavement improves before the steep descent. Ride with caution and be on the lookout for hazards.

Points of Interest
• **Harbourville (14.1 km)** This is a lovely fishing community with two working wharves protecting its harbour.

Berwick–Harbourville Cue Sheet

Dist	Type	Note	Next
0.0	○	Start of route	0.0
0.0	⚑	(Start) Berwick: 210 Commercial St; head north on Commercial St/NS-360	5.1
5.1	↑	Continue straight on NS-360 N	9.0
14.1	→	NS-360 N turns slightly R and becomes Long Point Rd (signs for Morden/Turner Brook/Long Point Rd)	11.2
25.3	←	L onto NS-221 E	3.2
28.5	→	R onto NS-360 S	5.1
33.6	○	End of route	0.0

ANNAPOLIS VALLEY

42 Canning–Scots Bay

MAP 15

Start Point

Canning: parking lot at intersection of Main St. and Seminary Ave.

Summary

Challenging hills; unpaved roads; winery; beach access; coastal ride.

Distance (km)	Duration	Max Grade +	Elevation Gain (m)	Unpaved
49.1	1:59/2:55	11.5	555	6% (3 km)

Description

This is a spectacular ride that follows along both the Minas Basin and the Bay of Fundy. You will pass wineries, orchards, and old barns, and have the opportunity to make some exceptional side trips. Be prepared for one challenging uphill on a dirt road and a very steep descent on pavement. The views along this ride are incredible, and well worth the effort.

After leaving Canning, you will head out to Kingsport and then to Medford, where you will see the many orchards the Valley is known for. The next section along the coast is unlike any other in the province, with views of red-hued cliffs eroding into the Minas Basin. After tackling an unpaved ascent, enjoy riding the 5 km downhill into Scots Bay on good roads where you will have a spectacular view of the iconic Cape Split. After exploring the beach, come back the way you came, and stop at the look-off to take in the panoramic view of the area—easily one of the best views of the Valley. The last leg of the trip takes you on a steep descent before coming back into Canning.

Ride Considerations

- These are mostly quiet roads, but they can get busy on weekends with people driving out to Kingsport, Blomidon Park, and Cape Split. Stay alert on the roads, especially during nice days and on weekends.
- This area is active farmland, so you may encounter farming equipment on the road while cycling; give a wide berth as you pass, and signal your intent.
- There is a very steep and twisty road (9.4% grade) coming down the North Mountain after passing the look-off; ride with caution.
- Fog can sometimes linger on the top of North Mountain, changing the temperature considerably; often, there is a noticeable wind as well.
- Check the tides if you want to go swimming or walk the beach, as many beaches will not be accessible at high tide. More importantly, the water can rise very quickly and can trap unsuspecting beach-walkers.

ANNAPOLIS VALLEY

The Canning–Scots Bay route offers a spectacular ride that follows along both the Minas Basin and the Bay of Fundy. (PAUL ILSLEY)

Side Trips/Variations

- **Longspell Road (5.1 km)** Cruise down a dirt road and check out this area's version of cottage country; access it by heading east at the intersection of Main Street and Medford Road (2 km return trip).

- **Blomidon Provincial Park** Keep riding past Houston Beach (14.0 km) for a spectacular ride along the coast. At Blomidon, you can walk the beach and/or hike the trails at the top of the hill. Getting to the park by road requires going up a very steep hill, so unless you are planning on hiking at the top (or are looking for some punishment), the best option is to park your bike at the bottom and hike up the trail to see the fantastic view (an approximately forty-minute round trip). This is a 10 km return trip from the turnoff.

Canning–Scots Bay Cue Sheet

Dist	Type	Note	Next
0.0	♀	Start of route	0.0
0.0	⚑	(Start) Canning: parking lot at intersection of Main St and Seminary Ave; head east on Main St/NS-221	4.8
4.8	←	L onto Main St	0.3
5.1	↑	Continue onto Medford Rd	3.4
8.5	←	L onto N Medford Rd	1.3
9.8	→	R onto Jackson Barkhouse Rd	1.0
10.8	→	R onto Pereau Rd	3.2
14.0	←	L onto Stewart Mountain Rd (unpaved road)	3.0
17.0	→	R onto NS-358 N (signs for Scots Bay)	8.4
25.4	←	L onto Wharf Rd	0.3
25.7	↩	Scots Bay Provincial Park; turnaround point	0.2
25.9	→	R onto NS-358 S	12.8
38.7	←	L to stay on NS-358 (towards Canning)	5.3
44.0	←	L onto Main St/NS-221	5.1
49.1	♀	End of route	0.0

- **Cape Split** Make this trip into a multi-sport adventure by riding to—and then hiking—Cape Split. This is one of the most popular hikes in Nova Scotia; it includes a walk through hardwood forests out to an incredible view of the famous Cape. Plan for three to five hours to hike the trail. Access it by keeping on the road past Scots Bay (25.4 km), following signs to the park (8 km return trip).

Points of Interest
- **Blomidon Estate Winery (2.3 km)** Take a tour around the vineyards of an award-winning winery.
- **Kingsport Beach (4.3 km)** A beautiful and popular beach, with good swimming when the tide is up. This is a great place for a beach walk to check out the red cliffs the area is known for; there is also a seasonal snack shop here. Access immediately past the turnoff to Main Street.
- **Houston Beach (14.0 km)** This is a nice spot to have a quick dip before heading up the mountain; access it by heading east on Stewart Mountain Road instead of heading up the mountain toward Scots Bay.
- **Scots Bay Provincial Park (25.7 km)** There is a spectacular rocky beach here with amazing views of Cape Split and Scots Bay.
- **The Look-Off (38.7 km)** Grab an ice cream and take in one of the best views of the Annapolis Valley.

 **Starrs Point Loop**   MAP 15

ANNAPOLIS VALLEY

Start Point
Port Williams: parking across from 1003 Kars St.

Summary
Some challenging hills; some rough roads; coastal views; dykes; local food/drink.

Distance (km)	Duration	Max Grade +	Elevation Gain (m)	Unpaved
48.0	2:10/3:12	5.5	326	—

Description
This is considered a "classic" by the local cyclists. It's a route that guides you through active farmland, following alongside the dykes that were built by the Acadians over three hundred years ago. Along the way, you will ride through the Village of Canning, past Kingsport Beach, and past abundant orchards and expansive farms.

This is an area that is increasingly known for its local food and drink offerings. Make some time to stop and take tours, and maybe bring a bike bag so you can take some goodies home with you. When you finish this tour, you'll find many options for food and drink in Port Williams or nearby Wolfville.

Ride Considerations

- Some of the roads on this route are in poor condition, but they are quiet roads that allow for manoeuvrability.
- This area is active farmland, so you may encounter farming equipment on the road while cycling; give a wide berth as you pass, and signal your intent.

Side Trips/Variations

- Combine this route with 42 **Canning–Scots Bay** to add an additional 31 km to the ride.

Points of Interest

- **Prescott House Museum (3.2 km)** Visit the restored home where Charles Prescott cultivated Nova Scotia's apple industry from 1811 to 1859.
- **Blomidon Estate Winery (14.5 km)** Take a tour around the vineyards of an award-winning winery.
- **Kingsport Beach (16.0 km)** A beautiful and popular beach, with good swimming when the tide is up. This is a great place for a beach walk to check out the red cliffs the area is known for; there is also a seasonal snack shop here. Access immediately past the turnoff to Main St.
- **Planters Ridge Winery (43.1 km)** Visit this artisanal winery and take a tour of the vineyards.
- **Foxhill Cheesehouse (44.2 km)** Stop at this sixth-generation family farm that makes and sells its own cheese and delicious gelato.

Starrs Point Loop Cue Sheet

Dist	Type	Note	Next
0.0	◉	Start of route	0.0
0.0	⚑	(Start) Port Williams: parking across from 1003 Kars St; head north on Kars St/Terry Creek Rd	0.1
0.1	→	R onto Starrs Point Rd	2.3
2.4	←	L to stay on Starrs Point Rd	1.4
3.8	←	L onto Church St	1.1
4.9	→	R to stay on Church St	0.6
5.5	→	R onto Wellington Dyke Rd	2.3
7.8	→	R onto Canard St	1.7
9.5	←	L onto Saxon St	2.1
11.6	→	R onto Canning Aboiteau Rd	1.2
12.8	→	R onto NS-221 E	4.1
16.9	←	L onto Main St	0.3
17.2	↑	Continue onto Medford Rd	3.4
20.6	←	L onto N Medford Rd	1.3
21.9	←	L onto Jackson Barkhouse Rd	0.1
22.0	→	R onto N Medford Rd	1.5
23.5	←	L onto Pereau Rd	3.9
27.4	→	R onto Main St/NS-221 W	2.4
29.8	←	L onto Hillaton Rd	1.0
30.8	→	R onto Saxon St	2.9
33.7	←	L onto Middle Dyke Rd	1.2
34.9	←	L onto NS-341 E	0.1
35.0	→	R onto Middle Dyke Rd	2.9
37.9	←	L onto Church St	7.1
45.0	↑	Continue onto Magee Rd	1.1
46.1	→	R onto Starrs Point Rd	1.8
47.9	←	L onto Kars St/Terrys Creek Rd	0.1
48.0	◉	End of route	0.0

Variation: Starrs Point Loop Extension (79.9 km, Map 15)

There is a variation on this route that takes you to the picturesque fishing village of Halls Harbour by heading up and over North Mountain.

This variation makes for a 79.9 km total ride.

Starrs Point Loop Extension Cue Sheet

Dist	Type	Note	Next
0.0	○	Start of route	0.0
0.0	▶	(Start) Port Williams: parking across from 1003 Kars St; head north on Kars St/Terry Creek Rd	0.1
0.1	→	R onto Starrs Point Rd	2.3
2.4	←	L to stay on Starrs Point Rd	1.4
3.8	←	L onto Church St	1.1
4.9	→	R to stay on Church St	0.6
5.5	→	R onto Wellington Dyke Rd	2.3
7.8	→	R onto Canard St	1.7
9.5	←	L onto Saxon St	2.1
11.6	→	R onto Canning Aboiteau Rd	1.2
12.8	→	R onto NS-221 E	4.1
16.9	←	L onto Main St	0.3
17.2	↑	Continue onto Medford Rd	3.4
20.6	←	L onto N Medford Rd	1.3
21.9	←	L onto Jackson Barkhouse Rd	0.1
22.0	→	R onto N Medford Rd	1.5
23.5	←	L onto Pereau Rd	3.9

Dist	Type	Note	Next
27.4	→	R onto Main St/NS-221 W	5.1
32.5	↑	Continue onto Black Hole Rd	4.9
37.4	↑	Slight L to continue onto Gospel Woods Rd	6.5
43.9	→	R onto NS-359 N	10.5
54.4	←	L onto Brow of Mountain Rd	2.1
56.5	↑	Continue onto NS-359 S (signs for Kentville)	4.4
60.9	←	L onto NS-221 E	3.3
64.2	→	Slight R onto Centreville Rd	0.6
64.8	→	R onto Middle Dyke Rd	2.0
66.8	←	L onto NS-341 E	0.1
66.9	→	R onto Middle Dyke Rd	2.9
69.8	←	L onto Church St	7.1
76.9	↑	Continue onto Magee Rd	1.1
78.0	→	R onto Starrs Point Rd	1.8
79.8	←	L onto Kars St/Terrys Creek Rd	0.1
79.9	○	End of route	0.0

45 Wolfville Wine Tour (RT)

MAP 17

Start Point
Wolfville: parking lot across from Willow Ave. and Main St.

Summary
Some challenging hills; farmland; wineries; water views.

Distance (km)	Duration	Max Grade +	Elevation Gain (m)	Unpaved
29.4	1:20/1:57	9.5	362	17% (5 km)

Description
Wolfville and the surrounding area are front and centre in Nova Scotia's burgeoning wine industry. The word has gotten out about the area's excellent soil and unique microclimate, with new vineyards opening regularly. The concentration of wineries provides an excellent opportunity for a cycling tour into the heart of the Gaspereau Valley, truly one of the gems of Nova Scotia.

This tour starts in Wolfville and takes you on the 40 **Harvest Moon Trailway** out to Grand Pré, touring beside dykes and active farmland so unique that the landscape was designated a UNESCO World Heritage Site in 2012. After the rail trail, the route takes you up over the ridge and into the Gaspereau Valley, where you will follow along the Gaspereau River. You are now in farming country, so stop in to the farm markets and see what's growing locally. You will you have the option to stop at four more wineries before you leave the Valley, tackling a steep climb to get you up onto Ridge Road. Enjoy the incredible view out toward Port Williams, Canning, and Cape Blomidon as you finish your ride back into Wolfville.

Ride Considerations
- Trunk 1 is the only paved option if you want to avoid the rail trail between Wolfville and Grand Pré; be aware that this is a busy section of road with no shoulders and it is not recommended; avoid it during peak hours.
- Most of the roads in the Gaspereau Valley are not usually high-traffic, but they are the main routes to get through the area; try to avoid them during peak hours.
- The Gaspereau area is active farmland, so you may encounter farming equipment on the road while cycling; give a wide berth as you pass, and signal your intent.
- Make a note of the wines you enjoyed in order to pick them up later at the wineries or at the NSLC; talk to the wineries about the best way to do this.
- If you want to tour the wineries you visit, it is advised to call in advance to find out when tours are offered or to make appointments.

ANNAPOLIS VALLEY

Enjoy the incredible view out toward Cape Blomidon as you finish your ride on the Wolfville Wine Tour route. (KIMBERLY SMITH)

- The final descent into Wolfville has some rough sections of road; stay alert to hazards.

Side Trips/Variations
- Connect this trip to ㊸ **Starrs Point Loop**, adding two more wineries (Planters Ridge and Blomidon Estate).
- Extend this trip by riding the ㊻ **Wolfville Area: Winery, Brewery, and Distillery Tour**. This route will take you farther along the South Mountain, adding craft breweries and distillers to your itinerary.

Points of Interest
- **Lightfoot & Wolfville Vineyards (0.6 km)** Access off the trail; look for signs.
- **Mercator Vineyards (2.3 km)** Access off of the trail; look for signs.
- **Grand Pré Historic Site (4.3 km)** Access where Harvest Moon Trailway ends at Grand Pré Road.
- **Grand Pré Winery (5.1 km)** Access it by heading west on Trunk 1 where it intersects with Grand Pré Road; the winery is just ahead on your right. Return the way you came, continuing south on Grand Pré Road. Be very careful coming out of the winery, as it is a busy road with a blind corner.
- **Luckett Vineyards (8.8 km)** Get ready to climb a steep hill for this one.
- **L'Acadie Vineyards (13.6 km)** 310 Slaytor Rd.
- **Gaspereau Vineyards (16.1 km)** 2239 White Rock Rd.
- **Benjamin Bridge Winery (18.2 km)** 1966 White Rock Rd.

ANNAPOLIS VALLEY

Wolfville Wine Tour (RT) Cue Sheet

Dist	Type	Note	Next
0.0	⊙	Start of route	0.0
0.0	⚑	(Start) Wolfville: parking lot across from Willow Ave and Main St; head east on Harvest Moon Trailway	4.2
4.2	➡	R onto Grand Pré Rd	3.2
7.4	➡	R onto Gaspereau River Rd	0.1
7.5	⬅	L onto Grand Pré Rd	1.3
8.8	↩	Luckett Vineyards	1.2
10.0	⬅	L on Gaspereau River Rd	1.5
11.5	⬅	Follow the s-curve, slight L to stay on Gaspereau River Rd	1.6
13.1	⬅	L onto Slayter Rd	2.0

15.1	➡	R onto Greenfield Rd	0.6
15.7	⬅	L to stay on Greenfield Rd	0.3
16.0	⬅	L onto White Rock Rd	4.7
20.7	➡	R onto Ridge Rd	6.1
26.8	↑	Continue onto Highland Ave	1.7
28.5	➡	R onto Main St/NS-1 E	0.1
28.6	⬅	L onto Elm Ave	0.2
28.8	➡	R onto Harvest Moon Trailway	0.3
29.1	↑	Straight on Harvest Moon Trailway	0.3
29.4	⊙	End of route	0.0

46 Wolfville Area: Winery, Brewery, and Distillery Tour (RT)

MAP 16

Start Point
Wolfville: parking lot across from Willow Ave. and Main St.

Summary
Some challenging hills; farmland; local food/drink.

Distance (km)	Duration	Max Grade +	Elevation Gain (m)	Unpaved
76.0	3:27/5:04	10.1	755	11% (8 km)

Description
Refer to **45 Wolfville Wine Tour** *for the first part of this ride. This route continues on at 20.7 km, staying on White Rock Road instead of heading north on Ridge Road.*

This ride takes the Wolfville Wine Tour and extends it, eventually bringing you through to Port Williams, where you will add breweries and distilleries to your itinerary. Instead of heading up Ridge Road to head back to Wolfville, continue on White Rock Road where, for the next 17 km, the ride will be a long, gradual ascent, with some occasional moments of respite. The climb will be worth it when you crest the hill north of Tupper Lake and see the incredible view of the Annapolis

Valley. This is the high point of the ride—in terms of both the achievement and your ascent.

The next leg of the ride is a beautiful 8.2 km descent on undulating hills down the South Mountain and into Cambridge. Continue north until you hit Belcher Street, which will take you into Kentville. Next stop is Port Williams, where you will find more places to visit and drinks to sample. Consider stopping here for some food before finishing up the journey back to Wolfville via the ㊵ Harvest Moon Trailway.

Ride Considerations:
- Refer to ㊺ Wolfville Wine Tour for ride considerations.
- When coming off the mountain and into Cambridge (44.1 km), there is a crosswalk 100 m away to help with crossing the often-busy Trunk 1.
- Be careful coming through Kentville, as Belcher Street can be quite busy and you will be coming through a main intersection; you will get back onto side roads after 2 km.

Side Trips/Variations
- In Cambridge, you have the option to get onto the ㊵ Harvest Moon Trailway, which will take you all the way back to Greenwich/Wolfville on a rail trail. Access it by heading east on the trail soon after crossing Trunk 1 (44.7 km). There are no wineries between here and Greenwich, so you will not miss out on the tour. If you want to continue the tour into Port Williams, head north on Route 358 where the trail intersects in Greenwich; otherwise, continue east, back to Wolfville.

Points of Interest: Refer to ㊺ Wolfville Wine Tour for points of interest on the first 20.7 km of the ride.
- **Maritime Express Cider Company, Kentville (59.5 km)** Access this by heading south into Kentville and following the one-way street to 325 Main Street.
- **Planters Ridge Winery (68.8 km)** 1441 Church St.
- **Barrelling Tide Distillery (70.6 km)** Access it by heading east on Starrs Road and going down Parkway Drive.
- **Sea Level Brewery (71.0 km)** 980 Terrys Creek Rd.
- **Wayfarers Brewery (71.0 km)** 1116 Kars St.
- **Church Brewing Company** 329 Main St., Wolfville.
- **Annapolis Cider Company** 388 Main St., Wolfville.
- **Paddy's Pub** 460 Main St., Wolfville.

Wolfville Area: Winery, Brewery, and Distillery Tour (RT) Cue Sheet

Dist	Type	Note	Next
0.0	●	Start of route	0.0
0.0	⚑	(Start) Wolfville: parking lot across from Willow Ave and Main St; head east on Harvest Moon Trailway	4.2
4.2	→	R onto Grand Pré Rd	3.2
7.4	→	R onto Gaspereau River Rd	0.1
7.5	←	L onto Grand Pré Rd	1.2
8.7	↰	Luckett Vineyards	1.2
9.9	←	L onto Gaspereau River Rd	1.5
11.4	←	Follow the s-curve, slight L to stay on Gaspereau River Rd	1.6
13.0	←	L onto Slayter Rd	2.1
15.1	→	R onto Greenfield Rd	0.6
15.7	←	L to stay on Greenfield Rd	0.3
16.0	←	L onto White Rock Rd	11.4
27.4	→	R onto Canaan Ave/Canaan Mountain Rd	0.4
27.8	←	L onto English Mountain Rd	8.2

36.0	←	L onto Prospect Rd	4.9
40.9	→	Prospect Rd turns slightly R and becomes Cambridge Rd/Cambridge Mountain Rd	2.9
43.8	→	R onto Riverside Dr	0.3
44.1	↑	Continue onto Cambridge Rd	3.1
47.2	→	R onto Brooklyn St	12.3
59.5	↑	Continue onto Belcher St	2.0
61.5	←	L onto Middle Dyke Rd (signs for Chipmans Corner)	2.1
63.6	→	R onto Church St	5.4
69.0	→	R onto Collins Rd	1.6
70.6	→	R onto Starrs Point Rd	0.2
70.8	←	L onto Kars St/Terrys Creek Rd	0.4
71.2	←	L onto NS-358 S	1.3
72.5	←	L onto Harvest Moon Trailway	3.3
75.8	↑	Straight on Harvest Moon Trailway	0.2
76.0	●	End of route	0.0

47 Gaspereau Valley

MAP 17

Start Point
Wolfville: parking lot across from Willow Ave. and Main St.

Summary
Challenging hills; unpaved/rough roads; remote area; swim spot.

Distance (km)	Duration	Max Grade +	Elevation Gain (m)	Unpaved
43.5	1:58/2:54	8.8	629	62% (27 km)

Description
This is a great ride with some challenging hills and lots of unpaved roads. From Wolfville, you will head into the Gaspereau Valley and then up onto the South Mountain through Lumsden Dam, Black River, and Five Corners. Head down into the Gaspereau once more before the final hill takes you to Grand Pré, where the ride finishes up on the ㊵ **Harvest Moon Trailway**, offering a nice cool-down as you make your way back to the start point.

Ride Considerations

- Signs are often missing on back roads; be prepared with maps, or download the route onto your phone or device.
- Cell service may be unavailable for portions of this ride.
- This is a gravel grinder ride with lots of rough, unpaved sections; ensure that your bike is suitable for these conditions.
- Greenfield Road, coming down into the valley (2.7 km), is in rough shape; ride with caution.
- Peck Meadow Road (21.9 km) is particularly rough; ride with caution.
- Be careful coming down Melanson Road (31.0 km) as there are lots of houses tucked away with the potential for cars and dogs to come out of hidden driveways.

Points of Interest

- **Lumsden Pond Provincial Park (12.7 km)** Stop at this popular swimming spot for a cool-down; there are outhouses and change rooms on-site.

Gaspereau Valley Cue Sheet

Dist	Type	Note	Next
0.0	◉	Start of route	0.0
0.0	⚑	(Start) Wolfville: parking lot across from Willow Ave and Main St; head east on Main St/NS-1	0.6
0.6	→	R onto Sherwood Dr	0.6
1.2	→	R onto Alline St	0.4
1.6	←	L onto Orchard Ave	0.1
1.7	→	R onto Pleasant St	0.2
1.9	←	L onto Gaspereau Ave	0.2
2.1	↑	Continue onto Greenfield Rd	2.2
4.3	→	R to stay on Greenfield Rd	0.6
4.9	→	R onto Allison Coldwell Rd	4.2
9.1	←	L onto Nowlan Mountain Rd	1.8
10.9	→	R onto Newtonville Rd	0.7
11.6	→	R onto Black River Rd	1.1
12.7	←	L onto Corkum and Burns Rd	2.8
15.5	←	L onto Deep Hollow Rd	1.7
17.2	→	R onto Davison St	0.3
17.5	←	Slight L onto Deep Hollow Rd	2.1
19.6	←	L to stay on Deep Hollow Rd	0.3
19.9	←	L onto Black River Rd	1.9
21.8	↑	Continue onto Peck Meadow Rd	9.2
31.0	←	L onto Melanson Rd	4.4
35.4	→	R onto Biggs Rd	1.0
36.4	→	R onto Hamilton Rd	0.6
37.0	←	L onto Grand Pré Rd	2.3
39.3	←	L onto Harvest Moon Trailway	4.2
43.5	◉	End of route	0.0

The Gaspereau Valley offers a great ride with challenging hills and gorgeous scenery.
(PAUL ILSLEY)

48 Bishopville–Sunken Lake

MAP 16

Start Point

Wolfville: parking lot across from Willow Ave. and Main St.

Summary

Challenging hills; unpaved/rough roads; remote area; steep descent.

Distance (km)	Duration	Max Grade +	Elevation Gain (m)	Unpaved
73.0	3:19/4:52	6.8	777	38% (28 km)

Description

This is an epic gravel grinder that is one of the favourites of the back road riding community. Ride on the ⓐ Harvest Moon Trailway out to Grand Pré, where you then head up over the ridge and into the Gaspereau Valley. Follow Gaspereau River Road out to Avonport, where you will get some beautiful views of the Minas Basin looking toward Cape Blomidon. Next, ride a mix of paved and unpaved roads to Hantsport, where you will head inland to Bishopville Road, starting your 11 km climb up the South Mountain. Explore the back roads on your way to, and then around, Sunken Lake, eventually coming down a steep hill back into the Gaspereau Valley. Tackle one more challenging hill up Ridge Road, where you will be rewarded with some incredible views before finishing your ride back into Wolfville.

Ride Considerations

- Signs are often missing on back roads; be prepared with maps, or download the route onto your phone or device.
- Cell service is likely to be unavailable for portions of this ride.
- This is a gravel grinder ride with lots of rough, unpaved sections; ensure that your bike is suitable for these conditions.
- The final descent on Highland Avenue coming into Wolfville is in poor condition; ride with caution.

Points of Interest

- **Avonport Beach (14.4 km)** Stop off at one of the more popular, but still fairly secret, saltwater beaches in the area; this is a great place to watch for shorebirds. Head north on Avonport Road to get to the beach.
- **Blue Beach (16.7 km)** This beach is known as a place where fossils can be found. Take a stroll on the beach and keep your eyes peeled; there is also a fossil museum here.

ANNAPOLIS VALLEY

- **Flat Rocks (25.3 km)** This is a local swimming hole, complete with a swinging rope. Continue on Bog Road instead of turning onto Old Post Road; the swim spot is just down the street, on the right-hand side.

Bishopville–Sunken Lake Cue Sheet

Dist	Type	Note	Next
0.0	◉	Start of route	0.0
0.0	⚑	(Start) Wolfville: parking lot across from Willow Ave and Main St; head east on Harvest Moon Trailway	4.2
4.2	→	R onto Grand Pré Rd	3.1
7.3	←	L onto Gaspereau River Rd	4.1
11.4	←	L onto Evangeline Trail/Oak Island Rd/NS-1 E	0.2
11.6	↑	At the roundabout, get the 2nd exit onto Oak Island Rd	1.1
12.7	→	R onto Avonport Station Rd	0.9
13.6	→	R onto Avonport Rd	0.3
13.9	←	L onto Bluff Rd	4.4
18.3	→	R onto Hutchinson Rd	1.5
19.8	←	L onto NS-1 E	2.6
22.4	→	R onto Willow St	0.1
22.5	→	Slight R onto Rand St	1.4
23.9	→	R onto Bog Rd	1.4
25.3	→	R onto Old Post Rd	1.3
26.6	←	Sharp L onto Bishopville Rd/Halfway River Rd	13.4
40.0	→	R onto Greenfield Rd	0.1
40.1	←	L onto Peck Meadow Rd	4.1
44.2	↑	Continue onto Black River Rd	1.9
46.1	→	R onto Deep Hollow Rd	0.3
46.4	→	R to stay on Deep Hollow Rd	2.2
48.6	↑	Continue onto Davison St	0.3
48.9	←	L onto Deep Hollow Rd	2.2
51.1	↑	Continue onto Sunken Lake Rd, then follow around Sunken Lake	11.6
62.7	←	L onto Deep Hollow Rd	1.1
63.8	→	R onto White Rock Rd	0.1
63.9	←	L onto Ridge Rd	6.2
70.1	→	R to stay on Ridge Rd	0.6
70.7	←	L onto Greenfield Rd	0.4
71.1	↑	Continue onto Gaspereau Ave	1.5
72.6	↑	Continue onto Harbourside Dr	0.1
72.7	→	R onto Harvest Moon Trailway	0.3
73.0	◉	End of route	0.0

The community of Avonport offers riders a beautiful view of the Minas Basin, plus a chance to cool off with a saltwater swim at Avonport Beach. (JAMIE ROBERTSON)

CYCLING ROUTES OF THE BAY OF FUNDY: MINAS BASIN

Route	Route Name	Distance (km)	Duration	Max Grade +	Elevation Gain (m)	Unpaved	Map
49	Windsor: Winery and Brewery Tour	23.9	1:04/1:35	4.8	148	—	18
50	Avondale Peninsula	21.7	0:59/1:26	3.5	208	—	18
51	Variation: Windsor–Avondale Peninsula	54.3	2:28/3:37	5.6	465	—	18
52	Kempt Shore	53.2	2:25/3:32	5.8	562	—	18
53	Noel Shore	78.3	3:33/5:13	6.8	699	7% (5 km)	19
54	Shubenacadie	48.9	2:13/3:15	4.9	459	12% (6 km)	19
55	Cobequid Trail (RT)	28.7	1:18/1:54	2.8	175	90% (26 km)	19
56	Blue Route: East Mountain–Pictou (RT)	112.4	5:06/7:29	5.3	846	6% (7 km)	26
57	Cobequid Mountains	84.8	3:51/5:39	5.4	855	33% (28 km)	20
58	Five Islands–Parrsboro	94.6	4:18/6:18	6.7	847	16% (15 km)	21
59	Parrsboro–River Hebert	93.3	4:14/6:13	6.4	562	10% (9 km)	21
60	Parrsboro–Cape Chignecto	49.6	2:15/3:18	12.0	649	—	22

Bay of Fundy: Minas Basin Regional Overview

This region encompasses the Minas Basin and Cobequid Bay, as well as the Bay of Fundy. It is an area that features massive tides and dramatic landscapes. The town of Windsor is located east of the Annapolis Valley and features many beautiful old century homes. This is also the gateway to the Avondale Peninsula, where you will find rolling hills, sprawling farmland, and tidal rivers. Take a tour around the Avondale Peninsula before heading up along the Kempt Shore on your way to Burntcoat Head, where you can see tides of up to 14.5 m.

Along the way, you will come to the Shubenacadie River, where you can watch the tidal bore—an impressively large wave caused by the funnelling of the tide as it enters the long, narrow, shallow inlet of the Shubenacadie River. The river changes direction, then rises 3 m, creating a dramatic wave. There are numerous companies here that will take people out in Zodiacs to ride the waves—it's an exhilarating (and very wet) ride.

On the other side of Cobequid Bay, you will find the Masstown Market, a bustling farm market where you can stock up on supplies before heading west along the shore to Economy. Stop in along the way at That Dutchman's Cheese Farm to sample locally made Gouda cheese. Parrsboro is the largest community along the

MINAS BASIN

north shore of the Minas Basin and is home to the Ship's Company Theatre, where there are more than seventy-five music and live theatre performances every year.

As you leave Parrsboro, you'll follow what has been dubbed the "Mini–Cabot Trail" for its many steep, challenging hills, and for the dramatic views around every corner. This exceptional coastline takes you along the most northwestern part of the province to Cape Chignecto—a rugged wilderness park known for its challenging hikes through deep valleys—and then northward to Joggins where you can visit a UNESCO site and explore the shoreline for ancient fossils.

This is "big country" and towns are few and far between. It is an area that feels ancient and isolated, providing a unique travel experience. The cycling in this part of the world takes some dedication because of the hills and the distances, but if you put in the effort, the rewards are great.

Minas Basin Bike Shops

- Bike Monkey (Truro) 902-843-7111
- Hub Cycle (Truro) 902-897-2482
- The Spoke and Note (Windsor) 902-306-1850

Minas Basin Emergency Services

- All Saints Springhill Hospital (Springhill)
- Hants Community Hospital (Windsor)
- Colchester East Hants Health Centre (Truro)
- South Cumberland Community Care Centre (Parrsboro)

49 Windsor: Winery and Brewery Tour

MAP 18

Start Point

Windsor: parking lot at 40 Water St.

Summary

Gentle hills; variable road conditions; local food/drink.

Distance (km)	Duration	Max Grade +	Elevation Gain (m)	Unpaved
23.9	1:04/1:35	4.8	148	—

Description

The Windsor area is part of the local food and drink movement that has blossomed in Nova Scotia—a trend that focuses on highlighting what is grown and produced in the region. Visitors can sip and nibble their way around the beautiful countryside here. This ride takes you on the back roads into Falmouth, crossing over the lazy Avon River to Windsor Forks, and continuing through farming country out toward Three Mile Plains before heading back to Windsor on Trunk 1.

Ride Considerations

- Some of the roads on this route are in poor condition; stay alert to vehicles when avoiding hazards.
- This area is active farmland, so you may encounter farming equipment on the road while cycling; give a wide berth as you pass, and signal your intent.
- Trunk 1 coming back into Windsor can be busy; try to avoid it during peak hours.

Side Trips/Variations

- Make the ride into a multi-sport adventure by going to Ontree, Canada's largest high-ropes park. Access it by heading south on Trunk 14 (10.5 km). Ski Martock Road will be on your left soon after you turn; follow this to your destination.

Windsor: Winery and Brewery Cue Sheet

Dist	Type	Note	Next
0.0	○	Start of route	0.0
0.0	⚑	(Start) Windsor: parking lot at 40 Water St; head west on Main Street/NS-1	2.0
2.0	←	Slight L onto Falmouth Back Rd	0.7
2.7	←	L onto Falmouth Dyke Rd	5.3
8.0	←	L onto Sangster Bridge Rd	2.5
10.5	←	L onto NS-14 N	2.5
13.0	→	Slight R onto Windsor Back Rd (signs for Three Mile Plains/Windsor Back Road)	5.3
18.3	←	L onto NS-1 W	4.1
22.4	←	L onto Wiley Ave	1.0
23.4	→	R onto Victoria St	0.1
23.5	←	L at the 1st cross street onto Stannus St	0.3
23.8	→	R onto Evangeline Trail/Water St/NS-1 E	0.1
23.9	○	End of route	0.0

MINAS BASIN

Points of Interest

- **Schoolhouse Brewery (Start/ Stop)** Originally one of the smallest breweries in the province, Schoolhouse Brewery has continued to grow and now has a great spot downtown with a nice outdoor deck close to the water.

Craft Producers

Do a bit of research before riding this route if you want to stop at more craft producers. New distilleries, cideries, breweries, and wineries open regularly.

- **Sainte-Famille Winery (7.0 km)** Take a tour at this well-established winery and buy a bottle to go.
- **Bent Nail Brewery/Bent Ridge Winery (11.8 km)** This small-batch winery and "pico-brewery" are located in the middle of one of the province's most popular U-pick orchards.

50 Avondale Peninsula

MAP 18

Start Point
Avondale: Avon River Museum, 17 Belmont Rd.

Summary
Some challenging hills; quiet roads; river views; local food/drink.

Distance (km)	Duration	Max Grade +	Elevation Gain (m)	Unpaved
21.7	0:59/1:26	3.5	208	—

Description
Something magical seems to happen when you cross the St. Croix River onto the Avondale Peninsula; the landscape suddenly changes and everything seems to be enveloped in an ethereal light. This is a special area that is often overlooked and is worth taking the time to explore. The Avondale Peninsula provides some beautiful, undulating hills, each with a view of water and farmland at the top. This is a short ride that is meant to be taken slow.

Ride Considerations
- This area is active farmland, so you may encounter farming equipment on the road while cycling; give a wide berth as you pass, and signal your intent.
- This is a hilly area with twisty roads and occasional blind spots; ride with caution.

MINAS BASIN

Side Trips/Variations

- Hike the community walking trails as a warm-up or cool-down from your ride; access via the Avondale Community Hall or at the Avondale Sky Winery.
- Combine this trip with **52 Kempt Shore** to add another 53 km.
- Consider heading up to Summerville for lunch; come back the way you came to complete the ride for a total of 57 km.

Points of Interest

- **Avon River Heritage Society Museum (Start/ Stop)** Learn some local history while taking in the grandeur of the tidal Avon River; there is a grassy area, a wharf, and a picnic area here.
- **Avondale Sky Winery (0.6 km)** Located at the beginning or end of your ride on Avondale Cross Road, 0.6 km from the start. Stop in for a wine tasting and enjoy some local food; check in advance for restaurant hours.

Avondale Peninsula Cue Sheet

Dist	Type	Note	Next
0.0	●	Start of route	0.0
0.0	⚑	(Start) Avondale: Avon River Museum, 17 Belmont Rd; head east on Belmont Rd	0.6
0.6	←	L onto Avondale Cross Rd	2.2
2.8	↑	Continue onto Belmont Rd	8.2
11.0	↑	Continue onto Glooscap Trail/NS-215 W	0.3
11.3	↑	Continue onto Lawrence Rd	0.1
11.4	→	R to stay on Lawrence Rd	2.5
13.9	↑	Continue onto Avondale Rd	7.0
20.9	↑	Continue straight up the hill on Avondale Rd	0.7
21.6	→	R onto Belmont Rd	0.1
21.7	●	End of route	0.0

 ## Variation: Windsor–Avondale Peninsula (54.3 km, Map 18)

Make this into a longer day by starting in Windsor and exploring some of the back roads.

From Windsor, follow Trunk 1 to Newport Corner and then head north on Route 215 through Brooklyn; at this point you can connect with, and ride, the **50** Avon Peninsula via Belmont Road. In Mantua, head south on Avondale Road, connecting with Trunk 14 that will bring you to Garlands Crossing; get onto Trunk 1 to finish the ride back into Windsor.

52 Kempt Shore

MAP 18

Start Point
Brooklyn: Newport and District Rink, 1240 Rte. 215.

Summary
Coastal and river views; undulating hills; swim spot; beach access; local food/drink.

Distance (km)	Duration	Max Grade +	Elevation Gain (m)	Unpaved
53.2	2:25/3:32	5.8	562	—

Description
The Kempt Shore is a lovely cycling route that hugs parts of both the St. Croix and Avon Rivers, as well as the southeast corner of the Minas Basin. The inland portion of the ride is equally nice, following undulating hills with quick, punchy climbs. This trip has a great swimming opportunity, as well a favourite local eatery; take your time on this one and enjoy exploring the roads less travelled.

Ride Considerations
- Route 215 around Brooklyn can get relatively busy; try to avoid it during peak hours.

Side Trips/Variations
- Combine this trip with ⑩ **Avondale Peninsula** to add another 21.7 km.
- Another option is to ride the Avondale Peninsula first, then head up to Summerville for lunch; return back along Route 215 to your vehicle, for a ride totalling 57.7 km.
- Extend this ride farther up the shore by first heading to Walton, and then coming back down through Cheverie and Summerville. In Cogmagun River (11.9 km), head north on Walton Woods Road, which will bring you into Walton. Head west on Route 215 to get on the route again in Cheverie (this makes a 72.3 km ride).

Points of Interest
- **Cheverie Beach and Camera Obscura (27.7 km)** Enjoy a nice picnic spot by a rocky beach and visit the camera obscura—a building designed to naturally project an image of the surrounding area through a small hole onto the floor—just up the road on the other side. Access it by turning east on Route 215 and travelling 1 km.

MINAS BASIN

- **Kempt Quarry (29.7 km)** Take a swim in an old gypsum quarry, where the water is a tropical aquamarine colour. Local lore suggests that, years ago, the quarry flooded so quickly that mining machinery was abandoned and still rests at the bottom.
- **Flying Apron Restaurant (35.3 km)** This unique gem sources local ingredients to prepare interesting and excellent food; there are also accommodations here. Call in advance for restaurant hours.
- **Walton Lighthouse** This option is only available if you take the extended route out to Walton. To access it, go east on Route 215 from Walton; you will see the lighthouse entrance in 200 m.

Kempt Shore Cue Sheet

Dist	Type	Note	Next
0.0	◉	Start of route	0.0
0.0	⚑	(Start) Brooklyn: Newport and District Rink, 1240 NS-215; head northwest on NS-215	0.9
0.9	←	Keep L to stay on Glooscap Trail/NS-215 E, follow signs for Walton	3.3
4.2	→	Slight R onto Old Walton Rd	0.4
4.6	→	R onto N River Rd	2.8
7.4	←	L onto Walton Woods Rd	4.5
11.9	←	Slight L onto Cogmagun Rd	6.3
18.2	→	R onto New Cheverie Rd	9.5
27.7	←	L onto Glooscap Trail/NS-215 W	24.6
52.3	→	Slight R to stay on Glooscap Trail/NS-215 W (signs for NS-14/Brooklyn/Windsor/Halifax)	0.9
53.2	◉	End of route	0.0

 **Noel Shore**

MAP 19

Start Point
South Maitland: Fundy Tidal Interpretive Centre, 9865 Rte. 236.

Summary
Some challenging hills; remote area; some rough roads; coastal and river views; tidal bore.

Distance (km)	Duration	Max Grade +	Elevation Gain (m)	Unpaved
78.3	3:33/5:13	6.8	699	7% (5 km)

Description
This is a big ride that starts by following the Shubenacadie River, which is known for its tidal bore. The route takes you out past Maitland and onto the Noel Shore, where it follows Cobequid Bay all the way to Burntcoat Head Provincial Park. After exploring the world's highest tides, head inland to Kennetcook before heading east and back to your starting point.

MINAS BASIN

Ride Considerations

- This area can feel a little remote at times, so come prepared; supplies can be picked up en route in Maitland (9.3 km) and in Kennetcook (52.9 km).
- Check the tide tables in advance (available online) if you are interested in seeing the tide at either of its extremes, or if you want to watch the tidal bore in action.
- The small section of unpaved road after Burntcoat Head can be avoided by heading east on Route 215 (38.5 km); then head south on Route 354 to join up with the route.

Noel Shore Cue Sheet

Dist	Type	Note	Next
0.0	●	Start of route	0.0
0.0	⚑	(Start) South Maitland: Fundy Tidal Interpretive Centre, 9865 NS-236	0.0
0.0	→	R onto Glooscap Trail/NS-236 W	1.0
1.0	→	R onto Glooscap Trail/NS-215 W (signs for Maitland/Windsor)	29.3
30.3	→	R onto Burntcoat Rd	8.2
38.5	↑	Continue onto Singer Rd	5.0
43.5	→	R onto NS-354 S	9.4
52.9	←	L onto NS-236 E (signs for Maltland/Truro)	17.9
70.8	→	R onto Rocks Rd/NS-236	6.2
77.0	→	R onto Glooscap Trail/NS-215 E/ (signs for Truro/Shubenacadie)	0.3
77.3	←	L onto Glooscap Trail/NS-236 E (signs for Truro/Princeport)	1.0
78.3	←	L back to your start point	0.0
78.3	●	End of route	0.0

Side Trips/Variations

- You can ride to Burntcoat Head and return the same way, keeping the whole ride near the water, for a total of 69.6 km.

Points of Interest

- **Fundy Tidal Interpretive Centre (Start/Stop)** There is a viewing deck here where you can watch the tidal bore, which is an impressively large wave caused by the funnelling of the tide as it enters the long, narrow, shallow inlet of the Shubenacadie River. Check with the centre to find out when the tidal bore happens so you can view this phenomenon either at the beginning or at the end of your ride.
- **Anthony Provincial Park (19.0 km)** This is a nice little picnic park with some beautiful views of the coast and of the Minas Basin.
- **Burntcoat Head Provincial Park (35.6 km)** Experience the vastness of the Bay of Fundy and the world's highest tides; this beach has an average tide of 14.5 m.
- **Summertime Treats (52.9 km)** Head into Kennetcook for a stop at the local ice cream stand before heading back on Route 236 East.

 **Shubenacadie**

MAP 19

Start Point

South Maitland: Fundy Tidal Interpretive Centre, 9865 Rte. 236.

Summary

Some challenging hills; some rough roads; river views; tidal bore.

Distance (km)	Duration	Max Grade +	Elevation Gain (m)	Unpaved
48.9	2:13/3:15	4.9	459	12% (6 km)

Description

The first half of this ride follows the mighty Shubenacadie River where you can stop and observe the river in its various tidal states. Ride a short section of unpaved road as you make your way to Stewiacke, then carry on to Shortts Lake; head west, back to the starting point, once you reach Pleasant Valley. Try and take note of the tide level before you leave, and again when you return from your ride, to see the tides in action.

Side Trips/Variations

• This ride has some sections of unpaved road. To stay on pavement, and to make a longer ride, take Route 215 south to Shubenacadie, then north on Trunk 2 until it meets with Route 289 West, or else connect back to the route by taking Shortts Lake West Road just past Alton.

Points of Interest

• **Fundy Tidal Interpretive Centre (Start/Stop)** There is a viewing deck here where you can watch the tidal bore, which is an impressively large wave caused by the funnelling of the tide as it enters the long, narrow, shallow inlet of the Shubenacadie River. Check in with the centre to find out when the tidal bore happens so you can view this phenomenon either at the beginning or at the end of your ride.

• **Caddell Rapids Lookoff (10.4 km)** This is a small picnic park that overlooks the Shubenacadie River and its impressive tides.

MINAS BASIN

Shubenacadie Cue Sheet

Dist	Type	Note	Next
0.0	📍	Start of route	0.0
0.0	🚩	(Start) South Maitland: Fundy Tidal Interpretive Centre, 9865 NS-236	0.0
0.0	←	L onto Glooscap Trail/NS-236 E	2.0
2.0	↑	Continue onto Pleasant Valley Rd/NS-289 E (signs for NS-102/Brookfield/Truro)	2.5
4.5	→	R onto Riverside Rd	13.9
18.4	→	R onto NS-2 S	1.0
19.4	←	L onto Main St E (signs for Stewiacke)	4.9
24.3	←	L onto Alton Rd	5.9
30.2	↑	Continue onto Shortts Lake West Rd	6.6
36.8	→	R onto Cement Plant Rd	0.3
37.1	←	L onto Pleasant Valley Rd/NS-289 W	9.8
46.9	↑	Continue straight onto Glooscap Trail/NS-236 W (signs for NS-215/Maitland/Windsor)	2.0
48.9	→	R, back to your start point	0.0
48.9	📍	End of route	0.0

 Cobequid Trail (RT)

MAP 19

Start Point
Truro: trailhead, beside 210 Willow St.

Summary
Easy ride; rail trail; unpaved roads; water views; kid-friendly.

Distance (km)	Duration	Max Grade +	Elevation Gain (m)	Unpaved
28.7	1:18/1:54	2.8	175	90% (26 km)

Description
This is an easy ride out of Truro that uses the Cobequid Trail and some quiet, unpaved roads. This route has some nice sections along the water with great views of the Salmon River as it runs out into Cobequid Bay. This is a relaxing ride, just minutes outside downtown Truro.

Ride Considerations
- If you are riding with children and want to stay on the rail trail, turn around at Shore Road and go back the way you came. Shore Road and Black Rock Road are both quiet dirt roads, but there is a 2 km stretch on Route 236 that is residential, with speeds of 60–80 kmh. Choose your route according to your group's level of comfort.

MINAS BASIN

Cobequid Trail (RT) Cue Sheet

Dist	Type	Note	Next
0.0	📍	Start of route	0.0
0.0	▸	(Start) Truro: trailhead, beside 210 Willow St; head west on the Cobequid Trail	9.8
9.8	→	R onto Shore Rd	4.6
14.4	←	L onto Black Rock Rd	2.8
17.2	←	L onto Glooscap Trail/NS-236 E	1.7
18.9	←	L onto Shore Rd	0.0
18.9	→	R onto Cobequid Trail	9.8
28.7	📍	End of route	0.0

Victoria Park

This is a three thousand–acre woodland park in the heart of Truro, featuring old-growth forests, tumbling waterfalls, and deep ravines. The area has a mountain bike park with over 40 km of trails suitable for all levels of experience and there are many hard-packed trails for all types of bicycles to get around the various parts of the park. There is easily a day's worth of cycling and exploring to do in this area.

56 Blue Route: East Mountain–Pictou (RT)

MAP 26

Start Point
East Mountain: carpool parking lot, beside 689 Pictou Rd.

Summary
Challenging hills; some bike lanes; rail trail; water views.

Distance (km)	Duration	Max Grade +	Elevation Gain (m)	Unpaved
112.4 (return)	5:06/7:29	5.3	846	6% (7 km)

Description
This ride is part of the Blue Route, Nova Scotia's provincial cycling network, and was the first official section opened. The route connects East Mountain with the town of Pictou through a combination of low-traffic roads, bicycle lanes, and well-maintained rail trail. As you leave East Mountain, the ride starts with a few challenging climbs to get over Mount Thom; then you will be treated to a gradual descent of nearly 19 km. After cycling past Salt Springs Provincial Park, the ride heads onto Route 376 toward Lyons Brook, an exceptional section of the route that is lined with beautiful old trees and farmland, and that offers views of the West River of Pictou. Get on the Jitney Trail, just past Lyons Brook, which takes you straight into the town of Pictou. To get home, head back the way you came.

MINAS BASIN

Side Trips/Variations

- To make this ride shorter, and to avoid the big hills, ride the route between Salt Springs Provincial Park and Pictou—a beautiful ride with very little elevation (46 km return).
- To make a shorter route that starts near Truro, ride from East Mountain to Salt Springs Provincial Park (66 km return); the ride back to East Mountain consists of a long, challenging climb.
- To avoid the rail trail section of the ride, bypass the turnoff (53.0 km) and follow the signs into Pictou.

Blue Route: East Mountain–Pictou (RT) Cue Sheet

Dist	Type	Note	Next
0.0	📍	Start of route	0.0
0.0	⚑	(Start) East Mountain: carpool parking lot, beside 689 Pictou Rd; head east on Pictou Rd/NS-4	37.8
37.8	←	L onto NS-376 N	15.1
52.9	→	Slight R onto Jitney Trail/Trans-Canada Trail	3.3
56.2	↩	Town of Pictou; turnaround point	3.3
59.5	←	Slight L onto NS-376 S	15.1
74.6	→	R onto NS-4 W (signs for Trans-Canada Highway/NS-104/Salt Springs/Truro)	37.8
112.4	📍	End of route	0.0

Points of Interest

- **Salt Springs Provincial Park (33.0 km)** A sheltered picnic park with basic amenities.
- **Uncle Leo's Brewery (50.6 km)** Stop and stock up at a local brewery that makes an assortment of quality craft beers.

 # 57 Cobequid Mountains

MAP 20

Start Point
Debert: Masstown Market, 10622 Trunk 2.

Summary
Challenging hills; remote area; unpaved/rough roads.

Distance (km)	Duration	Max Grade +	Elevation Gain (m)	Unpaved
84.8	3:51/5:39	5.4	855	33% (28 km)

Description
This inland route takes you on a section of the Blue Route, leaving from the Masstown Market and heading north into the Cobequid Mountains. Get ready for a solid 16 km climb as soon as the ride starts, then enjoy coming down the other side of the mountain into the Wentworth Valley. This area is full of hardwoods,

MINAS BASIN

and is particularly exceptional when the fall colours arrive (late September, early October). Ride through the valley and then head west, into some remote back roads with a series of challenging hills. The rest of the route is a combination of paved and unpaved road, with a 20 km stretch that is mostly downhill, taking you back to the Masstown Market to finish the ride.

Ride Considerations

- This route can get pretty remote; ensure that you have adequate supplies.
- Many of the back roads are in rough shape, but they are fairly quiet, allowing for manoeuvrability.
- Signs are often missing on back roads; be prepared with maps, or download the route onto your phone or device.
- Cell service is likely unavailable for portions of this ride.
- This is a gravel grinder ride with lots of rough, unpaved sections; ensure that your bike is suitable for these conditions.

Cobequid Mountains Cue Sheet

Dist	Type	Note	Next
0.0	◉	Start of route	0.0
0.0	⚑	(Start) Debert: Masstown Market, 10622 NS-2; head behind Masstown Market to NS-4 W	0.3
0.3	←	L onto NS-4 W	28.8
29.1	←	L onto Valley Rd	8.3
37.4	←	L onto Wentworth Collingwood Rd	9.6
47.0	←	L onto Westchester Rd	9.3
56.3	←	Slight L to stay on Westchester Rd	12.2
68.5	←	L onto Mines Bass River Rd	0.1
68.6	→	Slight R onto Station Rd	3.5
72.1	←	L onto E Village Rd	2.4
74.5	←	L to stay on E Village Rd	2.3
76.8	→	R onto NS-4 E	7.8
84.6	→	R into Masstown Market	0.2
84.8	◉	End of route	0.0

Points of Interest

- **Tunnel (8.6 km)** Stop to check out this large tunnel with flowing water through it, where McElmon Brook flows down toward the Folly River. This is a subtle gem that is often missed by cars speeding by; it is also a good place to cool down on a hot day.
- **Wentworth Provincial Park (29.0 km)** This is slightly off the route, but it is a nice picnic park along the water and it offers basic amenities. Access it by staying on Trunk 4 for 300 m after the turnoff to Wentworth Collingwood Road.

MAP 21

58 Five Islands–Parrsboro

Start Point
Five Islands Provincial Park: 618 Bentley Branch Rd., Trunk 2.

Summary
Challenging hills; remote area; unpaved/rough roads; coastal views.

Distance (km)	Duration	Max Grade +	Elevation Gain (m)	Unpaved
94.6	4:18/6:18	6.7	847	16% (15 km)

Description
This is a long ride through big country that makes you work for your views. The ride starts from Five Islands Provincial Park and follows the coast for 10 km before heading inland, where there will be a long, tough, 15 km climb up an unpaved road. As you make your ascent, you will pass rolling hills covered in blueberry bushes, and when you finally reach the top you will be rewarded with a stunning view of the hills of Cumberland County. The road turns to pavement at East Mapleton, followed by a fantastic 15 km descent toward Southampton. From this point, the ride is a series of rolling hills and paved roads back to Parrsboro. The final stretch is along the coast, providing a series of punchy hills that take you all the way back to Five Islands Provincial Park.

Ride Considerations
• Many of these roads are unpaved or in rough shape; ride with caution.
• This ride can get fairly remote; be sure to have adequate supplies.

Side Trips/Variations
• Starting this ride in Parrsboro and skipping the leg to Five Islands Provincial Park will reduce the ride by 20 km. We suggest you go counter-clockwise from either start point to avoid coming down 15 km of rough, unpaved road.

Points of Interest
• **Five Islands Provincial Park (Start/Stop)** This is a beautiful campground and park that features 90 m high sea cliffs; explore the beaches, dig for clams, and walk on the ocean floor.

Five Islands–Parrsboro Cue Sheet

Dist	Type	Note	Next
0.0	📍	Start of route	0.0
0.0	🚩	(Start) Five Islands Provincial Park: 618 Bentley Branch Rd, NS-2; head out of park on Bentley Branch Rd	3.0
3.0	←	L onto NS-2 N	7.0
10.0	→	R onto Lynn Rd	21.0
31.0	←	L onto NS-2 S (signs for Parrsboro)	9.2
40.2	←	L to stay on NS-2 S (signs for Parrsboro)	25.2
65.4	←	L onto Glooscap Trail/NS-2 S (signs for Truro)	0.0
65.4	←	L onto NS-2 S	26.2
91.6	→	R onto Bentley Branch Rd	3.0
94.6	📍	End of route	0.0

59 Parrsboro–River Hebert

MAP 21

Start Point
Parrsboro: 4049 Eastern Ave.

Summary
Some challenging climbs; remote area; unpaved/rough roads; river views.

Distance (km)	Duration	Max Grade +	Elevation Gain (m)	Unpaved
93.3	4:14/6:13	6.4	562	10% (9 km)

Description
It's hilly in this area and towns are far apart, making for long, challenging rides. This route takes you north out of Parrsboro, riding through some beautiful countryside on your way to the town of River Hebert. The highlight of the ride is on the peninsula, where you will follow the River Hébert, passing by vast farmland and some fantastic views of the water. The ride back is another inland route, finishing up on the same stretch of road you started on.

Ride Considerations
- Many of the back roads are in rough shape, but they are fairly quiet, allowing for manoeuvrability.
- This ride can get fairly remote; be sure to have adequate supplies.
- Cell service is likely unavailable for portions of this ride.
- There is one 9 km section of unpaved road that cannot be avoided if you are doing the loop.

Side Trips/Variations
- To make a shorter ride, park in the vicinity of Newville Lake (13.7 km) to make the loop approximately 63 km. This area is somewhat isolated; it's best to avoid leaving valuables in your vehicle.

Parrsboro–River Hebert Cue Sheet

Dist	Type	Note	Next
0.0	◉	Start of route	0.0
0.0	⚑	(Start) Parrsboro: 4049 Eastern Ave; head west on NS-2 N	0.0
0.0	→	R to stay on NS-2 N	14.4
14.4	←	L onto Boars Back Rd	19.9
34.3	↑	Continue onto NS-242 E	1.2
35.5	↑	Continue straight onto NS-242 E/ Taylor Rd	1.6
37.1	←	Slight L onto Lower Maccan Rd	13.7
50.8	←	L onto Lower Maccan Rd/NS-242 E	0.8
51.6	→	R onto NS-302 S (signs for Southampton/Parrsboro)	16.4
68.0	↑	Continue straight onto NS-2 S	25.2
93.2	←	L onto Glooscap Trail/NS-2 S (signs for Truro)	0.1
93.3	◉	End of route	0.0

MINAS BASIN

60 Parrsboro–Cape Chignecto

MAP 22

Start Point

Parrsboro: 4049 Eastern Ave.

Summary

Many steep, challenging hills; somewhat remote; coastal views; beach access.

Distance (km)	Duration	Max Grade +	Elevation Gain (m)	Unpaved
49.6 (one way)	2:15/3:18	12.0	649	—

Description

This route has been dubbed the "Mini–Cabot Trail" for its many steep, challenging hills and for the dramatic views that are unveiled around every corner. Take some time to explore this dramatic landscape as you cycle the ever-rolling hills of the coast, stopping in at rocky and muddy beaches along the way to gaze out to the Minas Basin and the Bay of Fundy. At the western end of the ride, take some time to cycle around Advocate Harbour and walk on the impressive driftwood beach that spans all the way to the entrance of Cape Chignecto Provincial Park. Enjoy many different views as you return the way you came, finishing up back in Parrsboro the next day. This is a challenging ride in a beautiful area; it is worth the effort—and affords some solid bragging rights.

Ride Considerations

- This ride is usually done over two days, with an overnight in Advocate or Parrsboro. Most people will enjoy taking their time to enjoy the views and the beaches along the way, and to explore both Advocate and Parrsboro.

Side Trips/Variations

- **Wards Falls (9.2 km)** This is a popular 6 km hike that takes you to a spectacular waterfall. There will be a sign off Parrsboro Shore Road, not far out of Parrsboro; ride your bike until you see the hiking trail. Be aware that signage to the falls is not always reliable.
- **Cape d'Or** Visit a lighthouse that is now a hostel and a fine-dining restaurant; it also provides a view of the most spectacular sunsets in the area. Access it by taking Back Street (43.1 km), just east of Advocate Harbour. Get onto Cape d'Or Road and follow this until the end. Be aware that a return trip will include 10 km of rough, unpaved roads with some steep sections.

MINAS BASIN

Points of Interest

- **Age of Sail Heritage Museum (21.4 km)** Stop into this small museum to learn about the local history and its connection with sailing.
- **Spencers Island (37.6 km)** This is a nice little beach area with camping. There is also a seasonal/occasional restaurant here called Spencer's Island Beach Café; be sure to call first if you are planning to eat here.
- **Wild Caraway Restaurant (45.2 km)** This is an excellent restaurant that is a destination unto itself. The owners are known for serving carefully crafted local dishes in a casual setting. Reservations are highly recommended.
- **West Advocate Beach (48.8 km)** There is a beautiful driftwood beach here that provides a fantastic view of Cape Chignecto. Access it by heading down Advocate Beach Road for 800 m.
- **Cape Chignecto Provincial Park (49.6 km)** This park is a hidden gem; take some time to walk the beaches and explore some of the trails. There is a challenging 60 km hiking trail here, considered by many to be one of the best-kept backcountry secrets in the province.

Parrsboro–Cape Chignecto Cue Sheet

Dist	Type	Note	Next
0.0	●	Start of route	0.0
0.0	▩	(Start) Parrsboro: 4049 Eastern Ave; head west on NS-2 N	0.0
0.0	→	R to stay NS-2 N	0.1
0.1	←	L onto King St	0.7
0.8	→	R onto Western Ave	1.7
2.5	↑	Continue onto Smith Hollow Rd	0.7
3.2	←	L onto Parrsboro Shore Rd/NS-209 W (signs for Diligent River)	34.4
37.6	←	L onto Spencers Island Rd	1.5
39.1	←	Slight L onto NS-209 W	8.8
47.9	←	L onto W Advocate Rd	1.7
49.6	●	End of route	0.0

The Peggys Cove lighthouse is what many people envision when they think of Nova Scotia. (PAUL NEWTON)

A sign outside the Tide Cycles bike shop in Bear River. (ADAM BARNETT)

At Blomidon Provincial Park, you can walk the beach and/or hike the trails at the top of the hill.
(KIMBERLY SMITH)

Cyclists pass under the image of a fox painted on an overpass on the Rum Runners Trail.
(BRIANNE STEINMAN)

Many of the cycling routes in Nova Scotia offer riders a view of the ocean. (DOUG BROWN)

Cycling on Cape Sable Island is all about the beaches, back roads, and working wharfs. (ADAM BARNETT)

The Rum Runners Trail has changed the way people travel by bicycle on the South Shore for the better. (SWEET RIDE CYCLING)

The Celtic Shores Coastal Trail takes cyclists up the coast by way of a converted railway bed, parallel to the stretch of road known as the Ceilidh Trail. (BICYCLE NOVA SCOTIA)

The Train Station Inn in Tatamagouche is a unique place to stop for a meal, or to stay overnight. (SHERRY HUDSON, PRESENCE PHOTOGRAPHY)

The Wolfville Wine Tour route takes cyclists along the scenic Gaspereau River. (JAMIE ROBERTSON)

Many of the cycling routes in Nova Scotia will take cyclists to hidden gems like this secluded swim spot off the beaten path. (ADAM BARNETT)

The western side of Cape Breton island will take cyclists through the Margaree Valley, known for salmon fishing along the Margaree River. (PAUL NEWTON)

Nova Scotia's back roads often take riders along active farmland. (SWEET RIDE CYCLING)

The Cabot Trail is known for lobster and crab fishing; pick up some lobster on your way and have a lobster boil on the beach. (KRISTEN DICK)

The final stretch leading to Meat Cove on Cape Breton Island is a 7 km ride on unpaved roads that hug the coastline, making for some incredible views. (SHEENA MASON)

The Rum Runners Trail provides a chance to ride away from traffic, and provides many relaxing vistas along the way. (BICYCLE NOVA SCOTIA)

CYCLING ROUTES OF THE NORTHUMBERLAND SHORE

Route	Route Name	Distance (km)	Duration	Max Grade +	Elevation Gain (m)	Unpaved	Map
61	Amherst Shore	75.1	3:24/5:00	4.5	527	—	23
62	Pugwash–Oxford	51.2	2:19/3:24	5.6	432	—	23
63	Fox Harbour Loop	37.6	1:42/2:30	2.8	207	—	23
64	Tatamagouche–Malagash	56.2	2:33/3:44	4.8	347	—	24
65	Tatamagouche–Wentworth Valley	69.9	3:10/4:39	5.7	503	—	24
66	Hippie Dippie	51.9	2:21/3:27	3.8	331	—	24
67	Cape John	52.6	2:23/3:30	2.9	271	—	25
68	Caribou Island	74.0	3:21/4:56	4.4	537	—	25
69	Gully Lake Preserve	82.1	3:43/5:28	9.5	870	46% (38 km)	26
70	Melmerby Beach	37.6	1:42/2:30	7.3	389	—	26
71	Museum of Industry (RT)	6.0	0:16/0:24	5.3	39	100% (6 km)	26
72	Antigonish: Cape George	75.4	3:25/5:01	8.7	833	—	27
73	Barneys River–Arisaig Loop	81.4	3:42/5:26	5.6	606	—	27
74	Beaver Mountain–Addington Forks	29.0	1:19/1:56	11.2	314	—	27

Northumberland Shore Regional Overview

The Northumberland Shore is known for comfortable ocean swimming—the waters here are easily the warmest in the province. This is beach country, as is evident from all the campgrounds and provincial parks along the shore. Wherever you are travelling in these parts, be sure to bring your beachwear; there will be ample opportunities to get into the water and laze on the sand.

Just as this area is known for its warm waters, it's also known for its warm summer climate—an ideal climate in which to grow grapes. Stop by the Jost winery for a tasting, and see about getting a tour of their facilities. You can also rent bikes here to explore the Malagash Peninsula and to visit the impressive Blue Sea Beach Provincial Park with its wide, sandy beach and extensive dune system. The nearby towns of Tatamagouche and River John are both lovey and offer a collection of small businesses and attractions. Although it is hard to envision now, these coastal communities were once home to a booming shipbuilding industry. These days you'll find a number of active fishing wharves and farms; this is an area known for its quiet roads, secret waterfalls, and swim spots. Heading inland from here will take you into the Wentworth Valley, which sits nestled in the Cobequid

Mountains. Travel through this area in the fall when the colours are changing—it rivals any other location in the province for impressive foliage.

Following the coastline will take you to the unique and somewhat exotic Caribou Island, where you can cycle along narrow spits of land and visit beaches on your way to the lighthouse at the point. Travel to the steel town of New Glasgow, the commercial hub of northeastern Nova Scotia, and home to nearby Melmerby Beach. Just when you thought the beaches couldn't get any better, this gem offers warm waters, boardwalks, and expansive views. Even farther along the coast is Cape George, considered one of the classic rides of Nova Scotia. The coastline here gets hilly and challenging, and takes you around the Cape to visit the lighthouse that looks over St. Georges Bay toward the Mabou Highlands of Cape Breton.

Touring around this part of the province in the summertime is a delight: it's all about taking it slow, visiting beaches, and checking out the small towns along the way. Enjoy the beauty of the Northumberland Shore and discover the "tropics" of Nova Scotia.

Additional Notes

- This is cottage country and there is often a lot of traffic on Trunk 6, which is the main road along the coast. Pay close attention on this road, and look out for camper-vans and trailers, especially on weekends and warm summer days; try to it avoid during peak hours.

Northumberland Shore Bike Shops

- Highland Bike Shop (Antigonish) 902-735-3320
- Pictou County Cycle (New Glasgow) 902-928-0331
- The Bicycle Specialist (Amherst) 902-660-3393

Northumberland Shore Emergency Services

- Cumberland Regional Health Centre (Amherst)
- Lillian Fraser Memorial Hospital (Tatamagouche)
- Aberdeen Hospital (New Glasgow)
- North Cumberland Memorial Hospital (Pugwash)
- St. Martha's Regional Hospital (Antigonish)

61 Amherst Shore

MAP 23

NORTHUMBERLAND SHORE

Start Point
Amherst: 98 Victoria St. East.

Summary
Some challenging hills; some rough roads; beach access; coastal views.

Distance (km)	Duration	Max Grade +	Elevation Gain (m)	Unpaved
75.1	3:24/5:00	4.5	527	—

Description
This route follows some nice rolling terrain out of Amherst and toward the Northumberland Strait, where the water is warm and the beaches are plentiful. After 25 km, you will hit the coast, which offers some nice riding and beautiful views. Cross the bridge into Northport, then head south on a lovely stretch of road that follows the Shinimicas River, passing by farms and pastures. Finish the ride inland on rolling hills all the way back to Amherst.

Ride Considerations
- The ride on the coast takes you on Route 366, which can get very busy in the summertime, especially on nice days and the weekends. Stay alert on this road and be aware of camper-vans and trailers.
- The last leg of this trip is on Trunk 6, which can get busy; try to avoid it during peak hours.

Points of Interest
- **Tidnish Dock Provincial Park (25.6 km)** A small picnic park with a rocky beach; access it by turning down Tidnish Head Road for 200 m.
- **Amherst Shore Provincial Park (36.6 km)** Another nice park that has camping areas among hardwood trees, along with beach access.

Amherst Shore Cue Sheet

Dist	Type	Note	Next
0.0	♀	Start of route	0.0
0.0	⚑	(Start) Amherst: 98 Victoria St East; head east on Victoria St/NS-6	3.7
3.7	←	L onto Sunrise Trail, NS-366	36.9
40.6	→	R onto Shinimicas Rd	8.2
48.8	→	Slight R onto NS-6 W	26.3
75.1	♀	End of route	0.0

62 Pugwash–Oxford

Start Point
Pugwash: 10308 Durham St.

Summary
Fairly easy ride; some challenging hills; some rough roads; river views.

Distance (km)	Duration	Max Grade +	Elevation Gain (m)	Unpaved
51.2	2:19/3:24	5.6	432	—

Description
This is a nice ride following along either side of the River Philip. After leaving Pugwash follow Trunk 6 west to Port Philip. As you head up the river, the east side is fairly easy going, except for one long, challenging climb of 2.5 km, which then makes for a nice descent into Oxford. Heading north, the west side of the river is relatively flat and has nice water views as you cycle to Port Howe, where you will then head east on Trunk 6 back to your starting point.

Ride Considerations
• The section from Pictou to Port Philip is on Trunk 6, which can be a busy road; try to avoid it during peak hours.

Side Trips/Variations
• This ride can start in either Pugwash or Oxford.
• To shorten the ride, skip the back-and-forth between Pictou and Port Philip; this will take 14 km off your distance.

Pugwash–Oxford Cue Sheet

Dist	Type	Note	Next
0.0	●	Start of route	0.0
0.0	⚑	(Start) Pugwash: 10308 Durham St; head west on Durham St/NS-6	0.2
0.2	←	L onto NS-6 W	6.7
6.9	←	L onto NS-321 S (signs for Oxford/Springhill)	18.6
25.5	→	R onto Lower Main St/NS-204 W (signs for Amherst)	17.3
42.8	→	R onto NS-6 E (signs for Pugwash/Wallace/Sunrise Trail)	8.1
50.9	→	R to stay on NS-6	0.3
51.2	●	End of route	0.0

Fox Harbour Loop

MAP 23

Start Point
Pugwash: 10308 Durham St.

Summary
Easy ride; some busy roads; coastal views; beach access.

Distance (km)	Duration	Max Grade +	Elevation Gain (m)	Unpaved
37.6	1:42/2:30	2.8	207	—

Description
Take an easy day trip from Pugwash to explore a portion of the Northumberland Shore. The highlight of this trip is the Gulf Shore Provincial Park, where there is a fantastic beach with warm water for swimming.

Ride Considerations
- The last stretch of this ride is on Trunk 6, which can get busy; try to avoid it during peak hours. To avoid this section, head west on North Wallace Road (20.5 km) to Wallace Bay; expect rough conditions.

Side Trips/Variations
- This trip can be combined with a trip out to Malagash to visit the Jost Winery, with the option to cycle around the Malagash Peninsula. To visit the winery, head east on Trunk 6 when you enter Wallace (22.2 km). See 64 Tatamagouche–Malagash for more details.

Points of Interest
- Gulf Shore Provincial Park (4.6 km) This is a good-sized picnic park with a fantastic beach for swimming.

Fox Harbout Loop Cue Sheet

Dist	Type	Note	Next
0.0	◉	Start of route	0.0
0.0	⚑	(Start) Pugwash: 10308 Durham St; head east on NS-6	0.1
0.1	←	L onto Church St (signs for Sunrise Trail/Pugwash Point/Gulf Shore)	1.3
1.4	→	Church St turns slightly R and becomes Gulf Shore Rd	13.6
15.0	↑	Continue onto Ferry Rd	7.2
22.2	→	R onto NS-6 W	15.4
37.6	◉	End of route	0.0

Busy Season

The Gulf Shore Road is heavily populated with cottages and campgrounds and can get very busy in the summertime, especially on nice days and on weekends. Stay alert on this road and be aware of camper-vans and trailers.

Tatamagouche–Malagash

MAP 24

Start Point

Tatamagouche: North Shore Recreation Centre, 30 Blair Ave.

Summary

Some rough roads; coastal views; winery; beach access.

Distance (km)	Duration	Max Grade +	Elevation Gain (m)	Unpaved
56.2	2:33/3:44	4.8	347	—

Description

Take a trip out to Malagash Peninsula to visit Jost Vineyards and to experience great views of Tatamagouche Bay. After visiting the winery, follow the mostly inland route along North Shore Road. There are not a lot of water views on this section, but there is a great park en route that provides beach access, where you can explore the dunes and go for a swim. Head around the point and enjoy the southern part of the peninsula that has beautiful water views and better road conditions. Finish by connecting back to Trunk 6 and back to Tatamagouche.

Ride Considerations

- The north side of the Malagash Peninsula has some very rough roads. To avoid these, or to make the trip shorter, take Smith Road (20.8 km) across the peninsula, taking approximately 22 km off the total distance.
- Trunk 6 is a main road, and can be fairly busy; try to avoid it during peak hours.

Points of Interest

- **Jost Vineyards (20.8 km)** Take some time to visit the largest winery in Nova Scotia. Access it by heading down Smith Road and then immediately turning onto Vintage Lane.
- **Blue Sea Beach Provincial Park (28.2 km)** This park has a beautiful wide, sandy beach with an extensive dune system; there is also a change house, a picnic area, and a boardwalk to the beach.

Tatamagouche–Malagash Cue Sheet

Dist	Type	Note	Next
0.0	📍	Start of route	0.0
0.0	🚩	(Start) Tatamagouche: North Shore Recreation Centre, 30 Blair Ave; head west on Blair Ave	0.1
0.1	→	R onto Lake Rd	0.2
0.3	←	L onto Main St/Sunrise Trail (signs for NS-6 W/Wallace/Pugwash)	14.6
14.9	→	R onto North Shore Rd (signs for Horton Point/Malagash Mine/North Shore Rd)	2.7

17.6	→	R to stay on North Shore Rd	3.2
20.8	←	L onto North Shore Rd	5.9
26.7	←	L onto Blue Sea Rd	6.0
32.7	→	R onto Malagash Rd	10.6
43.3	←	L to stay on Malagash Rd	2.3
45.6	←	L onto NS-6 E	10.3
55.9	→	R onto Lake Rd	0.2
56.1	←	L onto Blair Ave	0.1
56.2	📍	End of route	0.0

65 Tatamagouche–Wentworth Valley   MAP 24

Start Point
Tatamagouche: North Shore Recreation Centre, 30 Blair Ave.

Summary
Challenging hills; remote area; some coastal views.

Distance (km)	Duration	Max Grade +	Elevation Gain (m)	Unpaved
69.9	3:10/4:39	5.7	503	—

Description
This is a big ride that starts out following Tatamagouche Bay, then heads deep into the Wentworth Valley. Try to ride this route in the fall when the colours are changing; the Wentworth Valley is full of hardwood trees, making for an incredible sight. A section of this route is also part of the Blue Route, Nova Scotia's provincial cycling network.

Leave from Tatamagouche toward Wallace, then head inland, down into the Wentworth Valley. Just before Wentworth Station, the route heads east on Route 246. You will have a steady 11 km climb before coming down on the other side of the hill, with a nearly 15 km descent back into Tatamagouche.

Ride Considerations
- This route can get pretty remote; ensure that you have adequate supplies.
- The roads between Wallace and Wentworth Centre are low-traffic, but they are also twisty and hilly, with numerous blind spots; ride with caution.

Points of Interest

- **Wentworth Provincial Park (43.3 km)** This is slightly off the route, but is a nice picnic park along the water with basic amenities. Access it by staying on Trunk 4 for 300 m after the turnoff to Route 246.

Tatamagouche–Wentworth Valley Cue Sheet

Dist	Type	Note	Next
0.0	📍	Start of route	0.0
0.0	⚑	(Start) Tatamagouche: North Shore Recreation Centre, 30 Blair Ave; head west on Blair Ave	0.1
0.1	→	R onto Lake Rd	0.2
0.3	←	L onto Main St/Sunrise Trail (signs for NS-6 W/Wallace/Pugwash)	18.5
18.8	←	L onto NS-307 S (signs for Wentworth/Folly Lake/NS-4)	19.4
38.2	←	L onto NS-4 E	4.8
43.0	←	L onto NS-246 E (signs for NS-6/Sunrise Trail/Tatamagouche)	24.7
67.7	↑	Continue onto Maple Ave	1.4
69.1	←	L onto Blair Ave	0.8
69.9	📍	End of route	0.0

66 Hippie Dippie

MAP 24

Start Point
Tatamagouche: North Shore Recreation Centre, 30 Blair Ave.

Summary
Challenging hills; remote area; swim spot.

Distance (km)	Duration	Max Grade +	Elevation Gain (m)	Unpaved
51.9	2:21/3:27	3.8	331	—

Description
This is a nice tour of the Tatamagouche area, originally inspired by an annual fall ride put on by the Tatamagouche Brewing Company, and named after one of their craft beers. The roads are quiet, the pavement is in good condition, and the scenery is fantastic as you pass by expansive farmland and cross multiple rivers.

Ride Considerations
- This route can sometimes feel fairly remote; ensure that you have adequate supplies.

Side Trips/Variations
- You have the option to take the rail trail back to Tatamagouche for the final leg of the ride. Head west on the trail at 37.6 km; there is no sign, but the trail is distinctive and has open gates.

Points of Interest
- **The Falls (Waughs River) (23.0 km)** This is a local favourite, with multiple waterfalls and interesting rock formations; the water here is cold and fast-moving. To access, head down Power House Road at the intersection of Route 256 and Route 311; at the turn-around point, there is a path through the woods that leads to the swimming hole.

Hippie Dippie Cue Sheet

Dist	Type	Note	Next
0.0	⦿	Start of route	0.0
0.0	⚑	(Start) Tatamagouche: North Shore Recreation Centre, 30 Blair Ave; head east on Blair Ave	0.8
0.8	➡	R onto Maple Ave	1.4
2.2	↑	Continue onto NS-246 W	8.9
11.1	⬅	L onto Balmoral Rd/NS-256 E (signs for The Falls/West Branch/Central New Annan)	0.8
11.9	↰	Slight L to stay on Balmoral Rd/NS-256 E	11.1
23.0	➡	R onto NS-256 E/NS-311 S (signs for Truro)	0.2

23.2	⬅	L onto Balmoral Rd/NS-256 E (signs for McBains Corporation/Lyons Brook)	7.8
31.0	⬅	L onto NS-326 N (signs for Denmark/Brule)	8.0
39.0	⬅	L onto Upper River John Rd	7.9
46.9	↑	Continue straight onto NS-311 N (signs NS-6/Tatamagouche)	2.7
49.6	↑	Merge onto Main St/Sunrise Trail (signs for NS-6 W/Wallace/Amherst)	2.0
51.6	⬅	L onto Lake Rd	0.2
51.8	⬅	L onto Blair Ave	0.1
51.9	⦿	End of route	0.0

This bridge, on a section of the Trans-Canada Trail near Tatamagouche, takes cyclists over the Waughs River. (SHERRY HUDSON, PRESENCE PHOTOGRAPHY)

67 Cape John

MAP 25

NORTHUMBERLAND SHORE

Start Point
River John: School St.

Summary
Coastal views; fishing wharf.

Distance (km)	Duration	Max Grade +	Elevation Gain (m)	Unpaved
52.6	2:23/3:30	2.9	271	—

Description
This trip starts out in the very beautiful, and highly spirited, town of River John. The first leg is a highlight of the route, with an easy ride on excellent roads along Cape John. At the tip of the cape you'll find an active fishing wharf—a great place to have a picnic and take in the view. Going back the way you came, the route then gets onto Trunk 6, riding through the community of Seafoam before heading inland at Tony River. The last stretch of the ride is along a quiet road, which takes you back to River John.

Ride Considerations
- Fifteen kilometres of this ride is on Trunk 6, which is a busy road, especially on weekends and on warm, sunny days; stay alert on this section and beware of camper vans and trailers.

Side Trips/Variations
- To make this a shorter trip, head out to Cape John and back for a total of 18.6 km; this is the highlight of the ride.

Points of Interest
- **Cape John Wharf (9.1 km)** Follow a beautiful section of road to the end, where you will find a working fishing wharf.
- **Seafoam Lavender Company (26.1 km)** Stop by and roam through fields of lavender.

Cape John Cue Sheet

Dist	Type	Note	Next
0.0	📍	Start of route	0.0
0.0	🚩	(Start) River John: School St; head north on School St	0.1
0.1	→	R onto NS-6 E (signs for Pictou)	1.0
1.1	←	L onto Cape John Rd	8.0
9.1	↩	Turnaround point	8.0
17.1	←	L onto NS-6 E	15.0
32.1	→	R onto Meadowville Station Rd	6.2
38.3	→	R onto River John Rd	2.8
41.1	→	R to stay on River John Rd	10.4
51.5	←	L onto NS-6 W	0.9
52.4	←	L onto River John Station Rd	0.1
52.5	→	Slight R onto School St	0.1
52.6	📍	End of route	0.0

68 Caribou Island

MAP 25

Start Point
Pictou: 87 Caladh Ave.

Summary
Coastal views; beach access.

Distance (km)	Duration	Max Grade +	Elevation Gain (m)	Unpaved
74.0	3:21/4:46	4.4	537	—

Description

This route takes you out of Pictou along a coastal route to the very beautiful, and somewhat exotic, Caribou Island. The ride out of Pictou is full of undulating hills, with beach stops along the way. Once you get to Caribou Island, take your time and enjoy roads that are in excellent shape and a landscape that is constantly being rearranged by wind, weather, and tides. Be sure to visit the lighthouse and take in the view toward Prince Edward Island. The trip finishes inland on a quiet back road, providing one long, last hill before taking you downhill back to Pictou.

Ride Considerations
• There is a 4.4 km section of the ride on Trunk 6, which is a busy road; try to avoid it during peak hours.

Side Trips/Variations
• To make the ride shorter, skip over the Caribou Islands and take off 20 km; this is not recommended, as it is an incredibly beautiful and unique area.
• Another option for a shorter ride is to come back to Pictou by heading east on Trunk 6 at 45.4 km; this is a busy road, and should be avoided during peak hours. This would make the route a total of 60.6 km.
• For a much shorter ride, exploring Caribou Island only, park at the Waterside Beach Provincial Park, cycling to Caribou Lighthouse and back on quiet roads, for a ride totalling 18 km.

Points of Interest
• **Caribou-Munroes Island Provincial Park (8.2 km)** Stop in to walk along the beach, swim in the warm waters, and take a hike out to Munroes Island.
• **Caribou Lighthouse (29.9 km)** Head to the end of the road to check out this beautiful lighthouse and get a glimpse of the ferry as it travels between PEI and Nova Scotia.

Caribou Island Cue Sheet

Dist	Type	Note	Next
0.0	◉	Start of route	0.0
0.0	⚑	(Start) Pictou: 87 Caladh Ave; head north on Market St	0.1
0.1	→	R onto Water St	0.2
0.3	←	L onto Coleraine St	0.1
0.4	→	R onto Denoon St (signs for PEI Ferry)	1.0
1.4	↑	Continue onto Beeches Rd	1.2
2.6	↑	Continue onto Three Brooks Rd	12.7
15.3	→	R onto Shore Rd	5.0
20.3	→	Slight R onto Caribou Island Rd	9.7
30.0	↰	Caribou Lighthouse; turnaround point	9.6
39.6	→	Sharp R onto Shore Rd	5.8
45.4	→	R onto Sunrise Trail/NS-6 W (signs for River John/Tatamagouche)	4.4
49.8	←	L onto Meadowville Station Rd	6.2
56.0	←	L onto River John Rd	12.9
68.9	→	R onto Harris Rd	1.6
70.5	←	Slight L onto Jitney Trail	3.5
74.0	→	R toward Market St	0.0
74.0	←	Sharp L onto Market St	0.0
74.0	◉	End of route	0.0

69 Gully Lake Preserve

MAP 26

Start Point
Westville: Irving Station, 2500 Trunk 4.

Summary
Challenging hills; remote area; rough/unpaved roads; swim spot.

Distance (km)	Duration	Max Grade +	Elevation Gain (m)	Unpaved
82.1	3:43/5:28	9.5	870	46% (38 km)

Description
This is a classic gravel grinder, taking you on a mix of paved and unpaved roads through nice countryside and beautiful farmland. Along the way, you will have some challenging climbs getting to the Gully Lake Wilderness Area; afterward, you will be treated to a 7.5 km downhill that follows along a meandering stream. The northern part of the ride is gorgeous, with lots of shaded roads, gullies, and one-lane bridges; it also takes you by a fantastic swimming hole, where you can cool off before the final stretch. Coming down Fitzpatricks Mountain rewards you with a 7 km descent before you finish the last few kilometres on the way back to your starting point.

Ride Considerations

- Signs are often missing on the back roads; be prepared with maps, or download the route onto your phone.
- This a remote area; ensure that you have adequate supplies.
- Cell service is likely to be unavailable for portions of this ride.
- This is a gravel grinder ride with lots of rough, unpaved sections; ensure that your bike is suitable for these conditions.

Side Trips/Variations

- **Gully Lake Wilderness Area (40.3 km)** You have the option here to go hiking along the Juniper Head Trail, a 3.3 km hike through a mix of hardwood and softwood forest; access directly off the road.
- **Craig's Way Nature Walk (56.1 km)** This is a 1.5-hour hike through a beautiful, mature forest located in the Cobequid Mountains; you'll find a swimming hole nearby, across the bridge.

Points of Interest

- **MacKay Brook Falls (56.1 km)** There is a parking spot just after the bridge where you will see a path going down to the water. There are a number of little waterfalls here, and a fantastic swimming hole.

Gully Lake Preserve Cue Sheet

Dist	Type	Note	Next
0.0	●	Start of route	0.0
0.0	⚑	(Start) Westville: Irving Station, 2500 NS-4; head west on Truro Rd/NS-4	0.0
0.0	→	R onto NS-4 W	5.1
5.1	←	L onto Pleasant Valley Rd (signs for NS-104/NS-289/Union Centre)	0.4
5.5	→	R onto Ross Rd	3.6
9.1	→	R onto Pleasant Valley Rd	2.1
11.2	→	Slight R onto Millbrook Rd	12.1
23.3	←	L onto W River East Side Rd	0.4
23.7	→	R onto W River Station Rd	0.1
23.8	←	L to stay on W River Station Rd	0.1
23.9	→	R onto Cove Rd	7.5
31.4	↑	Continue onto Mt Thom Rd	2.5
33.9	→	R onto School Rd	1.5
35.4	→	R onto NS-4 E	1.3
36.7	←	L onto Glen Rd	11.7
48.4	←	L onto Dalhousie Rd	0.1
48.5	→	R onto Loganville Rd	4.6
53.1	→	R onto MacBeth Rd	5.3
58.4	→	R onto Elmfield Rd	4.2
62.6	←	L onto Millsville Rd	0.3
62.9	→	R onto New Rd	3.0
65.9	←	L onto Four Mile Brook Rd	0.6
66.5	→	R onto Rod MacKay Rd	3.3
69.8	→	R onto NS-376 S	1.8
71.6	←	L onto NS-4 E (signs for Trans-Canada Highway/NS-104/Alma/New Glasgow)	10.5
82.1	←	L onto Truro Rd/NS-4 E	0.1
82.1	●	End of route	0.0

70 Melmerby Beach

MAP 26

Start Point
New Glasgow: 271 Glasgow St.

Summary
Some challenging hills; coastal views; beach access.

Distance (km)	Duration	Max Grade +	Elevation Gain (m)	Unpaved
37.6	1:42/2:30	7.3	389	—

Description
This is a fantastic route that takes cyclists from the heart of New Glasgow to the shores of the Northumberland Strait and on to the white sands of Melmerby Beach. Leave the New Glasgow core and head north toward Trenton. Soon afterward, the ride heads east on Egypt Road, giving you a first glimpse of the beauty and solitude of Pictou County; this road is in good condition and will take you past multiple farms on fun, undulating hills. Head east on Pictou Landing Road to Little Harbour, then stop by the local general store, where, during the May to June lobster season, you can grab freshly cooked lobster. The next stretch of road takes you to Melmerby Beach, a perfect spot to go for swim; take a stroll on the beach and eat the lobster you picked up on the way.

Go back the way you came, then turn south on Woodburn Road; you will need to take a sharp right when you reach Glenfalloch Road, and then a quick left onto Frasers Mountain Branch Road. This quiet stretch of road will bring you right back to town, so relax and enjoy passing through one of the highest elevations in the county, providing 360-degree views of the surrounding countryside. As a final flourish, enjoy a fast 3.6 km descent into New Glasgow.

Ride Considerations • Be cautious leaving and re-entering New Glasgow; there can be a lot of traffic. The ride out to Trenton is also on a busy road, but it is wide and has shoulders. Try to avoid the downtown area during peak hours.

Side Trips/Variations

- Extend this ride by heading west on Pictou Landing Road (4.9 km) and following the shore to Little Harbour, where you will join back up with the ride. This will add 17.7 km.
- There is a nice walking trail that takes you to the end of the point at Melmerby Beach. To access, go to the end of the road to the gate, where you will access the trail (4 km return). Most of this route can also be done by bicycle if the conditions are dry.

Points of Interest

- **Powells Point Provincial Park (11.7 km)** This is a nice picnic park; take a break here and sit by the water on a quiet inlet.
- **Melmerby Beach (19.0 km)** An impressive white sand beach with warm waters; one of the most majestic provincial beaches.

Melmerby Beach Cue Sheet

Dist	Type	Note	Next
0.0	◉	Start of route	0.0
0.0	⚑	(Start) New Glasgow: 271 Glasgow St	0.0
0.0	←	L onto Glasgow St	0.2
0.2	→	R onto MacLean St	0.1
0.3	←	L onto Archimedes St/NS-4 W	0.4
0.7	↑	Continue straight onto N Provost St/NS-348 N	4.2
4.9	→	R onto Egypt Rd (signs for Hillside Road/Egypt Road)	6.5
11.4	→	R onto Pictou Landing Rd/NS-348 N (signs for Little Harbour/Melmerby Beach)	1.8
13.2	↑	Continue straight onto Little Harbour Rd/NS-289 E (signs for Kings Head/Melmerby Beach)	5.8
19.0	↩	Melmerby Beach Provincial Park; turnaround point	4.1
23.1	←	Sharp L onto Woodburn Rd	5.0
28.1	→	R onto Glenfalloch Rd	0.6
28.7	←	L onto Frasers Mountain Branch Rd	3.1
31.8	→	R onto Frasers Mountain Rd	3.6
35.4	↑	Continue onto Mountain Rd	1.4
36.8	←	L onto Temperance St	0.2
37.0	→	R onto Dalhousie St	0.3
37.3	←	L onto Glasgow St	0.3
37.6	◉	End of route	0.0

Museum of Industry (RT) (6 km, Map 26)

There is a nice recreational path that follows the west side of the river out of New Glasgow and heads south toward Stellarton. Follow this popular trail to the Museum of Industry, an excellent museum that uses interactive exhibits to explain locomotives, steam engines, and coal mining technology.

This is a kid-friendly ride because it is all off the road; be aware of other users on the trail such as walkers, joggers, and other cyclists. Return to New Glasgow the way you came.

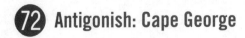

72 Antigonish: Cape George

MAP 27

Start Point
Antigonish: 303 Main St.

Summary
Challenging hills; coastal views; remote area; some rough roads; lighthouse; local food/drink; beach access.

Distance (km)	Duration	Max Grade +	Elevation Gain (m)	Unpaved
75.4	3:25/5:01	8.7	833	—

Description
This is a classic route, and one that is on many cyclists' bucket lists. It is a demanding ride that will take you around the hilly and rugged Cape George, providing dramatic views of Cape Breton across St. Georges Bay. Visit the Cape George Lighthouse, then take on one more challenging climb before you head west along the Northumberland Strait, where the terrain will continue to be hilly, but with less extreme grades. In Malignant Cove, head inland for the final stretch back to your starting point. This is a great ride; prepare to be challenged on this one.

Ride Considerations
- Ride with caution when entering and leaving Antigonish; try to avoid downtown during peak hours.
- It can get surprisingly windy on the coast, especially going around Cape George; bring appropriate layers.
- The road to the Cape George Lighthouse is 700 m long, on loose gravel.
- Some sections along the Northumberland Strait are in rough shape; call the local bike shop for updates.
- At the end of the ride, the road starts to get busier in Sylvan Valley (73.3 km); stay alert when coming back into residential and commercial traffic.

Side Trips/Variations
- Combine this with 73 Barneys River–Arisaig to make this into an epic 125 km ride.

Points of Interest
- **Crystal Cliffs Beach (14.9 km)** A nice sandy beach close to the road; access via Crystal Cliffs Farm Road.
- **Cape George Lighthouse (34.4 km)** Take in the incredible view of St. Georges Bay while taking a well-deserved rest; there are also many walking trails to explore here.

NORTHUMBERLAND SHORE

Antigonish: Cape George Cue Sheet

Dist	Type	Note	Next
0.0	♀	Start of route	0.0
0.0	←	(Start) Antigonish: 303 Main St; head east on Main St/NS-4	0.8
0.8	↑	Continue straight on NS-337	53.9
54.7	←	Sharp L onto NS-245 E (signs for North Grant/Antigonish)	20.5
75.2	←	L onto Main St/NS-4 E	0.2
75.4	♀	End of route	0.0

 Barneys River–Arisaig

MAP 27

Start Point
Antigonish: 303 Main St.

Summary
Challenging hills; remote area; some rough roads; coastal views; lighthouse; local food/drink.

Distance (km)	Duration	Max Grade +	Elevation Gain (m)	Unpaved
81.4	3:42/5:26	5.6	606	—

Description
This is the mirror image to the ⑫ Antigonish: Cape George route. It's a longer route that starts with a long, gradual climb coming out of Antigonish before heading west through Marshy Hope and north to Lower Barneys River. For the next 25 km, you will follow the Northumberland Strait, taking on some fun, punchy hills. Start heading inland at Malignant Cove, encountering a 9 km climb before the last section that takes you downhill and back into Antigonish.

Ride Considerations
- This route travels along the Trans-Canada Highway for 5 km, from Marshy Hope to Upper Barneys River. This is a busy road with fast-moving highway traffic, but it does have a wide paved shoulder with a rumble strip separator; there is no alternative route.
- Some sections along the Northumberland Strait are in rough shape; call the local bike shop for updates.

- At the end of the ride, the roads starts to get busier in Sylvan Valley (79 km); stay alert when coming back into residential and commercial traffic.
- Ride with caution when entering and leaving Antigonish; try to avoid downtown during peak hours.
- It can get surprisingly windy on the coast; bring appropriate layers.

Side Trips/Variations
- Combine this with **72 Antigonish: Cape George** to make it into an epic 125 km ride.

Points of Interest
- **Steinhart Distillery (51.5 km)** Stop by and sample the gin and vodka at this innovative distillery.
- **Arisaig Provincial Park (52.6 km)** A nice place to stop and learn about the local geology; there is also a short hiking trail down to the shoreline.
- **Arisaig Lighthouse (53.5 km)** Visit a lighthouse and grab a snack at the seasonal eatery located here.

Barneys River–Arisaig Cue Sheet

Dist	Type	Note	Next
0.0	●	Start of route	0.0
0.0	⚑	(Start) Antigonish: 303 Main St; head west on Main St/NS-4	0.9
0.9	→	R onto James St/NS-4 W	0.6
1.5	→	R onto Old Hwy 104/NS-4 W	2.1
3.6	↑	At the roundabout, continue straight onto NS-4	15.7
19.3	→	R onto Trans-Canada Hwy/NS-104 W (signs for Trans-Canada Highway/New Glasgow)	5.3
24.6	→	R toward Bear Brook Rd	0.0
24.6	←	L onto Bear Brook Rd	0.7
25.3	→	R onto Barneys River Rd	10.7
36.0	→	R onto Shore Rd/NS-245 E	24.7
60.7	↗	Stay R on NS-245	20.5
81.2	←	L onto Main St/NS-4 E	0.2
81.4	●	End of route	0.0

74 Beaver Mountain–Addington Forks (29 km, Map 27)

There is a small 5.8 km offshoot of this ride that will take you to a provincial park over an intense 11% grade; it is a steep 2 km climb, with an equally long and steep descent into the park. Access this side trip at 13.3 km by heading south on Beaver Mountain Road and staying on this road after the overpass until you reach the park.

This can be done as a 29 km ride on its own from Antigonish by following Addington Forks Road out of town until you get onto Beaver Meadow Road; continue on to the park. Take Trunk 4 to get back to Antigonish on the north side of the highway.

CAPE BRETON ISLAND: REGIONAL OVERVIEW

There is something undeniably unique about the island of Cape Breton. The air feels cleaner up here; the mountains are taller; the dances are more rambunctious; the coastline is more raw. There is a glimmer in the air in this part of the world, which you can see when looking into the eyes of those who live here. And with the mix of Celtic, Mi'kmaw, Acadian, and African-Nova Scotian cultures on the island, the history runs deep with stories that are rich and plentiful. Culture and tradition are important here; you can feel that when you're participating in events around the island.

The routes in this book take you all the way around the island, giving you the full range of landscapes, coastlines, and cultural experiences. Starting at the southwest end of the island, the Celtic Shores Coastal Trail takes you up the coast by way of a converted railway bed, parallel to the stretch of road known as the Ceilidh Trail. The spirit of music is strong on this part of the island; ceilidhs and kitchen parties are part of the cultural fabric. If you get a chance, be sure to check out a dance in one of the many community halls; they are often open to the public and are a great way to connect with the musical heritage of the area.

Coming into Mabou, you get your first taste of the highlands, which continue on up the coast into the Cape Breton Highlands. These hills are an extension of the Appalachian mountain chain that starts down in Georgia and runs all the way along the eastern edge of North America. Although they are smaller here, the hills are impressive, especially along the coast, where they often slope directly down into the ocean. Take your time touring through Cape Breton Highlands National Park and enjoy the dramatic views around every corner; bring along good footwear, as there are plenty of excellent hikes.

The western side of the island will take you through the Margaree Valley, known for salmon fishing along the Margaree River, and into Chéticamp, an Acadian fishing village, where you can hear the traditional language still being spoken. In the middle of the island is the Bras d'Or Lake, an inland sea made up of both fresh and salt water, surrounded by high hills and low mountains.

The eastern side of the island has plenty of great cycling routes; many follow the coast and visit some of the rugged industrial coal mining areas that have long been an integral part of Cape Breton's economy. This is also where you can visit Fortress of Louisbourg, the site of a French settlement founded in 1713, which is said to be the largest reconstruction project in North America. At the southern end of Cape Breton is Isle Madame, where Acadian culture thrives in an active fishing community; here you will also find the stunning Point Michaud Beach, next to the charming town of St. Peters.

Cape Breton is an island that offers up many adventures and is best experienced by bicycle. It takes some time and effort to get there, but once you arrive, you won't be disappointed. If possible, set aside a few extra days so you can take the time to explore and discover the island at your own pace.

Additional Notes

- Cape Breton is known for excellent camping and parks; be prepared for trailers and camper vans on your travels, especially around the Cabot Trail.
- The Celtic Colours Festival is an excellent, island-wide music festival that happens every year around the beginning of October. This also makes it an excellent time to visit to see the fall colours. Be aware that after the festival, most seasonal businesses shut down for the winter, making it more challenging to find accommodations and restaurants.
- Cellphone reception around the island can be a challenge, depending on your provider; this is especially true in the highlands.
- If you are travelling any of the routes around Sydney, be aware that there is an excellent multi-use trail that connects Sydney and Glace Bay.
- When travelling through the Chéticamp area, be sure to heed any wind warnings in the forecast. The area is known for "Les Suêtes"—very strong southeast winds that have been recorded at up to 200 kmh. These can be dangerous if you are riding the roads or hiking in exposed areas.
- The weather in the highlands can be very different than in the rest of the province; it has been known to snow in the highlands as late as June and as early as September. If you are cycling in northern Cape Breton, be sure to plan accordingly and check forecasts.

Cycling in Cape Breton offers riders a chance to experience a range of landscapes, coastlines, and cultural experiences—and to take in the rich landscape of the highlands. (KRISTEN DICK)

Cape Breton Island Bike Shops

- Framework Cycle & Fitness (Sydney) 902-567-1909
- Highland Bike Shop (Port Hawkesbury) 902-625-5930
- Velo Max (Chéticamp) 902-224-7944

Cape Breton Island Emergency Services

- Eastern Memorial Hospital (Canso)
- Victoria County Memorial Hospital (Baddeck)
- Sacred Heart Community Health Centre (Chéticamp)
- Buchanan Memorial Hospital (Neils Harbour)
- New Waterford Consolidated Hospital (New Waterford)
- Glace Bay Hospital (Glace Bay)
- Northside General Hospital (North Sydney)
- Cape Breton Regional Hospital (Sydney)
- Strait Richmond Hospital (Cleveland, Richmond County)

CYCLING ROUTES OF CAPE BRETON ISLAND: THE CABOT TRAIL

Route	Route Name	Distance (km)	Duration	Max Grade +	Elevation Gain (m)	Unpaved	Map
75	The Cabot Trail	298.6	3–4 days	14.0	3578	—	28
76	Big Baddeck Loop	24.3	1:06/1:37	5.3	255	—	28/31
77	Big Spruce–Hunters Mountain	18.7	0:51/1:14	6.9	226	—	28/31
78	Margaree Valley	25.5	1:09/1:42	3.6	188	—	28/30
79	Acadian Loop	29.0	1:19/1:56	6.7	286	—	28/30
80	Meat Cove	56.9	2:35/3:47	7.3	825	25% (14 km)	28
81	White Point	31.6	1:26/2:06	5.4	458	—	28
82	St. Anns–North River	44.4	2:01/2:57	6.0	399	—	28/31

Cape Breton Island: The Cabot Trail Regional Overview

Planning is the key to an enjoyable and invigorating ride around the Cabot Trail. Here are some tips that will help you make the most of your journey as you explore this beautiful part of the world.

Be Prepared
- Pack as lightly as possible; steep hills are easier when you are carrying less weight.
- Prepare for all types of weather. Outside July and August, the weather can be unpredictable, especially up in the highlands. (It has been known to snow in June and September.)
- Be prepared for wind. The Chéticamp area, in particular, is known for "Les Suêtes"—southeasterly winds that can come in with incredible force. Check weather forecasts and always carry a windbreaker and an extra layer.
- Plan ahead for accommodations, for places to pick up supplies, or if you intend to eat out, as there are long stretches of road where there are few or no amenities. (See **Services Available Around the Cabot Trail** on page 163 for more details.)
- Bring lots of water; access can sometimes be sparse between towns. Don't assume water is potable at campgrounds or rest areas; always check in advance.

- Stay alert to wildlife and watch for animals on the roads. Also, be prepared for the possibility that you could encounter a bear, a moose, or a coyote; it's not highly likely but it's good to take precautions. The Chéticamp Visitor Centre is an excellent place to learn what to do if you encounter local wildlife.
- This area is known for lobster and crab fishing; seafood is available fresh when in season. Ask for it when you go out to eat or pick some up and have a lobster boil on the beach.
- Bring hiking shoes or boots to take advantage of the many options for a hike or a quick walk to a beach or a waterfall along the way.
- Take your time. Some people will rush through the ride as its own challenge, but the sweetness of the highlands is best savoured by going slow. There are many incredible viewpoints along the ride, in addition to beaches, walking trails, and cultural experiences.

Getting to Baddeck

The easiest way to get there is to rent a car or van that has enough room for your bicycle; any rental company should be able to guide you through what you will need. The drive to Baddeck from Halifax takes approximately three and a half hours.

If you are flying in to the Halifax Stanfield International Airport, are not planning to rent a car, and need to get yourself and your bike to the Cabot Trail, you have limited options. We suggest you do some research online; a few suggestions are listed below. Be sure to also research whether these companies can guarantee that they will take your bike, whether there is an extra cost, whether it needs a bike bag or box, or whether you need to take your bicycle apart.

- **Maritime Bus** The closest this bus service will get you to the Cabot Trail is Wagmatcook (15 km to Baddeck, or 6.6 km to the Cabot Trail). Bikes must have a protective bag or box, there is a $5 fee, and you may need to remove your front wheel. Bikes get low priority, so they may be put onto the next bus if there is not enough room. Call well in advance to confirm route, schedules, and availability: **1-800-575-1807**.
- **Nova Shuttle** This service hits several points in Halifax before leaving from the airport at 8:30 AM; it arrives in Baddeck at 12:30 P.M. Bikes are accepted, but wheels must be able to come off. Mention that you are travelling with a bicycle when you make reservations: **1-800-898-5883**.
- Search online for "Shuttles from Halifax to Sydney/Baddeck." Call around to make arrangements that work with your plans. Most shuttles cost around $70 per person.

Bike Rentals

If you are renting a car and driving to Cape Breton, you have lots of options for renting a bicycle from one of the many bike shops or tour companies around the province. Call around for rates and availability (see **Appendix A: Bike Shops** and **Appendix B: Bike Tours and Rentals**).

There are only a few businesses that offer multi-day bicycle rentals in Cape Breton. When in doubt, call the local bike shops for advice. If you are coming into Sydney by plane or ferry, ask about the possibility of getting a shuttle to Baddeck; Framework Cycle sometimes offers this service.

- Highland Bike Shop (Port Hawkesbury) **902-625-5930**
- Velo Max (Chéticamp) **902-224-7944**
- Pedallers by the Bay (Baddeck) **902-818-8504**
- Eagle Eye Outfitters (Inverness) **902-258-5893**
- Framework Cycle and Fitness (Sydney) **902-567-1909**

Luggage Transfers/Tours

If you are looking to ride from inn to inn and don't want to carry your luggage, you can call around to see about getting luggage transfers, but options are limited. Velo Max will sometimes do transfers. They will also likely be up to date on any other services available.

The following Nova Scotia adventure companies offer guided and self-guided trips around Cape Breton. They will sometimes provide luggage transfer, but that is usually based on how busy the season is, and whether there are vehicles and drivers available. Call to find out whether their services fit with your plans:

- Freewheeling Adventures **1-800-672-0775**
- Pedal and Sea Adventures **1-877-777-5699**
- Eastwind Cycle **1-866-447-7468**
- Cabot Trail Adventures **1-902-383-2552**

Bike Shops

The Cabot Trail doesn't have many choices in terms of places to get your bike repaired. Your best option if you need extra parts or work done to your bicycle is to stop by the Highland Bike Shop in Port Hawkesbury before heading north: **902-625-5930**.

Velo Max Cycling **(902-224-7944)** is based in Chéticamp, and although they do not have a retail shop, they offer bike repairs by appointment, as well as roadside assistance for stranded cyclists. Call for assistance or to make an appointment. Velo Max has also been in the process of setting up "parts depots" around the trail—locations that are stocked with bicycle parts and accessories to help with repairs and common issues. The first location at the Belle Côte Gas Bar proved successful, and there are plans to open another one around Cape North.

Supplies/Restaurants/Accommodations

You will sometimes have to travel fairly long distances without amenities along the Cabot Trail. Accommodations can fill up quickly, so call well ahead of your trip to ensure a reservation. Many businesses in this area are seasonal, meaning they could be closed if you are travelling outside peak season (late June to early September). If you are at all unsure, call ahead to make sure that what you need is open.

There are many places to camp along the Cabot Trail, including campgrounds in the Cape Breton Highlands National Park, and other private campgrounds outside the park boundary. Accommodations are also available in motels and B & Bs in populated areas. A quick internet search will provide a number of options.

Services Available Around the Cabot Trail

Town/Area	Km	Supplies	Restaurant(s)	Accommodations
Baddeck	Start/Stop	X	X	X
North East Margaree	40.0		X	X
Margaree Forks	47.4	X		
Margaree Harbour	61.5	X	X	X
Chéticamp	83.8	X	X	X
Pleasant Bay	127.4		X	X
Cape North/Dingwall	157.6	X	X	X
Neils Harbour	179.0	X	X	
Ingonish	194.5	X	X	X
Wreck Cove Area	227.70	X		X
North Shore Area	244.70		X	X

Important Checkpoints

- **Chéticamp (84.0 km)** The first major town after leaving Baddeck.
- **Chéticamp Visitor Centre (92.0 km)** This is the main information centre for the Cape Breton Highlands National Park, where you can purchase a pass and learn more about the area.
- **MacIntosh Brook Campground (130.3 km)** The last refuge before tackling the North Mountain; there is shelter here with wood stoves and running water. (Water may or may not be potable.)
- **Ingonish (194.5 km)** The next major town after Chéticamp.
- **Englishtown Ferry decision point (253.5 km)** Decide here whether to head south on Route 312 and take the Englishtown Ferry, or to continue on the Cabot Trail around St. Anns Bay.

75 The Cabot Trail

MAP 28

Start Point
Baddeck: Visitor Information Centre, 454 Shore Rd.

Summary
Multi-day ride; very challenging hills; coastal ride; some rough roads; swim spots; beach access; local food/drink.

Distance (km)	Duration	Max Grade +	Elevation Gain (m)	Unpaved
298.6	3–4 days	14.0	3578	—

Description
The Cabot Trail is a jewel in Nova Scotia's crown, considered by many to be one of the world's best cycling routes. This multi-day tour will take you through the Cape Breton Highlands National Park, along the edge of spectacular cliffs, through old-growth forests, and along two very different, yet equally stunning, coastlines. This is a challenging trip that requires good fitness—or at least a lot of determination.

The best season for this trip is usually between late June and early September. No matter when you go, be aware that the weather can change dramatically, and very quickly—especially in the highlands, so be prepared. Consider riding this in the fall (late September or early October), when the air is a little bit cooler but the whole landscape is a kaleidoscope of colour as the leaves in the hardwood forests turn to red, yellow, and orange. This is considered the shoulder season, so the roads are a little quieter, but note that many seasonal shops and services might be shut down.

The route can be done in both directions, with the trip traditionally leaving from Baddeck. The notes and cue sheet for this ride are for the clockwise direction. This choice takes into consideration the prevailing winds, the best views, and the gentler climb of Cape Smokey.

Route Overview
1   Leaving Baddeck, cycle to the base of Hunters Mountain, where you will encounter the first challenging climb.
2   Stop for refuelling at the Dancing Goat Café in beautiful Margaree, then follow the east side of the Margaree River to the coast. Ride north along the coast to Chéticamp, where you'll get your first glimpse of the highlands.
3   Stock up in Chéticamp, as there are limited supplies and amenities until Ingonish on the eastern side. This is often where people will stop for the first night, having travelled 84 km.

4 Visit the Chéticamp Visitor Centre to get passes for the park and to ask any questions about the area, then head into the highlands, where you will take on the first of the big climbs.

5 French Mountain is a challenging climb with incredible views to help ease the pain. The descent down MacKenzie Mountain on the other side is very twisty and steep; ride with caution.

Cyclists will want to take advantage of the many opportunities to stop and take a refreshing dip as they cycle the Cabot Trail. (KRISTEN DICK)

6 Ride into Pleasant Bay, then tackle the North Mountain, a climb with a maximum grade of 14%. (You've got this.) Enjoy a fast descent on the other side as you make your way to Cape North and Dingwall.

7 After Dingwall, get off the Cabot Trail and take White Point Road for a fun detour to follow the coast and ride some punchy hills. The views here are amazing and there is an option for a great side trip to White Point, where there is a beach and a nice hiking trail.

8 Enter into Neils Harbour on a gratifying 4 km descent, coming into the harbour in full glory. Eat at the Chowder House; grab an ice cream; check out the lighthouse.

9 Ingonish has all the amenities and some nice attractions. Visit the Keltic Lodge for a meal, to stay the night, or to check out their walking trails; stop by Ingonish Beach, a popular white sand beach.

10 Ride a fairly gradual ascent up Cape Smokey. Stop at the picnic park at the top to take in the view. Ride with caution down Smokey Mountain, a very steep and twisty road.

11 Ride the undulating hills through Wreck Cove, North Shore, and Indian Brook.

12 Continue along the Cabot Trail around St. Anns Bay and North River, where you will find a number of artisanal craft shops.

13 The ride will intersect with the Trans-Canada Highway, and there will be a 9 km stretch on a busy road with wide paved shoulders.

14 Get off the highway for the last section and ride Route 205 along Baddeck Bay back to the start point.

Big Climbs

There are lots of climbs to keep you challenged on this ride, but these three particular mountains will test your limits:

- French Mountain (101.8 km)
- North Mountain (131.7 km)
- Cape Smokey (213.2 km)

		Distance (km)	Avg Grade (%)	Max Grade (%)	Elevation (m)
French	Ascent	9	5.6	13.4	444
	Descent	7.9	−5.6	−13.8	−383
North	Ascent	5.4	8.7	14.0	403
	Descent	6.4	−7.9	−15.3	−415
Smokey	Ascent	6.8	3.3	10.6	267
	Descent	5.8	−4.7	−14.9	−279

Ride Considerations

- This ride occasionally leaves the Cabot Trail to take advantage of some quieter roads and hilly coastal riding; this doesn't significantly alter the overall distance. You can always choose to stay on the Cabot Trail and avoid the alternate routes.
- Alternate routes:
  1 Leave Baddeck via Margaree Road
  2 Follow the east side of the Margaree River
  3 Ride the coast through White Point
  4 Finish off on Route 205 into Baddeck.
- This is a challenging ride with three very steep and long mountain climbs; know your limits.
- The Cabot Trail is a popular route for both cars and campers; stay alert to traffic, especially in the high season (from the end of June through early September).
- Moose are common in this part of Nova Scotia; these are very big animals that you don't want to run into on a steep descent. Stay alert to wildlife, especially when you're coming down the mountains.
- Long sections of this trail do not have amenities and are considered remote; ensure that you have adequate supplies, and plan your route accordingly. (See **Services Available Around the Cabot Trail** for more details.)
- Not all campgrounds have water available; carry lots of water and plan accordingly. The most reliable places for water are in the communities of Chéticamp, Cape North, Neils Harbour, and Ingonish.

- Cellular coverage is not always available; if using a phone for navigation, download maps and route information beforehand.
- Riding through Cape Breton Highlands National Park requires a pass; purchase one at the Chéticamp Visitor Centre. The cost is approximately $8 and is valid until 4 PM the next day.
- If taking the Englishtown Ferry (253 km), call in advance to ensure that it is running as scheduled: **902-929-2404**.
- There is a 9 km section of the ride on Highway 105 east of Englishtown. This is a busy road with fast-moving highway traffic, with wide paved shoulders; there is no alternative route.
- Contact Cape Breton Highlands National Park to find the most up-to-date information about the route and campgrounds: **902-224-2306**.

Side Trips/Variations

Depending on how much time you have, you might be tempted to do some side trips as you pedal around the trail. If you are driving, you may want to do some smaller rides along the way. Below is a list of routes in the book that can be accessed directly off the Cabot Trail.

76 Big Baddeck Loop
77 Big Spruce–Hunters Mountain
78 Margaree Valley
79 Acadian Loop
80 Meat Cove
81 White Point
82 St. Anns–North River

Points of Interest
- **Alexander Graham Bell Museum (Start/Stop)** Stop in and learn about the man who invented the telephone, among other things. This is an impressive museum with many interactive displays.
- **Lake-O-Law Provincial Park (33.3 km)** This is a great picnic area with some basic amenities and a lovely lake for swimming.
- **Dancing Goat Café (40.6 km)** Serves amazing food and excellent coffee.
- **Chéticamp Visitor Centre (92.0 km)** This is the entrance to the park; it includes many exhibits about the park, the geology and wildlife of the surrounding highlands, and the area's history.
- **Skyline Trail (107.5 km)** Take a walking detour to the most popular hike on the Trail. It is an easy walk and it gets very busy, especially on weekends, but the view at the end is spectacular. (This is the top of the first big climb; there are washrooms here.)

- **North Highlands Community Museum and Culture Centre (156.4 km)** Learn about the history and heritage of northern Cape Breton.
- **White Point Hiking Trail (side trip, 170.6 km)** The way down is steep and curvy (and fun). At the bottom you will find a nice beach, and a bit further along you can access the hiking trail out to White Point. Although the climb is steep coming back up (over 1 km at 8.3% grade), it's a worthy 2.4 km diversion.
- **Neils Harbour Chowder House (178.9 km)** This place is pretty much famous; stop in and enjoy some fresh seafood from the area.
- **Keltic Lodge (204.4 km)** This resort features a historic main lodge that is a throwback to the era of 1950s railroad hotels. There is an excellent restaurant, and walking trails are free to use.

The Cabot Trail Cue Sheet

Dist	Type	Note	Next
0.0	◉	Start of route	0.0
0.0	⚑	(Start) Baddeck: Visitor Information Centre, 454 Shore Rd; head west on Margaree Rd	5.2
5.2	←	L after the bridge to stay on Margaree Rd	5.3
10.5	→	R onto Cabot Trail	37.2
47.7	→	R onto East Margaree Rd	0.4
48.1	←	L to stay on East Margaree Rd	13.4
61.5	↗	Slight R to get back onto Cabot Trail	99.6
161.1	←	L onto White Point Rd	9.5
170.6	↑	Continue straight onto New Haven Rd	7.3
177.9	→	Keep R to stay on New Haven Rd	1.9
179.8	←	L back onto Cabot Trail	73.7
253.5	→	R to stay on Cabot Trail	27.2
280.7	→	R onto Trans-Canada Hwy/NS-105 W (signs for Trans-Canada Highway/Baddeck)	8.8
289.5	←	L onto NS-205 W (signs for Baddeck)	9.1
298.6	◉	End of route	0.0

- **Ingonish Beach (204.7 km)** An impressive white sand beach; very popular on warm summer days.
- **Artisans (244.0 km)** There are a number of artisans and crafters between North Shore and St. Anns Bay.
- **Clucking Hen Café (244.8 km)** Stop in for some food and a cold drink; they make excellent sandwiches to go.
- **Swim spot (250.6 km)** This is accessed via a small paved road on the southwest side of a bridge, soon after passing Cabot Shores Wilderness Resort, with a path going down to the water at the end; look for it on your right-hand side after crossing the bridge. Walk up the river for some good swim spots away from the road.

76 Big Baddeck Loop

Start Point

Baddeck: Visitor Information Centre, 454 Shore Rd.

Summary

Smooth grades; low-traffic roads; river views.

Distance (km)	Duration	Max Grade +	Elevation Gain (m)	Unpaved
24.3	1:06/1:37	5.3	255	—

Description

This route has all the hallmarks of a "classic." It is easily accessible from Baddeck, but quickly takes you on quiet back roads, along both the west and east sides of Baddeck River. The combination of lush forest, rushing river, and rolling hills in this area provides a unique sense of calm and makes for a highly enjoyable ride.

Heading out of town you will cross the overpass and have a nice smooth ride downhill to the Baddeck Bridge. Across the bridge you will start a twisty uphill ride toward Uisge Bàn Falls Provincial Park along quiet roads. After crossing over the Baddeck River, you will be heading downriver, making for a sweet descent back toward Baddeck. Once you complete the loop it is a quick downhill run back to town.

THE CABOT TRAIL

Ride Considerations

- Bring hiking shoes if you want to hike to Uisge Bàn Falls.

Side Trips/Variations

- The Uisge Bàn Falls are a worthy addition to this ride. The hike will take you on a 1.5 km round trip through stunning hardwood forests to the 15 m high waterfall. Access it by turning onto North Branch Road (11.5 km) and following a 3.5 km unpaved road to the parking lot.

Big Baddeck Loop Cue Sheet

Dist	Type	Note	Next
0.0	◉	Start of route	0.0
0.0	⚑	(Start) Baddeck: Visitor Information Centre, 454 Shore Rd; head west on Margaree Rd	5.2
5.2	↑	Continue onto Westside Baddeck Rd	7.6
12.8	➡	R onto Big Baddeck Rd Extension	0.5
13.3	↑	Continue onto Big Baddeck Rd	9.9
23.2	⬅	L onto Margaree Rd	1.1
24.3	◉	End of route	0.0

Big Spruce—Hunters Mountain (18.7 km, Map 28/31)

There is a short ride not far from this route that starts off at Big Spruce Brewing (64 Yankee Line Road) and heads up and over Hunters Mountain. Start by heading north from the brewery on Yankee Line Road. At 7.1 km, head south on the Cabot Trail to go over Hunter's Mountain until you reach the Trans-Canada Highway, which you will follow west and back to the brewery.

Getting there from Baddeck:

1. Take the Trans-Canada Highway out of Baddeck (14.1 km one way).
2. Follow Margaree Road out of town (there is an unpaved section of road after Baddeck Bridge) to get to the base of Hunters Mountain to connect with the loop (10 km one way).

 Margaree Valley

MAP 28/30

Start Point
North East Margaree: Dancing Goat Café, 6289 Cabot Trail.

Summary
Easy ride; rough roads; river views; swim spot; local food/drink; kid-friendly.

Distance (km)	Duration	Max Grade +	Elevation Gain (m)	Unpaved
25.5	1:09/1:42	3.6	188	—

Description
The Margaree Valley is a very special place; it probably has something to do with the beautiful river winding through the valley and the abundant wildlife in the area. This ride starts and ends at the Dancing Goat Café, a local favourite due to its excellent food and coffee. Leaving the café, the ride takes you meandering through the valley, following both sides of the Northeast Margaree River. Keep your eyes open for local artisans selling their wares, and for people wading in the water, casting fishing lines in pursuit of elusive wild Atlantic salmon or trout.

Ride Considerations

- The roads here are in poor condition but are quiet, providing lots of room to avoid potholes and rough sections.

Side Trips/Variations

- Head west on the Cabot Trail from the Dancing Goat Café to ride the **79 Acadian Loop** (43.2 km return).

Points of Interest

- **Dancing Goat Café (Start/Stop)** Amazing food and excellent coffee.
- **Margaree Salmon Museum (0.9 km)** Learn about the history and importance of salmon fishing in the Margaree.
- **Swim spot (6.1 km)** Take some time for a dip in one of the local swimming holes. Access it by following the path heading north on the west side of the bridge on Crowdis Crossing Road.

Margaree Valley Cue Sheet

Dist	Type	Note	Next
0.0	●	Start of route	0.0
0.0	▶	(Start) North East Margaree: Dancing Goat Café, 6289 Cabot Trail; head west on Cabot Trail	0.5
0.5	→	Sharp R onto East Big Intervale Rd	0.7
1.2	←	L to stay on East Big Intervale Rd	1.0
2.2	←	L onto Cranton Crossing Rd	1.2
3.4	→	R onto West Big Intervale Rd	7.3
10.7	↑	Continue onto Hatchery Rd	4.1
14.8	→	R onto East Big Intervale Rd	0.8
15.6	←	L to stay on East Big Intervale Rd	0.9
16.5	←	L onto Egypt Rd	6.3
22.8	→	R onto Cabot Trail	2.7
25.5	●	End of route	0.0

 ## Acadian Loop
(29 km, Map 28/30)

There is a short, pleasant ride nearby that follows along both sides of a more westerly section of the Margaree River. The ride starts at Duck Cove Inn (10289 Cabot Trail) and follows the Cabot Trail north to Belle Côte, then turns inland and follows south on the east side of the river, then finishes the loop back on the Cabot Trail.

 **Meat Cove**

MAP 28

Start Point
Cape North: North Highlands Community Museum, 29243 Cabot Trail.

Summary
Difficult; challenging hills; unpaved roads; steep descents; beach access.

Distance (km)	Duration	Max Grade +	Elevation Gain (m)	Unpaved
56.9 (return)	2:35/3:47	7.3	825	25% (14 km)

Description
Meat Cove is on the northernmost tip of Cape Breton Island, and it feels like it with its wild, rugged beauty. This ride gives you a chance to experience the landscapes and seascapes that exist at the extreme fringes of the island, while you experience steep ascents and some very fast, sharp downhills.

The ride takes you along Aspy Bay (famous for its oysters) and takes you past the Cabots Landing Provincial Park before heading inland for your first big challenging hill, a nearly 4 km climb at an average 3.5% grade. Consider it a warm-up: you will do this up-and-down routine three more times before you finish the ride.

The final stretch leading to Meat Cove is a 7 km ride on unpaved roads that hug the coastline, making for some incredible views. Meat Cove boasts a pub with a deck that overlooks the water, giving you an opportunity for a break and a meal before the return trip, where you will go back the way you came.

This is a back-and-forth ride, so you can enjoy the views (and the hills) in reverse. Remember that the Cabots Landing beach is near the end of the ride, so you can dive into the ocean to wash off the sweat of the day.

Ride Considerations
- There are many challenging hills on this ride. Mind your speed coming downhill; there are lots of sharp turns with patches of gravel roads.
- Make note of the sharp left turn (at 15.4 km) onto Meat Cove Road at the Co-op.
- The roads on the Bay St. Lawrence peninsula are in rough condition; use with caution if you decide to take this route as a side trip.

Side Trips/Variations
- For a shorter ride, start at the Cabots Landing Provincial Park (36.5 km total).

THE CABOT TRAIL

- Take a trip out to Dingwall for a milder ride, or as a cool-down after your journey to Meat Cove. Follow Dingwall Road, riding alongside Dingwall Harbour to the Markland Inn, where you can get fresh seafood straight from Aspy Bay (8.6 km diversion).

Points of Interest

- **North Highlands Community Museum (Start/ Stop)** Learn about the history and heritage of Northern Cape Breton.
- **Cabots Landing Provincial Park (10.0 km)** This is an amazing 3 km white sand beach; make time to stop on one or both legs of your journey.

Meat Cove Cue Sheet

Dist	Type	Note	Next
0.0	●	Start of route	0.0
0.0	⚑	(Start) Cape North: North Highlands Community Museum, 29243 Cabot Trail; head north on Bay St Lawrence Rd	15.4
15.4	◀	Sharp L onto Meat Cove Rd	13.1
28.5	↩	Meat Cove; turnaround point	13.1
41.5	▶	Sharp R onto Bay St Lawrence Rd	15.4
56.9	●	End of route	0.0

Meat Cove is on the northernmost tip of Cape Breton Island. (AARON MURNAGHAN)

 **White Point**

MAP 28

Start Point
Neils Harbour: 90 Lighthouse Rd.

Summary
Challenging hills; coastal views; beach access; local food/drink.

Distance (km)	Duration	Max Grade +	Elevation Gain (m)	Unpaved
31.6	1:26/2:06	5.4	458	—

Description
Because the coastal part of this route isn't officially part of the Cabot Trail, cyclists sometimes pass it by. That is a shame, because it is an absolute gem that offers incredible views and challenging climbs with a fantastic side trip option.

Coming out of Neils Harbour, you will follow the Cabot Trail for a slow, gradual climb of approximately 9 km, followed by a 5 km descent to South Harbour. Here you will turn onto White Point Road, where the hills start getting steep and the roads more twisty; be ready for some challenging riding for the next 11 km. After tackling the coastal hills, you will be rewarded with a glorious 4 km downhill run, rounding a corner with a view of the shimmering ocean in the distance. Finish the ride with a well-deserved meal at the famous Neils Harbour Chowder House.

Ride Considerations
- This is a challenging ride; the distance is relatively short, but it will test your endurance. Bring lots of water for this one.
- Bring hiking shoes or sandals if you want to hike the trail at White Point (it's worth it).

Side Trips/Variations
- If you aren't intimidated by yet another hill, take some time to visit the community of White Point (22.9 km). The ride down is steep and curvy (and fun). At the bottom you will find a nice beach, and a bit further along you can access the hiking trail out to White Point. Although the climb is steep coming back up, over 1 km at 8.3% grade, it's a worthy diversion (2.4 km return).

THE CABOT TRAIL

Points of Interest

- **White Point Beach (side trip)** This is a nice little beach at the bottom of a steep descent.
- **White Point Hiking Trail (side trip)** Take some time to hike out to the end of White Point; it's rugged terrain, but an easy walking trail. (Less than 2 km round trip.)
- **Neils Harbour Chowder House (Start/ Stop)** Always amazing; local seafood at a genuine chowder house.

White Point Cue Sheet

Dist	Type	Note	Next
0.0	◉	Start of route	0.0
0.0	⚑	(Start) Neils Harbour: 90 Lighthouse Rd; head north on Lighthouse Rd	0.3
0.3	←	L onto New Haven Rd	0.9
1.2	→	R onto Cabot Trail	12.3
13.5	→	R onto White Point Rd	9.5
23.0	↑	Continue onto New Haven Rd	7.3
30.3	→	Keep R to stay on New Haven Rd	1.0
31.3	←	Slight L onto Lighthouse Rd	0.3
31.6	◉	End of route	0.0

 # 82 St. Anns–North River

MAP 28/31

Start Point

Englishtown: The Gaelic College, 51779 Cabot Trail.

Summary

Fairly easy ride; low-traffic roads; river views; local artisans.

Distance (km)	Duration	Max Grade +	Elevation Gain (m)	Unpaved
44.4	2:01/2:57	6.0	399	—

Description

This route follows St. Anns Bay and the North River, providing plenty of beautiful water views. Along the way you will pass a variety of local artisans selling their wares to the public. Most of the roads are fairly quiet and the hills are gently rolling. Taking the Englishtown Ferry across St. Anns Bay provides some incredible views, especially on a calm day. This is a nice mellow ride that should be savoured.

Ride Considerations

- This route requires taking the Englishtown Ferry across St. Anns Bay; call in advance to ensure the ferry is operational: **902-929-2404**.
- The last 4 km segment of this ride is on the Trans-Canada Highway; this is a busy road with fast-moving highway traffic, but with wide paved shoulders.

Side Trips/Variations

- Visit a swim spot and more artisans via a small diversion toward Ingonish. Head north on the Cabot Trail (at 26.1 km) instead of turning down toward Englishtown. The swim spot is on the southwest side of the bridge at approximately 3 km (go down a small side road to see the trail); continue farther along the road to visit more shops.

Points of Interest

- There are artisans' shops all along this route; some are open by appointment only.

St Anns–North River Cue Sheet

Dist	Type	Note	Next
0.0	○	Start of route	0.0
0.0	⚑	(Start) Englishtown: The Gaelic College, 51779 Cabot Trail; head west on Cabot Trail	26.1
26.1	→	R onto NS-312 S	6.8
32.9	↑	Get the ferry from St Anns Bay to Englishtown	0.2
33.1	→	R to stay on NS-312 S (NS-105/Baddeck/Sydney)	6.1
39.2	→	R onto Trans-Canada Hwy/NS-105 W (signs for Trans-Canada Highway)	4.1
43.3	→	R onto Cabot Trail	1.1
44.4	○	End of route	0.0

CYCLING ROUTES OF CAPE BRETON ISLAND: BEYOND THE CABOT TRAIL

Route	Route Name	Distance (km)	Duration	Max Grade +	Elevation Gain (m)	Unpaved	Map
83	Celtic Shores Coastal Trail (RT)	83.8	3:48/5:35	2.6	458	100% (84 km)	29
84	Lake Ainslie: Mabou–Nevada Valley (RT)	77.2	3:30/5:08	5.9	557	19% (15 km)	30
85	Inverness–Margaree Beach Tour (RT)	85.4	3:53/5:42	7.0	813	7% (6 km)	30
86	Washabuck Peninsula	56.5	2:34/3:46	8.1	593	—	31
87	Boularderie Island	80.6	3:39/5:22	5.1	677	20% (16 km)	32
88	Alder Point	17.1	0:46/1:08	3.7	116	—	32
89	New Victoria	37.0	1:40/2:28	3.8	241	—	33
90	Northern Coastal Industrial Loop	93.9	4:15/6:15	7.0	706	—	33
91	Variation: Donkin Loop	32.1	1:27/2:08	3.5	207	—	33
92	Hillside Loop	49.0	2:14/3:16	5.9	353	—	34
93	Variation: Marion Bridge–Grand Mira	50.4	2:17/3:21	3.6	318	23% (12 km)	34
94	Albert Bridge–Marion Bridge	29.3	1:19/1:57	3.2	203	—	34
95	Fortress of Louisbourg	42.9	1:57/2:51	8.0	377	—	34
96	Point Michaud	41.7	1:53/2:46	7.7	363	—	35
97	St. Peters: Cape George	64.6	2:56/4:18	8.0	663	—	35
98	Isle Madame	67.3	3:03/4:29	6.5	503	—	35

Cape Breton Island: Beyond the Cabot Trail Regional Overview

Please refer to the **Cape Breton Island Regional Overview on page 157.**

83 Celtic Shores Coastal Trail (RT)

MAP 29

Start Point
Troy Station: 1020–1142 Ceilidh Trail or Inverness: Miners Museum, 62 Lower Railway St.

Summary
Rail trail; mostly flat; good access points; wayfinding; coastal views; beach access; kid-friendly.

Distance (km)	Duration	Max Grade +	Elevation Gain (m)	Unpaved
83.8 (one way)	3:48/5:35	2.6	458	100% (84 km)

Description
This route is considered a "Destination Trail" by Tourism Nova Scotia—the first of its kind in the province—and it is a stellar example of the good work that can happen when a community comes together with a unified vision. The trail is on a converted railbed that extends from Port Hastings all the way up to Inverness, with a significant amount of the route on the coast. (The starting point for this trip is at Troy Station, as the section south to Port Hastings is often washed out and is not recommended.) This is one of the more visually stunning rail trails in the province and is located in an area rich in music, history, and culture.

The first part of the ride takes you into Judique, home of the Celtic Music Interpretive Centre—a great place to learn about local culture through the music and art that defines the region. It continues on to Port Hood, where you'll have access to a beautiful beach, the first of many that dot the coast. Next stop is Mabou, home of the lively Red Shoe Pub, where the trail heads inland for the final leg of the trip into Inverness, a lovely town, and the site of one of the most spectacular beaches on the island.

This is a fantastic cycling trip that can be used as a starting point for many other adventures on the island. Enjoy cycling the dynamic coast, get out and listen to some local music, and maybe stop in at one of the community halls to dance at a ceilidh.

Ride Considerations
- Read **Preparing to Ride: Packing Considerations** to learn more about packing and preparing for a long trip.
- The distance indicated is for a one-way trip.
- This route can be done from either direction; the cue sheets for this route description start at Troy Station.

The Celtic Shores Coastal Trail is considered a "Destination Trail" by Tourism Nova Scotia. The trail is on a converted railbed, and a significant amount of the route runs along the coast. (BICYCLE NOVA SCOTIA)

- Sections of the trail can be fairly remote and cellphone reception can't be guaranteed; ensure that you are adequately prepared.
- You always have the option to ride the parallel roads; just be aware that they can be busy and should be avoided during peak hours.

Celtic Shores Coastal Trail

Visit the official Celtic Shores Coastal Trail website for maps, more details, and the most up-to-date information about the trail celticshores.ca

- There is signage along the route indicating the many access points where you can get onto the trail or get off for amenities; visit the trail's website for more details.
- This trail is shared with OHVs, pedestrians, and horses; refer to **Road Safety: Etiquette** to learn more about how to share the trail with others.
- This is a rail trail, so be sure to have the appropriate tires for hard-packed gravel.
- Although this is a maintained rail trail, there can be variable trail surfaces; be prepared for sections that are soft or in rough condition. Contact the Celtic Shores Trail Association about any trail issues that should be taken care of.

Side Trips/Variations

- If you are cycling the whole route back and forth, consider riding the trail one way and then taking the Ceilidh Trail (Trunk 19) back to Troy Station. This option will provide an opportunity to visit the Glenora Distillery, the first single malt whisky producer in North America; you can also see more of the local communities. If taking Trunk 19, recognize that it is the main road for this side of the island; try to avoid it during peak hours.
- Get off the trail in Mabou (58 km) to visit the beautiful West Mabou Beach (access via Little Mabou Road) and/or follow along the north side of Mabou Harbour to get a taste of the Cape Mabou Highlands.

Points of Interest

- **Celtic Music Interpretive Centre, Judique (19.7 km)** Learn about Celtic music through exhibits and live performances; access via Baxters Cove Road, then head north on Trunk 19. After your visit, head north for 2 km for access back onto the trail.
- **Port Hood Station Provincial Park (38.2 km)** A day-use picnic park with a beautiful beach, not far off the trail; access from the Port Hood trail head/parking lot.
- **Red Shoe Pub, Mabou (58.2 km)** Take a small detour in Mabou to visit this popular pub owned by the Rankin Sisters, a beloved Cape Breton musical family. Enjoy local beer, live music, and great food. Access it by taking Trunk 19 north in Mabou where the trail crosses the road.
- **Inverness Beach, Inverness (83.8 km)** Walk the boardwalk and explore an incredible white sand beach. The famous Cabot Links golf course is also located here; it is the only official "links" course in Canada.

Suggested Itinerary (Rail and Road)

Kilometres are daily riding distances.

- **Day 1** Troy Station to Mabou (via the rail trail): Stop for lunch and visit the museum in Judique and then take some time at the beach in Port Hood. This is mostly coastal riding, except for the last leg between Port Hood and Mabou (58.3 km).
- **Day 2** Mabou to Inverness. If you're spending time in Mabou, consider taking a day to visit West Mabou Beach or to hike in the Cape Mabou Highlands. Otherwise, head to Inverness by taking the road through Nevada Valley, then take a fantastic ride around the nicest part of Lake Ainslie, and finish the final leg of the trip back on the rail trail (65.1 km). See **84 Lake Ainslie: Mabou–Nevada Valley** for more details.

- **Day 3** Ride the trail or road back to Troy Station: It's suggested to spend a day exploring Inverness and the surrounding area. There is an incredible beach just on the edge of town, golfing on the Cabot Links, and there are many shops and services to visit. See ㊿ **Inverness–Margaree** for a good day-long return cycling trip out of Inverness. Otherwise, when you are ready to turn around and head south, take the Celtic Shores Coastal Trail all the way back to Troy Station, or else return via Trunk 19, visiting the towns and attractions you missed on the way up (83.8 km).

Towns En Route (Accommodation and/or Amenities)
- Judique (22 km)
- Port Hood (38 km)
- Mabou (58 km)
- Inverness (84 km)

Bike Rentals
If you are driving to Cape Breton from Halifax or another location, there are a number of places where you can rent a bicycle along the way. If you are planning to rent on the island itself, we recommend you call around first to ensure you can find a suitable bike for your trip. See **Appendix A: Bike Shops** and **Appendix B: Bike Tours and Rentals** to review your options based on where and how you will be travelling.

Shuttles/Luggage/Getting around
Some cycling shops and businesses will shuttle cyclists and/or their luggage for a fee. It is best to call around to see if this option is available. If these businesses are unable to help, they may have up-to-date information about what is available.

Note
This ride has no cue sheet because there are no turns. Start by heading north from Troy Station and continue on to Inverness, staying on the trail the whole way, crossing the occasional road.

Nearby Bike Shops/Repairs/Rentals

- Highland Bike Shop (Port Hawkesbury) **902-625-5930**
- Velo Max (Chéticamp) **902-224-7944**

84 Lake Ainslie: Mabou–Nevada Valley (RT)

MAP 30

Start Point
Mabou: Mabou Hall, 11538 Trunk 19.

Summary
Undulating hills; rail trail option; lake views; water access.

Distance (km)	Duration	Max Grade +	Elevation Gain (m)	Unpaved
77.2	3:30/5:08	5.9	557	19% (15 km)

Description
Lake Ainslie is the largest freshwater body in the province; it is surrounded by deep glens and beautiful hardwood forests. The roads in this area are generally in good shape and fairly quiet, making for a fantastic cycling route.

Soon after leaving Mabou, you will get off the road and onto the Celtic Shores Coastal Trail for an easy ride in the woods for 15 km. In Strathlorne, you will get onto quiet roads and start to follow the northern part of Lake Ainslie on your way to Scotsville. At this point, the ride heads south on Route 395 for what is the nicest stretch of road on this trip.

The ride inland back to Mabou will take you through the Nevada Valley, where you can admire the hills in the distance while cycling past farms and homesteads. Finish off the ride with a nice descent back into town, where you can visit the pub to celebrate your day.

Ride Considerations
- If you only have time for one side of the lake, choose the east side; it has better roads, along with great views of the water and the hills and glens in the distance.

Side Trips/Variations
- If you want to avoid the rail trail, you can take Trunk 19 to Strathlorne Station where you can connect with Strathlorne Scotsville Road to continue the trip.
- For a shorter route around the lake, this trip can be done from Inverness in a similar manner by finishing the ride on the western side of the lake on West Lake Ainslie Road, instead of going through the Nevada Valley. This makes for a 66 km loop. See 85 Inverness–Margaree for more details.

- Visit Egypt Falls by taking Route 395 north from Scotsville (28.8 km) to Upper Margaree, then following Egypt Road to Pipers Glen Road. This is the widest waterfall in Cape Breton—an impressive sight. The hike down is short, but challenging, so be sure to have good shoes (12.4 km diversion).

Points of Interest

- **Glenora Distillery (13 km)** Visit the first single malt whisky producer in North America; they also serve food and have live music during peak season. (This is only available by taking Trunk 19 instead of the rail trail.)
- **MacDonald House Museum (35.4 km)** Get a sense of what it was like to live in this area at the turn of the twentieth century at this restored home that has an extensive collection of 1900s furniture and artifacts.
- **Trout Brook Provincial Park (40.2 km)** This is a great place for a picnic and for a swim in the waters of Lake Ainslie.

Lake Ainslie: Mabou–Nevada Valley (RT) Cue Sheet

Dist	Type	Note	Next
0.0	◉	Start of route	0.0
0.0	▮	(Start) Mabou: Mabou Hall, 11538 NS-19; head east on Ceilidh Trail/NS-19	1.0
1.0	→	R onto NS-252 E (signs for Brook Village/Whycocomagh)	2.2
3.2	←	L onto Celtic Shores Coastal Trail	15.4
18.6	→	R onto Strathlorne Scotsville Rd	10.3
28.9	→	R onto NS-395 S (signs for Trout River/Whycocomagh)	24.2
53.1	→	R onto NS-252 W (signs for Mabou)	23.1
76.2	←	L onto Ceilidh Trail/NS-19 S (signs for Port Hood/Canso Causeway)	1.0
77.2	◉	End of route	0.0

85 Inverness–Margaree Beach Tour (RT) MAP 30

Start Point
Inverness: Visitor Information Centre, 15756 Central Ave.

Summary
Some busy roads; some rough roads; undulating hills; coastal, river, and lake views; beach access.

Distance (km)	Duration	Max Grade +	Elevation Gain (m)	Unpaved
85.4	3:53/5:42	7.0	813	7% (6 km)

Description

Bring your beach towel and swimwear for this ride; it visits four white sand coastal beaches in the first 30 km, all of them easily accessible. You can start the day exploring Inverness Beach, then ride up the coast, slightly inland, until you start to see the water views north of Saint Rose. You will then have three fantastic beaches to visit before you reach Belle Côte. This ride also features some great views of the highlands off to the north before you head inland.

The second half of the ride will head south, along the east side of the Margaree River, following quiet roads dotted with farms and cottages. You will cycle through Southwest Margaree to Scotsville along a windy road with rolling hills and good pavement. Finish the ride by heading back toward the coast along the road, and then take the Celtic Shores Coastal Trail back into Inverness.

This ride covers a lot of different elements of Cape Breton. Take a full day so you have time to enjoy the beaches, the meandering Margaree River, and the views of Lake Ainslie.

Ride Considerations

- The road north from Inverness can be busy; try to avoid it during peak hours.

Side Trips/Variations

- To avoid the rail trail, continue on Strathlorne Scotsville Road (79.3 km) until you hit Trunk 19, then head north, back to Inverness.
- Visit Egypt Falls by following Egypt Road (65.9 km) to Pipers Glen Road. This is the widest waterfall in Cape Breton—an impressive sight. The hike down is short, but challenging, so be sure to have good shoes (6.4 km diversion).

Points of Interest

- **Inverness Beach (Start/Stop)** Start your ride close to home and visit this absolutely stunning beach.
- **Chimney Corner Beach (23.8 km)** Access via Chimney Corner Beach Road.
- **Whale Cove (28.6 km)** A gorgeous beach that you access directly from the road, which means it can sometimes be busy. Good views of the highlands begin at this point.
- **MacKinnons Beach/Margaree Harbour (32.0 km)** This little gem is tucked away down Margaree Harbour Village Road, just before you start to come inland. It has a cozy feel, with a breakwater helping to shelter the cove from waves and wind.

Inverness–Margaree Beach Tour (RT) Cue Sheet

Dist	Type	Note	Next
0.0	●	Start of route	0.0
0.0	▮	(Start) Inverness: Visitor Information Centre, 15756 Central Ave; head north on Central Ave/NS-19	11.8
11.8	←	L onto Shore Rd/NS-219 E (signs for Chimney Corner/Margaree Harbour)	20.5
32.3	←	L onto Cabot Trail (signs for Cheticamp/Pleasant Bay)	1.7
34.0	→	R onto East Margaree Rd	13.4
47.4	→	R to stay on East Margaree Rd	0.4

47.8	→	R onto Cabot Trail	1.3
49.1	←	L onto NS-19 S (signs for Inverness/Mabou/Port Hood)	7.9
57.0	←	L onto NS-395 S (signs for Scotsville/Whycocomagh)	11.8
68.8	→	R onto Strathlorne Scotsville Rd	10.3
79.1	→	R onto Celtic Shores Coastal Trail	5.9
85.0	→	R onto Ceilidh Trail/Central Ave/NS-19 N	0.4
85.4	●	End of route	0.0

86 Washabuck Peninsula

MAP 31

Start Point
Whycocomagh: east side of Little Narrows Ferry.

Summary
Fairly easy terrain; some rough roads; beach access.

Distance (km)	Duration	Max Grade +	Elevation Gain (m)	Unpaved
56.5	2:34/3:46	8.1	593	—

Description
This route gives you the chance to experience the gentle charm of Washabuck Peninsula, a fairly easy ride, except for one significant 3 km climb. Keep an eye out for the distinctive white gypsum hills around Plaster Cove, where you will also find a nice beach—perfect for a swim and a picnic.

Ride Considerations
- The ferry at Little Narrows is free for cyclists walking on; park on the mainland and take your bicycle across for the day. Ferry information: 902-294-0016.
- There are some very rough sections on the northeast part of the route, but the road gets better on the east side; the southeast portion of the ride has nice views and good pavement.

BEYOND THE CABOT TRAIL

Points of Interest

- **MacCormack Provincial Park (32.3 km)** This is a nice picnic park where you can have a rest and take in the view.
- **Iona Beach (33.1 km)** This is a conservation area with a small beach next to a wharf, perfect for a mid-ride swim.
- **Highland Village Museum (35.0 km)** Visit a living history museum and cultural centre that celebrates the Gaelic experience in Nova Scotia.

Washabuck Peninsula Cue Sheet

Dist	Type	Note	Next
0.0	◉	Start of route	0.0
0.0	⚑	(Start) Whycocomagh: east side of Little Narrows Ferry; head east on ferry	0.2
0.2	←	L onto Little Narrows Rd	8.0
8.2	→	R onto St Columba Rd	2.5
10.7	←	L onto Washabuck Rd	8.4
19.1	→	Slight R onto Gillis Point Rd	10.4
29.5	↑	Continue straight onto St Columba Rd	3.6
33.1	→	R onto NS-223 W (signs for Little Narrows)	23.2
56.3	←	L onto ferry ramp/NS-223 W (signs for Baddeck/Whycocomagh)	0.1
56.4	↑	Ferry back to your start point	0.1
56.5	◉	End of route	0.0

87 Boularderie Island

MAP 32

Start Point
Bras d'Or: Ultramar, 1283 Hwy. 105.

Summary
Gravel grinder; swim spot; punchy hills; water views; beach access.

Distance (km)	Duration	Max Grade +	Elevation Gain (m)	Unpaved
80.6	3:39/5:22	5.1	677	20% (16 km)

Description
If you are into gravel grinders and lots of hills, you'll like this one. This is a long ride, but it can be shortened up in a number of ways (all options are unpaved roads, and are listed below). Most of this route runs along the water and passes small communities and old farmsteads. You will encounter many challenging hills no matter which route you choose. Be prepared for various conditions, as unpaved roads can change from year to year and throughout the season.

Ride Considerations
- Bring lots of water for this ride; amenities are limited.
- Make sure you have your patch kit and pump; many of the roads are unpaved and it can get pretty remote near the southern tip.

Side Trips/Variations
- Cut across Calabash Road for a 39 km loop.
- Cut across Church Road for a 55 km loop.
- Cut across Steels Crossing Road for a 60.5 km loop.
- Cut across Matheson Road for a 71.7 km loop.
- Start at Calabash Road and do the southern loop for a 51 km loop.

Points of Interest
- **Graves Point Provincial Park (5.2 km)** This is a picnic park with access to the water.
- **Ross Ferry Marine Park (48.1 km)** A picnic park located where the ferry used to operate between Ross Ferry and Big Harbour, crossing the Great Bras d'Or Channel.

Boularderie Island Cue Sheet

Dist	Type	Note	Next
0.0	⦿	Start of route	0.0
0.0	⚑	(Start) Bras d'Or: Ultramar, 1283 NS-105; head west on Trans-Canada Hwy/NS-105	0.3
0.3	←	L onto Hillside Boularderie Rd	19.9
20.2	↑	Continue onto Kempt Head Rd	17.4
37.6	↑	Continue on Kempt Head Rd	23.5
61.1	→	R onto Trans-Canada Hwy/NS-105 E	1.9
63.0	←	L onto Old Route 5	9.7
72.7	↑	Continue onto Millville Hwy	4.5
77.2	←	L onto Trans-Canada Hwy/NS-105 E (signs for North Sydney/NL Ferry)	3.4
80.6	⦿	End of route	0.0

88 Alder Point

MAP 32

Start Point

Bras d'Or: 15 Alder Point Rd.

Summary

Easy ride; water views; fishing community.

Distance (km)	Duration	Max Grade +	Elevation Gain (m)	Unpaved
17.1	0:46/1:08	3.7	116	—

Description

This is a lovely route not far from Sydney and close to a couple of other small loops promoted by the Cape Breton Regional Municipality. It has some great water views as you make your way to the end of Alder Point Road, where you will come to a wharf and a small beach—a great spot for a rest and a picnic.

Points of Interest

- **Alder Point Wharf (7.4 km)** This is at the northernmost tip of the ride; it provides a beautiful view of Cape Smokey and a chance to witness the power of the tides where the strait meets the bay.

Alder Point Road takes cyclists to a lovely spot for a rest and a picnic. (ADAM BARNETT)

Alder Point Cue Sheet

Dist	Type	Note	Next
0.0	📍	Start of route	0.0
0.0	🚩	(Start) Bras d'Or: 15 Alder Point Rd; head north on Alder Point Rd	7.4
7.4	↰	Alder Point Wharf; turnaround point	2.2
9.6	←	L onto Schoolhouse Rd	1.3
10.9	↑	Continue onto Little Pond Rd	2.9
13.8	↑	Continue onto Main St	1.0
14.8	→	R onto Bras D'or Florence Rd/NS-305 N	2.2
17.0	←	L onto Alder Point Rd/NS-305 E	0.1
17.1	📍	End of route	0.0

 **New Victoria**

MAP 33

Start Point
Sydney: Neville Park, 199 Jameson St.

Summary
Coastal views; lighthouse.

Distance (km)	Duration	Max Grade +	Elevation Gain (m)	Unpaved
37.0	1:40/2:28	3.8	241	—

Description
This route provides some wonderful views of Sydney Harbour and is a classic ride for cyclists in the area. As you leave a commercial part of Sydney, you will head north toward New Victoria, quickly getting onto quieter roads. After 6 km, you will pass South Bar, where the road opens up to offer an expansive view of Spanish Bay, a lovely stretch of coast that looks out on fishing boats, the Newfoundland ferry (if you are lucky), and cliffs on the other side of the bay. After visiting the Low Point Lighthouse you can decide whether to come back the way you came or carry on to Scotchtown and River Ryan, where you will then head inland and back toward your starting point in Sydney.

Ride Considerations
• This route starts in Sydney and goes through a commercial area before getting onto roads with moderate traffic; try to avoid it during peak hours.

Side Trips/Variations
• To make this a longer trip (93.8 km), keep going to Glace Bay and beyond, following the notes for ⑨ **Northern Coastal Industrial Loop**.
• This route is shown as a loop, but it also makes a fantastic return trip; visit the lighthouse and come back the way you came (32.4 km return trip).

Points of Interest
• **Low Point Lighthouse (16.2 km)** Follow an unpaved 0.5 km road to get to this working lighthouse and take in the ruggedness of northern Cape Breton. Keep your eyes open for windmills as you look toward New Waterford.

New Victoria Cue Sheet

Dist	Type	Note	Next
0.0	📍	Start of route	0.0
0.0	🚩	(Start) Sydney: Neville Park, 199 Jameson St; head west on Jameson St	0.2
0.2	➡	R onto Victoria Rd/NS-28 E	14.3
14.5	⬅	L onto Browns Rd	0.7
15.2	➡	R onto Browns Rd Extension	0.6
15.8	⬅	L onto Lighthouse Rd	0.4
16.2	↩	Low Point Lighthouse; turnaround point	0.5
16.7	➡	R onto Browns Rd Extension	0.6
17.3	⬅	L onto Browns Rd	0.7

18.0	➡	R onto New Waterford Hwy/NS-28 W	1.0
19.0	⬅	L onto Daley Rd	2.4
21.4	⬆	Continue onto May St	1.1
22.5	➡	R onto Union Hwy/NS-28 E	1.8
24.3	➡	R onto Lingan Rd	11.5
35.8	➡	Slight R onto Fisher St	0.3
36.1	➡	R onto Henry St	0.2
36.3	➡	R onto Victoria Rd/NS-28 E	0.5
36.8	➡	R onto Jameson St	0.2
37.0	📍	End of route	0.0

90 Northern Coastal Industrial Loop

MAP 33

Start Point

Sydney: Neville Park, 199 Jameson St.

Summary

Some rough roads; coastal views; beach access.

Distance (km)	Duration	Max Grade +	Elevation Gain (m)	Unpaved
93.9	4:15/6:15	7.0	706	—

Description

Gear up for a long ride that starts from Sydney and follows the coast through what is considered Cape Breton's industrial region. This area has been known for its coal deposits since the 1720s, when French soldiers from the Fortress of Louisbourg first started extracting this valuable resource; coal has been mined here for more than 250 years.

This route will take you through a variety of terrain, weaving in and out of coastal roads and residential communities. Sometimes the view is like a postcard, with coastal cliffs and white sand beaches, while at other times the route feels gritty and urban. Along the way you will see a number of windmills—the updated version of industrial energy production. There are wind farms in the communities of Gardiner Mines, Lingan, Glace Bay, Donkin, and Bateston.

This is an epic ride that offers insight into the coal mining industry that is so deeply woven into Cape Breton's history.

Ride Considerations

- This ride goes through a combination of commercial, residential, and quiet coastal routes; be prepared for changes in traffic throughout your ride.
- Road conditions vary; be prepared for some rough roads.

Side Trips/Variations

- Make this a shorter ride by taking the multi-use path from Glace Bay to Sydney, for a 66 km loop.

Points of Interest

- **Low Point Lighthouse** Follow an unpaved 0.5 km road to get to this working lighthouse and take in the ruggedness of northern Cape Breton; access it by following Trunk 28 east past the turnoff (13.4 km), taking Browns Road, then Lighthouse Road.
- **Dominion Beach Provincial Park (24.6 km)** A beautiful white sand beach with boardwalks for strolling.
- **Cape Breton Miners Museum (31.6 km)** Take a small detour to visit this museum where you can learn about the mining history in Cape Breton through a variety of exhibits, and by taking an underground mine tour. The museum is located at 17 Museum St. in Glace Bay.
- **Big Glace Bay Beach (39.5 km)** This is a lovely beach located beside the Big Glace Bay Lake Migratory Bird Sanctuary.

Northern Coastal Industrial Loop Cue Sheet

Dist	Type	Note	Next
0.0	●	Start of route	0.0
0.0	⚑	(Start) Sydney: Neville Park, 199 Jameson St; head west on Jameson St	0.2
0.2	→	R onto Victoria Rd/NS-28 E	13.2
13.4	→	R onto Daley Rd	2.4
15.8	↑	Continue onto May St	1.1
16.9	→	R onto Union Hwy/NS-28 E	2.4
19.3	↑	Continue onto Seaside Dr	5.5
24.8	↑	Continue onto Mitchell Ave/NS-28 E	0.3
25.1	←	L onto Commercial St/NS-28 E (signs for Glace Bay)	0.7
25.8	→	R onto Kings Rd/NS-28 E	5.4
31.2	→	R onto Commercial St/NS-28 E	0.4
31.6	→	R onto Catherine St	0.8
32.4	←	L onto Park St	0.3
32.7	→	R onto Brookside St/Marconi Trail/NS-255 S	6.8
39.5	↑	Continue onto Donkin Hwy/No 6 Mines Rd	10.8
50.3	←	L onto Marconi Trail/NS-255 S (signs for Mira Gut/Main-à-Dieu)	16.2
66.5	→	R onto Hornes Rd/Marconi Trail/NS-255 S	8.6
75.1	→	R onto Hornes Rd	1.4
76.5	↑	Continue onto Old Hornes Rd	0.5
77.0	→	R onto NS-22 N	10.6
87.6	↑	At the roundabout, continue straight onto George St/NS-22 N	2.1
89.7	→	R onto Woodill St	0.3
90.0	↑	Continue onto St Peters Rd	0.4
90.4	←	L onto Hospital St	0.1
90.5	→	R onto Howe St	0.6
91.1	←	L onto Ashby Rd	0.0
91.1	→	R onto Whitney Ave	0.4
91.5	↑	Continue onto Victoria Rd/NS-28 E	2.2
93.7	→	R onto Jameson St	0.2
93.9	●	End of route	0.0

BEYOND THE CABOT TRAIL

Variation: Donkin Loop (32.1 km, Map 33)

Take a shorter tour of the Coastal Industrial Loop by starting in Donkin (304 Brookside St.) and following Route 255 east to Port Caledonia, then getting on Donkin Highway/Long Beach Road to Port Morien, home of the first coal mine in North America, which began production in 1720. Get onto Birch Cove Road in Port Morien and follow this west, and then north back to Donkin.

---

92 Hillside Loop

MAP 34

Start Point
Sydney: Framework Cycle & Fitness, 333 George St.

Summary
Challenging hills; some busy roads; river views.

Distance (km)	Duration	Max Grade +	Elevation Gain (m)	Unpaved
49.0	2:14/3:16	5.9	353	—

Description
This is an opportunity for a country ride that comes straight out of downtown Sydney. Most of the route is inland, but you will follow the beautiful Mira River for 14 km in the middle of your ride. The road coming out of Sydney can be busy during peak hours, but the other roads are relatively quiet.

Ride Considerations
• This ride starts and finishes in downtown Sydney; try to avoid cycling this section during peak hours.

Hillside Loop Cue Sheet

Dist	Type	Note	Next
0.0	📍	Start of route	0.0
0.0	🚩	(Start) Sydney: Framework Cycle & Fitness, 333 George St; head south on George St/NS-22	3.5
3.5	↑	At the roundabout, continue straight onto NS-22 S	13.1
16.6	→	R onto Hillside Rd	13.5
30.1	→	R onto Gabarus Hwy/NS-327 N	14.4
44.5	↑	At the roundabout, continue straight onto Alexandra St/NS-327	2.5
47.0	←	L to stay on Alexandra St/NS-327 N	0.2
47.2	→	R onto Argyle St	0.7
47.9	←	L onto George St/NS-22	1.1
49.0	📍	End of route	0.0

93 Variation: Marion Bridge–Grand Mira (50.4 km, Map 34)

To make this trip a "metric century," ride the Marion Bridge–Grand Mira route for an additional 50.4 km (note that this ride has 23% unpaved roads). Start in Marion Bridge (3966 Gabarus Highway) and head southwest on the north side of the Mira River by following Grand Mira North Road. At 25.5 km, head east and then north on Maceachern Road until turning onto Grand Mira Gabarus Road to stay along the water. Finally, get on Grand Mira South Road to finish the ride back into Marion Bridge.

 # 94 Albert Bridge–Marion Bridge MAP 34

Start Point
Albert Bridge: 4320 Louisbourg Hwy.

Summary
Some rough roads; river views.

Distance (km)	Duration	Max Grade +	Elevation Gain (m)	Unpaved
29.3	1:19/1:57	3.2	203	—

Description
This is a nice route that takes you on both sides of the Mira River. Finish the day off by cycling another 2.5 km to the Mira River Provincial Park (east of start/finish point, down Brickyard Road) so you can cool off in the water you've been eyeing for nearly 30 km.

Ride Considerations
- Expect rough conditions on the south side of the river (Brickyard Road).
- On the map it looks like you can head east, crossing over the river at the Mira Gut, but this bridge has been decommissioned.

Side Trips/Variations
- Continue riding down the river to Grand Mira on the 93 Marion Bridge–Grand Mira route for an additional 50.4 km, making this ride a gravel grinder. There are supplies available in both Albert Bridge and Marion Bridge.

Albert Bridge–Marion Bridge
Cue Sheet

Dist	Type	Note	Next
0.0	📍	Start of route	0.0
0.0	🚩	(Start) Albert Bridge: 4320 Louisbourg Hwy; head west on Trout Brook Rd	13.8
13.8	➡	R onto Gabarus Hwy/NS-327 N	0.4
14.2	➡	R onto Grand Mira Rd N/Hillside Rd	13.5
27.7	➡	R onto Louisbourg Hwy/NS-22 S	1.6
29.3	➡	R onto Trout Brook Rd	0.0
29.3	📍	End of route	0.0

95 Fortress of Louisbourg
(42.9 km, Map 34)

This National Historic Site is the largest reconstruction project in North America. The site is a partially reconstructed eighteenth-century fort, originally built by the French on a settlement founded in 1713. This is a really impressive place to visit and is worth the trip.

The route between Albert Bridge and Louisbourg has good pavement and decent shoulders, but it can be a busy road. From Albert Bridge, follow Trunk 22 south to the town of Louisbourg and then follow the signs to the Fortress of Louisbourg; come back the way you came. There are many amenities in the town of Louisbourg.

 **Point Michaud**

MAP 35

Start Point
St. Peters: 10004 Grenville St.

Summary
Easy ride; good roads; beach access.

Distance (km)	Duration	Max Grade +	Elevation Gain (m)	Unpaved
41.7 (return)	1:53/2:46	7.7	363	—

Description
Point Michaud is a stunning beach, conveniently located at perfect picnicking distance from the town of St. Peters. The roads are good for the majority of this ride, and they are relatively quiet. You will come around the corner to an impressive view of the ocean around L'Ardoise (11 km), and this view continues on and off for the rest of the ride. Enjoy your time at the beach and then head back the way you came.

Ride Considerations
- You have an option to turn this ride into a loop, but the road is unpaved after Point Michaud and can be very rough; there are also no more water views. To do this, follow Point Michaud Road to Grand River, taking Soldiers Cove Road to Trunk 4, and then head west back to St. Peters (52.7 km loop).

Points of Interest
- **Point Michaud Beach (20.9 km)**
  This is an outstanding beach that deserves some time for exploration; it is over 3 km long and is backed by sand dunes and cranberry bogs. It also makes for a great picnic spot.

Point Michaud Cue Sheet

Dist	Type	Note	Next
0.0	📍	Start of route	0.0
0.0	🚩	(Start) St. Peters: 10004 Grenville St; head east on Grenville St/NS-4	1.5
1.5	➡	R onto NS-247 S	19.4
20.9	↩	Point Michaud Beach; turnaround point	19.3
40.2	⬅	L onto NS-4 W (signs for Port Hawkesbury/Fleur-de-Lis Trail W)	1.5
41.7	📍	End of route	0.0

Point Michaud is a stunning beach; take some time to explore its sand dunes and cranberry bogs. (ADAM BARNETT)

97 St. Peters: Cape George

MAP 35

Start Point

St. Peters: 10004 Grenville St.

Summary

Challenging hills; some rough road; lake views.

Distance (km)	Duration	Max Grade +	Elevation Gain (m)	Unpaved
64.6	2:56/4:18	8.0	663	—

Description

This ride departs from St. Peters and follows around Cape George, hugging the Bras d'Or Lake for most of the journey. You will pass old farms and hardwood forests along the way; this is an exceptionally beautiful fall ride when the leaves start to change colour in late September.

Ride Considerations

- The roads range from excellent to poor throughout this ride and they are often narrow; these are secondary roads that don't see a lot of traffic, so there is usually adequate room for manoeuvring.

St. Peters: Cape George Cue Sheet

Dist	Type	Note	Next
0.0	◉	Start of route	0.0
0.0	⚑	(Start) St. Peters: 10004 Grenville St; head east on Grenville St/NS-4	0.1
0.1	←	L onto W Bay Rd/Pepperell St (signs for French Cove/Cape George/Roberta/Dundee)	36.1
36.2	←	L onto Black River Rd	9.6
45.8	←	L onto NS-4 E (signs for Saint Peters/Sydney/Fleur-de-lis Trail E)	15.5
61.3	→	R to stay on NS-4 E (signs for Sydney/Saint Peters/Fleur-de-lis Trail)	3.3
64.6	◉	End of route	0.0

 **Isle Madame**

MAP 35

Start Point
D'Escousse: 3281 Rte. 320.

Summary
Excellent roads; beach access; lighthouse.

Distance (km)	Duration	Max Grade +	Elevation Gain (m)	Unpaved
67.3	3:03/4:29	6.5	503	—

Description
Isle Madame is a French cultural region located on a beautiful island full of coves, inlets, and fishing villages off the most southeastern tip of Cape Breton. Everywhere around the island you will have constantly changing views of the water, depending on which bay you are facing. The roads are twisty, punchy, and sometimes very skinny; in other words: fun. On the first part of the ride you will be cycling through Rocky Bay, a beautiful area that is an old Irish settlement—a curious contrast to the French culture all around. When you head south, you will be riding out to the end of another island and a peninsula. Take some time to explore Petit-de-Grat, an island that has the feeling of a Newfoundland outpost with its unique layout of roads and houses. Stop for snacks or lunch in Arichat before finishing the rest of the loop on the western part of the island.

The roads here are all in excellent shape, which makes for enjoyable exploration of the many side roads, of which there are many. It is recommended that you make a full day out of this trip. Take your time; explore any roads that catch your interest, and enjoy the many beaches and other beautiful treats this area has to offer.

Side Trips/Variations
- Take off 12 km by leaving out the Cape Auguet section of the ride.
- Take off another 15 km by leaving out the Petit-de-Grat section.
- Take the road out to Janvrin Island to add another 21 km. This is a back-and-forth diversion that goes along marshes, and provides a different feel than the rest of the island. Watch for eagles riding the thermals as you go over the bridge. At 53.6km, head west on Maceachern Road, staying right at the intersection with Port Royal Road, then follow Janvrin Harbour Road out to the island.

BEYOND THE CABOT TRAIL

Points of Interest

- **Pondville Beach Provincial Park (12.7 km)** A sheltered white sand beach with excellent swimming.
- **Cape Auguet Lighthouse (37.2 km)** The ride down to the lighthouse is curvy and fun, and closely follows the shore the whole way.
- **LeNoir Forge Museum (45.1 km)** Stop in to learn about the rich history of this unique area.

Isle Madame Cue Sheet

Dist	Type	Note	Next
0.0	○	Start of route	0.0
0.0	⚑	(Start) D'Escousse: 3281 NS-320; head east on NS-320	0.5
0.5	↰	Slight L onto D'Escousse Cap La Ronde Rd	3.7
4.2	→	R onto Bona Rd/D'Escousse Cap La Ronde Rd	2.0
6.2	→	R onto Rocky Bay Rd	6.5
12.7	←	L onto Fleur-de-lis Trail/NS-320 E	3.4
16.1	←	L onto High Rd (signs for High Rd/Petit de Grat)	2.6
18.7	↑	Continue onto Little Anse West Arichat Rd/N Side Petit De Grat Rd	2.5
21.2	←	L onto S Side Petit De Grat Rd	2.6
23.8	↑	Continue onto Breakwater Rd	0.7
24.5	↩	Turnaround point	0.3
24.8	↑	Continue onto Breakwater Rd	2.6
27.4	↑	Continue onto S Side Petit De Grat Rd	0.3
27.7	→	R onto N Side Petit De Grat Rd	2.5
30.2	←	Slight L onto Little Anse West Arichat Rd/Veteran's Memorial Dr	0.9
31.1	←	L onto Robins Rd	1.6
32.7	←	Slight L onto Cape Auguet Rd	4.4
37.1	↩	Cap Auget Lighthouse; turnaround point	4.5
41.6	↑	Continue onto Robins Rd	1.6
43.2	←	L onto Little Anse West Arichat Rd/Veteran's Memorial Dr	5.6
48.8	←	L onto NS-206 W (signs for Lennox Passage/Louisdale)	9.6
58.4	→	R onto Fleur-de-lis Trail/NS-320 E (signs for D'Escousse)	6.6
65.0	←	Slight L onto Old Wharf Rd	2.3
67.3	○	End of route	0.0

Isle Madame is a beautiful island full of coves, inlets, and picturesque fishing villages. (ADAM BARNETT)

CYCLING ROUTES OF THE EASTERN SHORE

Route	Route Name	Distance (km)	Duration	Max Grade +	Elevation Gain (m)	Unpaved	Map
99	Guysborough: Tickle Loop	123.3	5:35/8:12	6.3	1250	—	36
100	Interval Loop	33.3	1:30/2:13	4.0	229	3% (1 km)	36
101	Sherbrooke Loop	39.5	1:47/2:38	6.9	320	20% (8 km)	37
102	Sober Island	26.1	1:11/1:44	3.9	220	13% (3.5 km)	37
103	Clam Harbour	44.0	2:00/2:57	4.4	357	—	38
104	Ostrea Lake	38.1	1:48/2:38	4.5	322	8% (3 km)	38
105	Musquodoboit Harbour (RT)	30.0	1:21/2:00	3.5	218	50% (15 km)	38
106	Three Fathom Harbour	41.3	1:52/2:45	5.4	293	2% (1 km)	38

Eastern Shore Regional Overview

When people think about Nova Scotia's fishing industry and the province's rugged, fog-laced coastlines, they are often conjuring up the Eastern Shore in their minds. There is a stark and often raw beauty to this part of the province, with its pristine wilderness and stunted trees. As you travel up the coast, the history of this traditional fishing area becomes evident everywhere you go, as you pass by the working wharves, the lobster traps drying in the sun, and the lighthouses that help guide fishing vessels home in rough waters. It can feel like you are stepping back in time here, when people lived off the bounty of the land and worked for their comforts.

The towns are spread out around these parts and the population is fairly low, so there are fewer cycling routes here than in some of the other parts of the province. But the routes here include incredible coastal beauty, along with some of the best beaches anywhere. Guysborough was often overlooked for its cycling potential until the Lost Shores Gran Fondo was created, bringing thousands of cyclists to the shores of this beautiful area. The longest route of the event includes a visit to Canso, the most northeastern tip of the mainland, and home to the Stan Rogers Folk Festival. This festival is named for the legendary musician whose songs reflected the Canadian—and particularly the east coast—experience; it brings in thousands of people ever year to camp out and celebrate roots, folk, and blues music.

Sherbrooke is a must-stop for anyone travelling along the Eastern Shore. It is home to Sherbrooke Village, a popular living history museum where you can immerse yourself in life in the year 1867; as you enter the village, you will feel as if time has stood still since then. The town of Sherbrooke is on the mighty St. Marys

River, one of the greatest salmon-producing rivers in Nova Scotia. This is a graceful, meandering river that tempts you to sit on its banks and watch the water flow.

The Eastern Shore is home to an ecologically unique stretch of shoreline known as the "100 Wild Islands." This is an archipelago of over one hundred islands made up of boreal rainforests, bogs, and barrens along a 250 km stretch of shoreline; it has been mostly undisturbed by humans for over ten thousand years. The area presents an opportunity to explore large sheltered coves with isolated beaches, to walk along dramatic coastlines, and to see some of the vast species of seabirds, songbirds, and shorebirds. This important area is now part of the protected Eastern Shore Islands Wilderness Area, which will help ensure that it remains in its pristine state for future generations.

As you tour the coastline you will come to some of the most popular beaches in the province. These are all a relatively short drive from Halifax and offer incredible white sand, as well as some excellent surfing. Clam Harbour is a pristine beach and is home to the annual Clam Harbour Beach Sandcastle Competition, where thousands come to watch and take part in creating elaborate and impressive sand castles. Martinique Beach is not far away and offers an expansive crescent beach—the longest sandy beach in Nova Scotia, at 5 km. Closer to the city, you will come to Lawrencetown Beach, another popular summer spot, and one that is connected with Cole Harbour via the ❷ **Shearwater Flyer and Salt Marsh Trail**, which allows cyclists to visit the beach from the city on a multi-use path.

This area is full of rich history, rugged coastline, and lovely communities. Take the time to visit the beaches and stop in at the museums along the way. If you are lucky, you may even get the chance to boil some lobsters on the shore for the full Eastern Shore experience.

Additional Notes

- This part of the province is known for being foggy, and it can come in quickly. Check the weather before you go and ensure that you bring adequate layers for warmth.
- There are not a lot of amenities east of Sheet Harbour. If you are cycling long-distance or need supplies, be sure to plan appropriately.
- Trunk 7 is the main road for this area. Be aware that this road gets busier during peak hours, especially as you get closer to Halifax.

Guysborough was often overlooked for its cycling potential until the Lost Shores Gran Fondo was created, bringing thousands of cyclists to the shores of this beautiful area.
(LOST SHORES GRAN FONDO)

Eastern Shore Bike Shops

Note: The nearest bike shops are at either end of the region, in Halifax Metro and Antigonish.

- Halifax Area Bike Shops see page 39
- Highland Bike Shop (Antigonish) 902-735-3320

Eastern Shore Emergency Services

- Guysborough Memorial Hospital (Guysborough)
- St. Mary's Memorial Hospital (Sherbrooke, Guysborough County)
- Eastern Shore Memorial Hospital (Sheet Harbour)
- Musquodoboit Valley Memorial Hospital (Middle Musquodoboit)
- Twin Oaks Memorial Hospital (Musquodoboit Harbour)

99 Guysborough: Tickle Loop

MAP 36

Start Point

Guysborough: Chedabucto Place Performance Centre, 27 Green St.

Summary

Long ride; challenging hills; remote; coastal views; fishing villages; lighthouse.

Distance (km)	Duration	Max Grade +	Elevation Gain (m)	Unpaved
123.3	5:35/8:12	6.3	1250	—

Description

This route is taken directly from the Lost Shores Gran Fondo, a popular event in the area that is growing every year. This is a big ride, but it can be shortened in a number of ways (see **Side Trips/Variations**). It takes you along two beautiful stretches of coastline, both with a very distinct feel.

The ride out of Guysborough is on good pavement and will quickly provide some water views as you cycle along mostly gentle rolling hills. After you take a break in Queensport to admire the lighthouse, you will be riding inland as you make your way to Canso, home of the Stan Rogers Folk Festival. After a quick loop through town, you are coming back the way you came until you hit Route 316 heading south. Once you get to Port Felix, you will hit another stretch of coast, where you will see fishing boats, a beautifully rugged landscape, and the stunted trees that have adapted to the unrelenting wind and sea-salt spray. At Larrys River, you will start to head inland for the final stretch back to Guysborough.

Ride Considerations

- If you do this whole ride, it will be a long day, and it can sometimes feel fairly remote; be sure to bring water and supplies.
- There is often a breeze coming off the ocean and it can get cool quickly, especially if fog rolls in; it is good to have a few layers handy, even on a nice summer day.

Side Trips/Variations

- Skip the ride out to Canso and take off 34 km (89 km total).
- Guysborough to Canso is an approximately 100 km return trip.
- Make this a shorter day by riding out to Queensport and back; this is a nice waterfront ride with long coasters and a few challenging hills (48 km).

EASTERN SHORE

Points of Interest

- **Queensport Lighthouse/Rest Area (23.7 km)** This is a good spot to rest and take in the view of the lighthouse just off the shore; this is also the turnaround point if you want to make this into the shorter ride mentioned above.

Guysborough: Tickle Loop Cue Sheet

Dist	Type	Note	Next
0.0	♀	Start of route	0.0
0.0	⚑	(Start) Guysborough: Chedabucto Place Performance Centre, 27 Green St; head west on Green St	0.4
0.4	←	L onto Marine Dr/NS-16 S	31.0
31.4	↑	Continue Straight on Marine Dr/NS-16 S	12.9
44.3	←	L onto Bennetts Lake Rd	0.4
44.7	↑	Continue onto Tickle Rd	1.5
46.2	→	R onto Tickle Rd/Union St	1.0

Dist	Type	Note	Next
47.2	↑	Continue onto Union St	1.2
48.4	←	L onto Roberts St	0.5
48.9	→	R onto Main St	0.6
49.5	↑	Continue straight on NS-16	15.8
65.3	←	L onto Marine Dr/NS-316 N	30.9
96.2	→	Sharp R onto Larrys River Rd	24.8
121.0	←	Slight L onto Marine Dr/NS-16 N (signs for Guysborough/Monastery)	1.9
122.9	→	R onto Green St	0.4
123.3	♀	End of route	0.0

This route, taken directly from the Lost Shores Gran Fondo, brings you along two beautiful stretches of coastline, both with a very distinct feel. (LOST SHORES GRAN FONDO)

100 Interval Loop

Start Point
Guysborough: Chedabucto Place Performance Centre, 27 Green St.

Summary
Easy ride; some unpaved roads; water views.

Distance (km)	Duration	Max Grade +	Elevation Gain (m)	Unpaved
33.3	1:30/2:13	4.0	229	3% (1 km)

Description
This is a nice, easy route with mostly flat terrain. The ride starts by leaving town along the Guysborough Harbour and has water views for the whole ride.

Ride Considerations
- Halfway through the ride there is 1 km of unpaved road; everything else is paved and in good condition.

Interval Loop Cue Sheet

Dist	Type	Note	Next
0.0	◉	Start of route	0.0
0.0	⚑	(Start) Guysborough: Chedabucto Place Performance Centre, 27 Green St; head east on Green St	0.5
0.5	←	L onto Main St/NS-16	6.1
6.6	↗	Slight R to stay on NS-16	1.5
8.1	←	Slight L onto N Riverside Rd	0.8
8.9	←	L to stay on N Riverside Rd	9.0
17.9	←	L onto Crossing Rd	0.7
18.6	←	L onto Antigonish Guysborough Rd	8.1
26.7	→	R onto Marine Dr/NS-16 S (signs for Guysborough)	6.1
32.8	→	R onto Green St	0.5
33.3	◉	End of route	0.0

EASTERN SHORE

Sherbrooke Loop

MAP 37

Start Point
Sherbrooke: 15 Main St.

Summary
Easy ride; water views; beach access.

Distance (km)	Duration	Max Grade +	Elevation Gain (m)	Unpaved
39.5	1:47/2:38	6.9	320	20% (8 km)

Description
This ride takes you along some beautiful stretches of water and gives you an opportunity to stop at the beach around the halfway point. Follow the St. Marys River out of town—a gorgeous, lazy river known for its salmon fishing. The ride continues on Marine Drive down to Port Hilford, where you will be on unpaved roads as you cut over to Sonora. Finish the ride by visiting Sherbrooke Village, a popular living history museum, where you can immerse yourself in what traditional Nova Scotian life would have been like in 1867.

Points of Interest
- **Port Hilford Beach (18.1 km)** Take a break and explore this nice expanse of beach; access it by staying on Route 211 for 100 m past the turnoff to Sonora Road.

Sherbrooke Loop Cue Sheet

Dist	Type	Note	Next
0.0	○	Start of route	0.0
0.0	⚑	(Start) Sherbrooke: 15 Main St; head east on Main St	0.1
0.1	↑	Continue straight onto NS-7 E	4.5
4.6	→	R onto Marine Dr/NS-211 E (signs for Port Bickerton/Country Harbour ferry/Canso)	13.5
18.1	→	R onto Sonora Rd	0.6
18.7	←	L to stay on Sonora Rd	3.0
21.7	→	R to stay on Sonora Rd	17.0
38.7	←	L onto Main St	0.3
39.0	→	R to stay on Main St	0.5
39.5	○	End of route	0.0

EASTERN SHORE

102 Sober Island

MAP 37

Start Point
Sheet Harbour: 23566 Trunk 7.

Summary
Some unpaved roads; hilly; coastal views.

Distance (km)	Duration	Max Grade +	Elevation Gain (m)	Unpaved
26.1	1:11/1:44	3.9	220	13% (3.5 km)

Description
This is a fun loop along rugged coastal inlets which give it a classic Eastern Shore feel. Follow along the edge of Sheet Harbour on your way to Sober Island via twisty roads with lots of little hills. After you cross the causeway onto Sober Island, you will have some fun ups and downs; the road feels a little bit like a roller coaster. After visiting Sober Island, head east toward Beaver Harbour where you get onto Trunk 7, finishing the ride with a few steady climbs on paved shoulders.

Ride Considerations
- Following Sober Island Road all the way to the end will take you into someone's driveway—so turn around before this, or be ready to wave and say hello.
- Trunk 7 can be busy; try to avoid it during peak hours. This section of road between Beaver Harbour and Watt Section has paved shoulders.

Side Trips/Variations
- You can choose to start this trip from Sheet Harbour, where there are more amenities (add 11 km).

Sober Island Cue Sheet

Dist	Type	Note	Next
0.0	📍	Start of route	0.0
0.0	🚩	(Start) Sheet Harbour: 23566 NS-7; head west on NS-7	0.1
0.1	←	L onto Beaver Harbour Rd/Sunset Dr	0.1
0.2	←	L onto Passage Rd	6.2
6.4	→	R onto Sober Island Rd	2.1
8.5	→	R onto Mozier Cove Rd	1.4
9.9	↩	Turnaround point	1.4
11.3	←	L onto Sober Island Rd	2.1
13.4	→	R onto Passage Rd	7.3
20.7	←	L onto NS-7 W	5.4
26.1	📍	End of route	0.0

103 Clam Harbour

MAP 38

Start Point
Lake Charlotte: 11470 Trunk 7.

Summary
Coastal views; good roads; beach access; fishing wharf.

Distance (km)	Duration	Max Grade +	Elevation Gain (m)	Unpaved
44.0	2:00/2:57	4.4	357	—

Description
Be sure to bring your beach gear for this ride; it will take you to Clam Harbour Beach Provincial Park, a beautiful and popular beach that is home to an impressive sandcastle competition every year. The beginning of this ride takes you on Trunk 7 for 8 km, but then gets onto quieter roads. Most of this route is on good roads, with undulating hills and lots of water views. Take the side trip down to a small fishing village in Little Harbour before heading to Clam Harbour for some time at the beach. This is a great loop with lots of Eastern Shore charm.

Ride Considerations
- Trunk 7 can be a busy road; try to avoid it during peak hours.
- The short road heading downhill to Clam Harbour Beach is loose gravel, so ride with caution.

Side Trips/Variations
- Skipping the leg to Little Harbour will reduce your distance by 7 km.

Points of Interest
- **The Deanery Project (11.9 km)** Stop into this community-run organization that offers educational programs related to forest stewardship, active transportation, and rural living.
- **Little Harbour (24.8 km)** This is home to a beautiful and active fishing wharf with impeccable charm.
- **Clam Harbour Beach Provincial Park (34.0 km)** A stunning white sand beach with a picnic area and boardwalk. This area can be foggy, even if it has been sunny for the rest of the ride, so come prepared.

EASTERN SHORE

Clam Harbour Cue Sheet

Dist	Type	Note	Next
0.0	📍	Start of route	0.0
0.0	🚩	(Start) Lake Charlotte: 11470 NS-7; head east on NS-7	8.1
8.1	→	R onto West Ship Harbour Rd	13.4
21.5	←	L onto Southwest Cove Rd	0.5
22.0	→	R onto Little Harbour Rd	2.8
24.8	↩	Turnaround point	2.8
27.6	←	L onto Southwest Cove Rd	0.5
28.1	←	L onto Clam Harbour Rd	4.8
32.9	←	L onto Beach Rd	0.9
33.8	↩	Clam Harbour Beach Provincial Park; turnaround point	0.9
34.7	↑	Continue onto Clam Harbour Rd	9.3
44.0	←	L onto NS-7 W	0.0
44.0	📍	End of route	0.0

The Deanery Project offers educational programs related to forest stewardship, active transportation, and rural living. (LYNNE PASCOE)

104 Ostrea Lake

MAP 38

Start Point
Head of Jeddore: 8990 Trunk 7.

Summary
Some unpaved roads; coastal views; lighthouse.

Distance (km)	Duration	Max Grade +	Elevation Gain (m)	Unpaved
38.1	1:48/2:38	4.5	322	8% (3 km)

Description
Enjoy a ride that takes you along Musquodoboit Harbour via twisty roads with plentiful water views and many driftwood beaches. This route will give you a good taste of the rugged beauty of the Eastern Shore, and is an easy day-drive from Halifax.

Ride Considerations
- Trunk 7 can be busy; try to avoid it during peak hours.
- At the turn-around point in Lower West Jeddore you will see a "No Maintenance Road" which is in rough shape. Although it does cut across the peninsula, it should only be tackled by adventurous souls with knobby tires.

Side Trips/Variations
- Skip the leg to Lower West Jeddore and take 11 km off your ride.
- If you want to avoid the gravel roads, it's recommended that you stay on the west side of the route, from Smith Settlement to Pleasant Point, and then come back the way you came (30 km return).

Points of Interest
- **French Point Lighthouse (13.6 km)** Head over to Kent Island to get a glimpse of a classic Nova Scotia lighthouse. (Please respect that this is private land.)

Ostrea Lake Cue Sheet

Dist	Type	Note	Next
0.0	◉	Start of route	0.0
0.0	⚑	(Start) Head of Jeddore: 8990 NS-7; head west on NS-7	1.1
1.1	←	L onto Ostrea Lake Rd	12.1
13.2	→	R onto Kent Rd	0.4
13.6	↴	French Point Lighthouse; turnaround point	0.4
14.0	←	L onto Ostrea Lake Rd/Pleasant Point	2.5
16.5	→	R onto Cross Rd/Ostrea Lake and West Jeddore Crossing Rd	3.2
19.7	→	R onto W Jeddore Rd/Lower West Jeddore Rd	5.4
25.1	↴	Turnaround point	12.0
37.1	←	L onto NS-7 W	1.0
38.1	◉	End of route	0.0

EASTERN SHORE

105   Musquodoboit Harbour (RT)

MAP 38

Start Point

Musquodoboit Harbour: Musquodoboit Trailway Trailhead, 67 Park Rd.

Summary

Rail trail; water views; easy ride; beach option; local food/drink; kid-friendly.

Distance (km)	Duration	Max Grade +	Elevation Gain (m)	Unpaved
30.0	1:21/2:00	3.5	218	50% (15 km)

Description

This route takes you on a combination of paved road and rail trail through the lush and beautiful Musquodoboit Valley. Staying off the road for the first portion of the ride allows you to relax and take in your surroundings as you enjoy the well-maintained rail trail. The second half of the ride is on the road, following the Musquodoboit River, which offers many beautiful water views. This is a relaxing ride with the option to visit Martinique Beach afterwards, or just grab some treats from one of the many offerings in Musquodoboit Harbour.

Ride Considerations

- There are a number of places to grab food in Musquodoboit Harbour; there is also a bank, a pharmacy, a brewery, and a post office.

Side Trips/Variations

- Choose to take the rail trail back and forth to avoid the roads; it is approximately the same distance.
- To make a longer route and to get in some beach time, visit Martinique Beach Provincial Park (25 km return); access it by heading south from Musquodoboit Harbour on East Petpeswick Road.
- There are some great hiking trails along the rail trail if you want to turn your day into a multi-sport adventure.

Musquodoboit Harbour (RT) Cue Sheet

Dist	Type	Note	Next
0.0	◉	Start of route	0.0
0.0	⚑	(Start) Musquodoboit Harbour: Musquodoboit Trailway Trailhead, 67 Park Rd; head north on trail	14.6
14.6	←	Sharp L onto NS-357 S	15.3
29.9	←	L onto Park Rd	0.1
30.0	←	L onto Musquodoboit Trailway	0.0
30.0	◉	End of route	0.0

EASTERN SHORE

106 Three Fathom Harbour

MAP 38

Start Point

East Lawrencetown: Lawrencetown Beach Provincial Park, 4348 Lawrencetown Rd.

Summary

Some busy roads; wharf; beach access.

Distance (km)	Duration	Max Grade +	Elevation Gain (m)	Unpaved
41.3	1:52/2:45	5.4	293	2% (1 km)

Description

This ride starts and finishes at Lawrencetown Beach—the perfect place for a post-ride swim. The first half of the route takes you along Porters Lake, with nice water views. After hitting Trunk 7 for a 4 km stretch, you will head down through Chezzetcook and Grand Desert, where you will be treated to some great coastal riding with lots of islands in the distance. Take some time to visit the marina and beach in Three Fathom Harbour; the road down has excellent pavement and is incredibly picturesque.

Ride Considerations

- A small part of this ride is on Trunk 7, which can be busy; try to avoid it during peak hours.

Side Trips/Variations

- You have the option to finish off the last 6 km on rail trail; access it by getting on the trail just past the intersection of Marine Drive and Causeway Road (35.8 km).
- Take Dyke Road (24.7 km) to visit a nice rocky beach with some interesting views; there are 100 m of unpaved road to get to the beach area.
- You can continue on past Lawrencetown Beach on the ❷ Salt Marsh Trail to extend this ride on rail trail. Take the trail toward Cole Harbour and enjoy the marshlands and wildlife while you make your way to Rainbow Haven Beach Provincial Park, another popular beach spot (26.4 km return).

Points of Interest

- **Lawrencetown Beach (Start/Stop)** This beach is well known for its surf, attracting all sorts of adventurers looking to catch the next perfect wave. The beach is beautiful and there are lots of amenities, including showers to wash off sweat or salt water.

- **Fishermans Beach (32.9 km)** Located at the end of a perfectly paved road in Three Fathom Harbour; explore the beach and check out the working wharf.
- **Viewpoint (40.2 km)** There is a hiking path heading up the hill at the intersection of Lawrencetown Road and Crowell Road. Halfway up the hill, you are high enough to take in the view; this is the best part of the hike.

Three Fathom Harbour Cue Sheet

Dist	Type	Note	Next
0.0	◉	Start of route	0.0
0.0	⚑	(Start) East Lawrencetown: Lawrencetown Beach Provincial Park, 4348 Lawrencetown Rd	0.0
0.0	→	R onto Lawrencetown Rd/Marine Dr/NS-207 E	1.2
1.2	←	L onto Crowell Rd/West Porters Lake Rd (signs for NS-107/NS-7/West Porters Lake/Crowell Road)	5.4
6.6	↑	Continue onto West Porters Lake Rd	6.7
13.3	→	R onto NS-7 E (signs for Musquodoboit Harbour/Antigonish)	3.4
16.7	→	R onto Stella Dr (signs for NS-207 W/West Chezzetcook/Lawrencetown/Marine Drive Trail)	0.3
17.0	→	R onto Marine Dr/NS-207 W (signs for West Chezzetcook/Lawrencetown/Marine Drive Trail)	0.6
17.6	←	L onto Shore Rd	3.8
21.4	←	L onto Marine Dr/NS-207 W	8.9
30.3	←	L onto Causeway Rd/Hawkins Island Rd	2.6
32.9	↻	Fishermans Beach; turnaround point	2.7
35.6	←	L onto Marine Dr/NS-207 W	5.7
41.3	◉	End of route	0.0

BIKE-FRIENDLY BUSINESSES

Bike Friendly Certification is a recognition and training program for businesses and institutions that support bicycle commuting, bicycle travel, and bicycle tourism experiences in Nova Scotia. Started in 2018, Bike Friendly Certification is a program delivered by Bicycle Nova Scotia.

Program Goals and Services

- Offer training and resources that help businesses and institutions become bike-friendly.
- Help bike-friendly businesses stand out and connect with customers.
- Recognize businesses and institutions that encourage employees to bike to work.
- Encourage communities to meet growing demand for bike-friendly amenities and services.

Benefits of Certification

The number of people who choose cycling for primary or occasional transportation, along with the number of people who choose to cycle while on vacation, is growing. Bicycle Nova Scotia helps businesses stand out as leaders in providing services for customers or employees who want to arrive by bike. Businesses can get certified for free; they will be mailed a Bike Friendly Certified window decal to decorate their storefronts, and will then be added to the online bicycling destination map. By working together, we can help make Nova Scotia a bike-friendly province and a top cycling destination.

Starting an Application

Whether you want to promote your bike-friendly workplace or you want to identify yourself as a destination for bicycle tourists, Bicycle Nova Scotia has a certification category designed for you. All businesses that can meet the basic program criteria are eligible for certification.

Visit the certification page and download the program guide to learn more about how to apply at **bikefriendlyns.ca**.

WOMEN ON WHEELS (WoW)

Women on Wheels (WoW) groups exist in many communities across Nova Scotia. Initially, the groups focused on building the bicycle skills of senior women, but it is not unusual now to find a WoW ride that includes women from six to seventy-six years old. Experience shows that regular, organized rides that are led by women encourage more women to ride—and when women ride, families do too. If you'd like to start a WoW group in your community, please contact Bicycle Nova Scotia and we'll help you start a group close to home.

For more information, visit bicycle.ns.ca/women-on-wheels-wow or visit the WoW NS Facebook group.

APPENDIX A: BIKE SHOPS

Name	Street	City/Town	Phone	Website
The Bicycle Specialist	198 Church Street	Amherst	902-660-3393	Facebook
Highland Bike Shop	258 Main Street	Antigonish	902-735-3320	Facebook
Oakhaven Bike Barn	7091 Trunk 1	Belleisle	902-665-5044	Facebook
Spin Your Wheels	252 Aberdeen Road	Bridgewater	902-530-7746	Facebook
Velo Max Cycling	PO Box 681	Chéticamp	902-224-7944	velomax.ca
The Bike Pedaler	25 Portland Street	Dartmouth	902-406-7773	Facebook
Cyclesmith	2553 Agricola Street	Halifax	902-425-1756	cyclesmith.ca
Giant Bicycle Halifax	5536 Sackville Street	Halifax	902-407-2462	gianthalifax.ca/ca
Halifax Cycles	3600 Kempt Road	Halifax	902-407-4222	halifaxcycles.com
Idealbikes	103 Chain Lake Drive	Halifax	902-444-7487	Idealbikes.ca
Long Alley Bicycles	6164 Quinpool Road	Halifax	902-404-9849	longalleybicycles.com
MEC	1550 Granville Street	Halifax	902-421-2667	mec.ca
Valley Stove and Cycle	353 Main Street	Kentville	902-542-7280	valleystoveandcycle.com
Lunenburg Bike Shop	151 Montague Street	Lunenburg	902-521-6115	lunenburgbikeshop.com
Sweet Ride Cycling	523 Main Street	Mahone Bay	902-531-3026	sweetridecycling.com
Pictou County Cycle	2619 Westville Road	New Glasgow	902-928-0331	pictoucountycycle.com
Trailside Bike Shop	263 Brookfield Mines Road	North Brookfield	902-298-5785	n/a
Highland Bike Shop	3 Water Street	Port Hawkesbury	902-625-5930	Facebook
Sportwheels Sports Excellence	209 Sackville Drive	Sackville	902-865-9033	sportwheels.ca
Vélo Baie Saint-Marie	9976 Hwy 1	Saulnierville	902-769-0221	velobsm.ca
Framework Cycle & Fitness	333 George Street	Sydney	902-567-1909	frameworkfitness.com
Bike Monkey	109 Robie Street	Truro	902-843-7111	bikemonkey.ca
Hub Cycle	33 Inglis Place	Truro	902-897-2482	hubcycle.ca
Train Station Bike and Bean	5401 St. Margarets Bay Road	Upper Tantallon	902-820-3400	bikeandbean.ca

Name	Street	City/Town	Phone	Website
The Spoke & Note	85 Water Street	Windsor	902-306-1850	thespokeandnote.ca
Banks Bikes	360 Main Street Suite 20	Wolfville	902-542-2596	banksbikes.ca
Mansers's Bike Shop	165 Pleasant Street	Yarmouth	902-742-0494	Facebook

APPENDIX B:
BIKE TOURS AND RENTALS

Name	Street	City/Town	Phone	Website
Keppock Mtn Recreation Area	193 Keppock Road	Antigonish	n/a	thekeppoch.ca
Pedallers By the Bay	n/a	Baddeck	902-818-8504	Facebook
Pedal and Sea	8384 St. Margarets Bay Road	Black Point	877-777-5699	pedalandseaadventures.com
Cabot Trail Adventures	299 Shore Road	Cape North	902-383-2552	cabottrailoutdooradventures.com
Atlantic Canada Cycling	n/a	Halifax	888-800-2498	atlanticcanadacycling.com
Eastwind Cycle	2433 Agricola Street	Halifax	866-447-7468	eastwindcycle.com
I Heart Bikes	1507 Lower Water Street	Halifax	902-406-7774	iheartbikeshfx.com
Ride East	n/a	Halifax	902-233-7083	rideeast.ca
Freewheeling Adventures	2118 Hwy 329	Hubbards	800-672-0775	freewheeling.ca
Eagle Eye Outfitters	15860 Central Avenue	Inverness	902-258-5893	eagleeyeoutfitters.ca
Liverpool Adventure Outfitters	4003 Sandy Cove Road	Liverpool	902-354-2702	liverpooladventureoutfitters.com
Moxie's Riverside Rentals	45 Blair Street	New Glasgow	902-923-2798	moxiesriversiderentals.com
Bras D'Or Lakes Inn	10095 Grenville Street	St. Peters	902-535-2200	brasdorlakesinn.com
Remember Adventures	365 Main Street	Tatamagouche	902-293-1533	rememberadventures.ca
Trail Flow Outdoor Adventures	n/a	Wolfville	902-300-9449	trailflow.ca

Nova Scotia has an abundance of hills that make riding in this province both challenging and rewarding. (DOUG BROWN)

Some routes in this book are labelled "gravel grinders," meaning they are on mostly unpaved or dirt roads. (SWEET RIDE CYCLING)

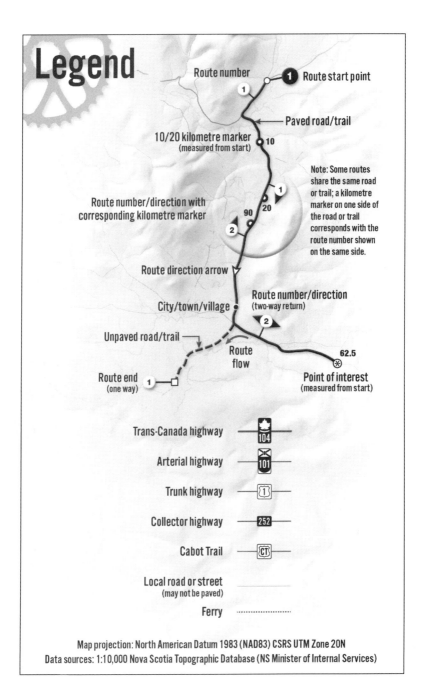

Legend

Route number

Route start point

Paved road/trail

10/20 kilometre marker
(measured from start)

Note: Some routes share the same road or trail; a kilometre marker on one side of the road or trail corresponds with the route number shown on the same side.

Route number/direction with corresponding kilometre marker

Route direction arrow

City/town/village

Route number/direction
(two-way return)

Unpaved road/trail

Route flow

Route end
(one way)

Point of interest
(measured from start)

62.5

Trans-Canada highway — 104

Arterial highway — 101

Trunk highway — 1

Collector highway — 252

Cabot Trail — CT

Local road or street
(may not be paved)

Ferry

Map projection: North American Datum 1983 (NAD83) CSRS UTM Zone 20N
Data sources: 1:10,000 Nova Scotia Topographic Database (NS Minister of Internal Services)

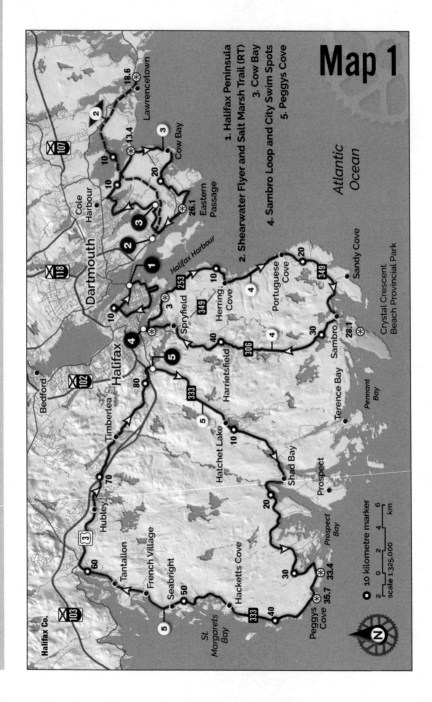

Map 1

1. Halifax Peninsula
2. Shearwater Flyer and Salt Marsh Trail (RT)
3. Cow Bay
4. Sambro Loop and City Swim Spots
5. Peggys Cove

Atlantic Ocean

scale 1:325,000

○ 10 kilometre marker

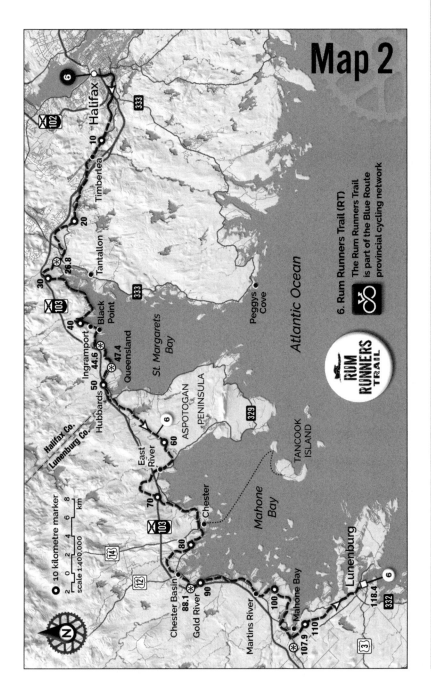

Map 2

333

102

Halifax

6

10

Timberlea

20

Tantallon

26.8

30

103

40

Black
Point

Ingramport

44.6

47.4

50

Hubbards

Queensland

St. Margarets
Bay

333

Peggys
Cove

Atlantic Ocean

ASPOTOGAN
PENINSULA

329

East
River

6

60

TANCOOK
ISLAND

70

103

Chester

Mahone
Bay

80

14

12

Chester Basin

88.1

Gold River

90

Martins River

100

Mahone Bay

107.9

110.1

3

Lunenburg

6

118.4

332

6. Rum Runners Trail (RT)

The Rum Runners Trail
is part of the Blue Route
provincial cycling network

RUM
RUNNERS
TRAIL

N

10 kilometre marker

km

8

6

4

2

0

2

scale 1:400,000

Halifax Co.

Lunenburg Co.

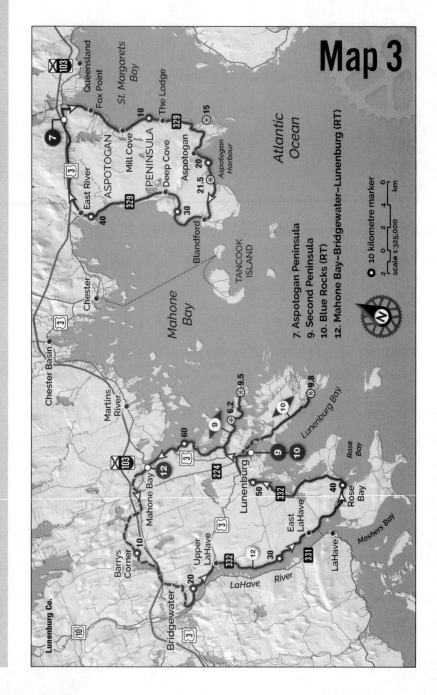

Map 3

Queensland

St. Margarets Bay

Fox Point

The Lodge

10

ASPOTOGAN
PENINSULA

Mill Cove

Deep Cove

Aspotogan

329

15

20

21.5

Aspotogan
Harbour

30

East River

40

329

Blandford

TANCOOK
ISLAND

Chester

Mahone
Bay

Chester Basin

Martins
River

Atlantic
Ocean

7. Aspotogan Peninsula
9. Second Peninsula
10. Blue Rocks (RT)
12. Mahone Bay–Bridgewater–Lunenburg (RT)

9.5

6.2

9.8

60

9

10

Lunenburg Bay

Mahone Bay

12

3

224

Lunenburg

9

10

Rose
Bay

50

332

40

Rose
Bay

3

Upper
LaHave

East
LaHave

Moshers Bay

Barrys
Corner

10

332

12

30

331

LaHave

20

LaHave   River

Bridgewater

3

1o kilometre marker

6
km
4
2
0
2
scale 1:325,000

N

103

7

3

103

10

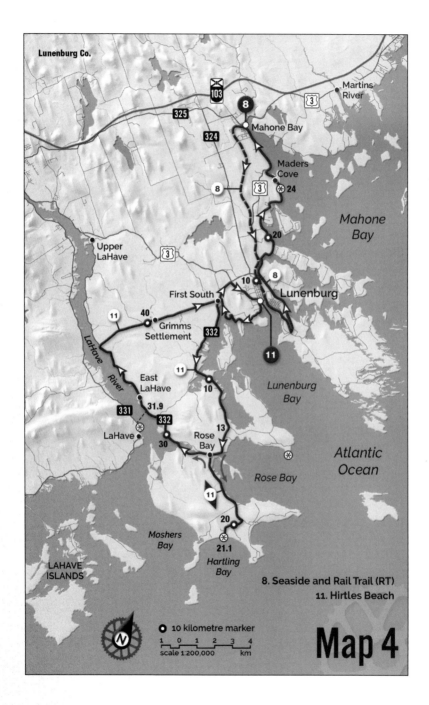

Lunenburg Co.

Martins
River

103

8

325

324

Mahone Bay

Maders
Cove

8

3

24

Mahone
Bay

20

Upper
LaHave

3

10

8

Lunenburg

First South

11

40

Grimms
Settlement

332

11

East
LaHave

10

Lunenburg
Bay

LaHave
River

331

31.9

332

LaHave

30

Rose
Bay

13

11

Atlantic
Ocean

Rose Bay

Moshers
Bay

11

20

21.1

Hartling
Bay

LAHAVE
ISLANDS

8. Seaside and Rail Trail (RT)
11. Hirtles Beach

Map 4

○ 10 kilometre marker

1 0 1 2 3 4
scale 1:200,000   km

N

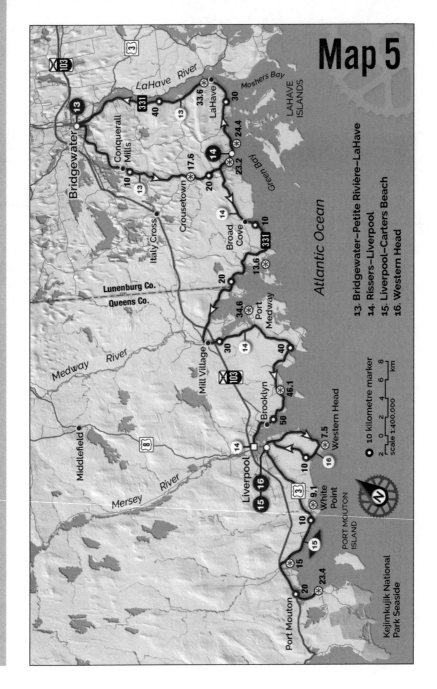

Map 5

Atlantic Ocean

LAHAVE ISLANDS

13. Bridgewater–Petite Rivière–LaHave
14. Rissers–Liverpool
15. Liverpool–Carters Beach
16. Western Head

LaHave River

Moshers Bay

Green Bay

Bridgewater

Conquerall Mills

Italy Cross

Crousetown

Broad Cove

LaHave

Lunenburg Co.
Queens Co.

Port Medway

Medway River

Mill Village

Brooklyn

Middlefield

Mersey River

Liverpool

Western Head

White Point

PORT MOUTON ISLAND

Port Mouton

Kejimkujik National
Park Seaside

⊙ 10 kilometre marker

scale 1:400,000

km

33.6
24.4
23.2
17.6
34.6
13.6
46.1
7.5
9.1
23.4

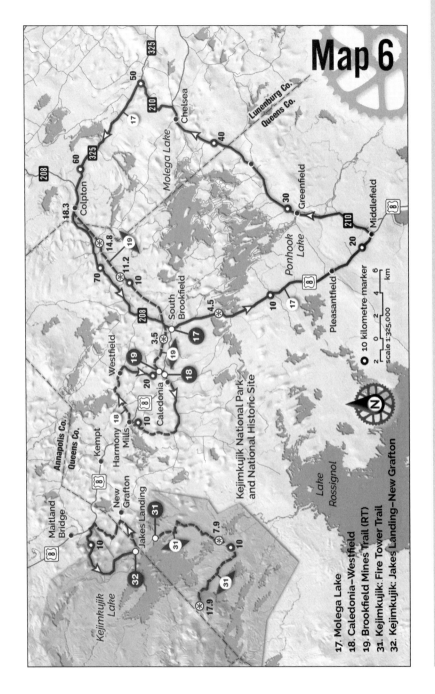

Map 6

ROUTE MAPS

17. Molega Lake
18. Caledonia–Westfield
19. Brookfield Mines Trail (RT)
31. Kejimkujik: Fire Tower Trail
32. Kejimkujik: Jakes Landing–New Grafton

10 kilometre marker

scale 1:325,000
km

Kejimkujik National Park
and National Historic Site

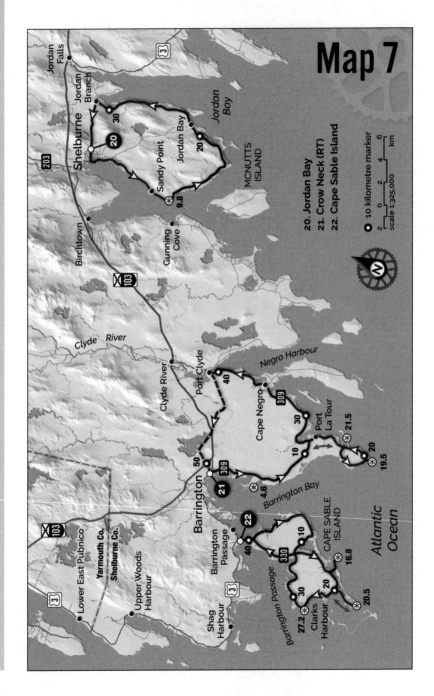

ROUTE MAPS

Map 7

Jordan Falls

Jordan Branch

Shelburne

30

20

Jordan Bay

20

Jordan Bay

Sandy Point

MCNUTT'S ISLAND

9.8

Gunning Cove

Birchtown

Clyde River

Clyde River

Port Clyde

Negro Harbour

40

309

Cape Negro

30

Port La Tour

21.5

10

20 19.5

50

309

21

4.6

Barrington Bay

Barrington

Barrington Passage

Yarmouth Co.
Shelburne Co.

Lower East Pubnico

Upper Woods Harbour

Shag Harbour

Barrington passage

22

40

330

10

CAPE SABLE ISLAND

16.8

30

20

Clarks Harbour

27.2

20.5

Atlantic Ocean

20. Jordan Bay
21. Crow Neck (RT)
22. Cape Sable Island

○ 10 kilometre marker

scale 1:325,000

km

N

224   Adam Barnett

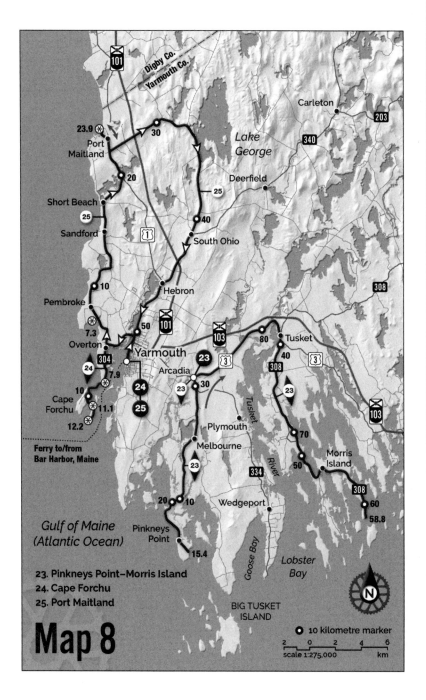

23.9 ⊛
Port
Maitland

30

Lake
George

Carleton

203

340

Deerfield

25

40

South Ohio

20

Short Beach
25

Sandford

10

Pembroke

7.3
Overton

24

304

7.9

Cape
Forchu

10

11.1

12.2

Hebron

50

101

103

80

Tusket

40

308

3

23

308

103

Yarmouth

23

3

Arcadia

24

23

30

25

23

Plymouth

70

Melbourne

50

Morris
Island

308

60

58.8

Ferry to/from
Bar Harbor, Maine

23

334

Wedgeport

Tusket
River

Goose Bay

Lobster
Bay

20

10

*Gulf of Maine
(Atlantic Ocean)*

Pinkneys
Point

15.4

23. Pinkneys Point–Morris Island
24. Cape Forchu
25. Port Maitland

BIG TUSKET
ISLAND

N

Map 8

O 10 kilometre marker

2 0 2 4 6
scale 1:275,000   km

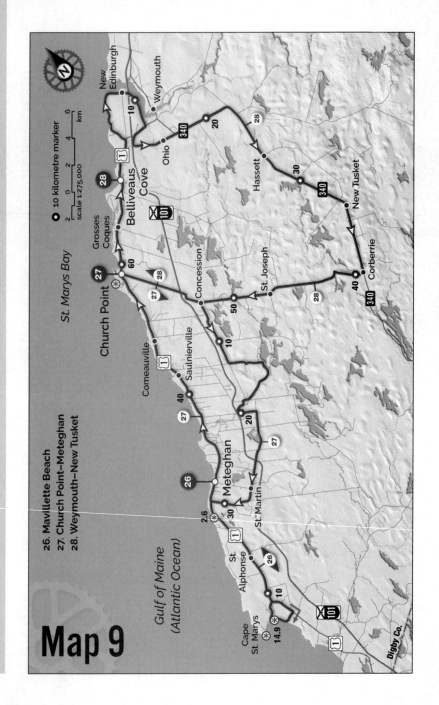

Map 9

Gulf of Maine
(Atlantic Ocean)

St. Marys Bay

Church Point

26. Mavillette Beach
27. Church Point–Meteghan
28. Weymouth–New Tusket

○ 10 kilometre marker

scale 1:275,000

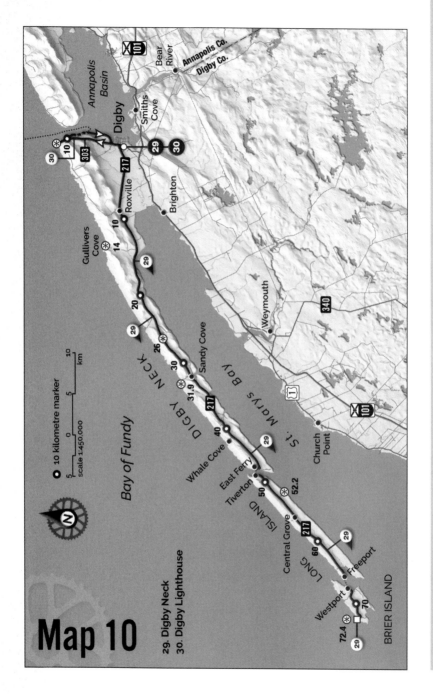

Annapolis Co.
Digby Co.

Bear River

Annapolis Basin

Smiths Cove

Digby

303

10

30

29

30

217

Roxville

Brighton

10

14

Gullivers Cove

29

20

29

26

30

31.9

Sandy Cove

217

Weymouth

340

DIGBY NECK

St. Mary's Bay

Bay of Fundy

40

Whale Cove

Church Point

62

East Ferry

Tiverton

50

52.2

ISLAND

60

217

29

Central Grove

Freeport

LONG

Westport

70

72.4

29

BRIER ISLAND

10 kilometre marker

km

scale 1:450,000

N

29. Digby Neck
30. Digby Lighthouse

Map 10

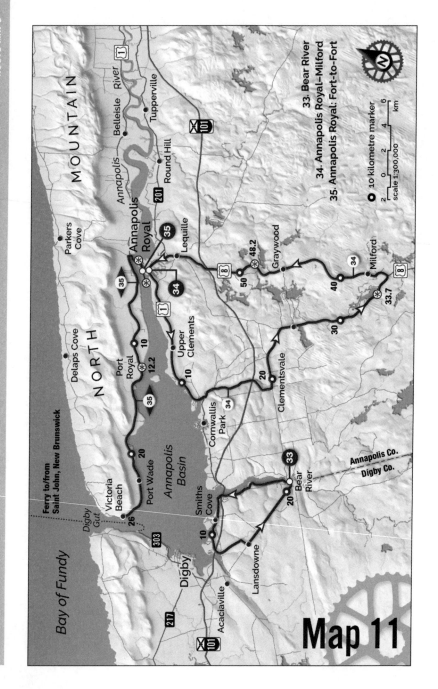

33. Bear River
34. Annapolis Royal–Milford
35. Annapolis Royal: Fort-to-Fort

N

● 10 kilometre marker

scale 1:300,000

km

MOUNTAIN

Belleisle River

Tupperville

Annapolis

Round Hill

NORTH

Parkers Cove

Annapolis Royal

Lequille

Graywood

Milford

Delaps Cove

Port Royal

Upper Clements

Clementsvale

Cornwallis Park

Bay of Fundy

Ferry to/from
Saint John, New Brunswick

Digby Gut

Victoria Beach

Port Wade

Annapolis Basin

Smiths Cove

Bear River

Digby

Acaciaville

Lansdowne

Annapolis Co.
Digby Co.

Map 11

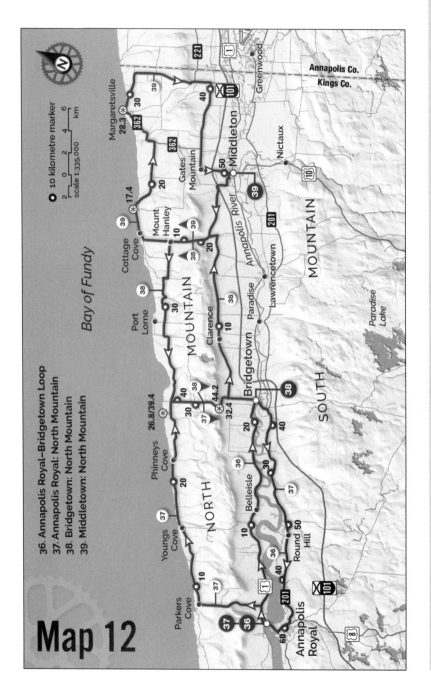

Map 12

36. Annapolis Royal–Bridgetown Loop
37. Annapolis Royal: North Mountain
38. Bridgetown: North Mountain
39. Middletown: North Mountain

Bay of Fundy

● 10 kilometre marker

scale 1:335,000

Annapolis Co.
Kings Co.

Greenwood

Margaretsville

Nictaux

Middleton

Gates
Mountain

Mount
Hanley

Cottage
Cove

Annapolis River

Port
Lorne

Lawrencetown

SOUTH   MOUNTAIN

Paradise
Lake

Clarence

Paradise

Bridgetown

NORTH   MOUNTAIN

Phinneys
Cove

Belleisle

Youngs
Cove

Round
Hill

Parkers
Cove

Annapolis
Royal

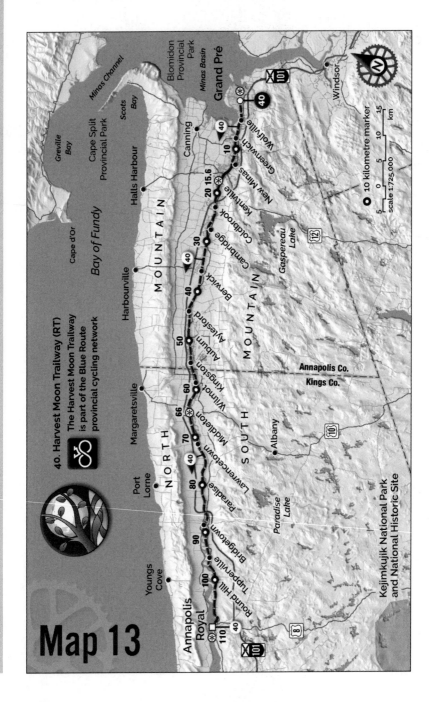

ROUTE MAPS

Map 13

40. Harvest Moon Trailway (RT)

The Harvest Moon Trailway is part of the Blue Route provincial cycling network

10 kilometre marker

scale 1:725,000

km

Bay of Fundy

Minas Basin

Minas Channel

Scots Bay

Greville Bay

Cape d'Or

Cape Split Provincial Park

Blomidon Provincial Park

Grand Pré

Windsor

Wolfville

Greenwich

New Minas

Kentville

Coldbrook

Cambridge

Berwick

Aylesford

Auburn

Kingston

Wilmot

Middleton

Lawrencetown

Paradise

Bridgetown

Tupperville

Round Hill

Annapolis Royal

Canning

Halls Harbour

Harbourville

Margaretsville

Port Lorne

Youngs Cove

NORTH MOUNTAIN

SOUTH MOUNTAIN

Gaspereau Lake

Paradise Lake

Albany

Annapolis Co.

Kings Co.

Kejimkujik National Park and National Historic Site

230   Adam Barnett

Map 14

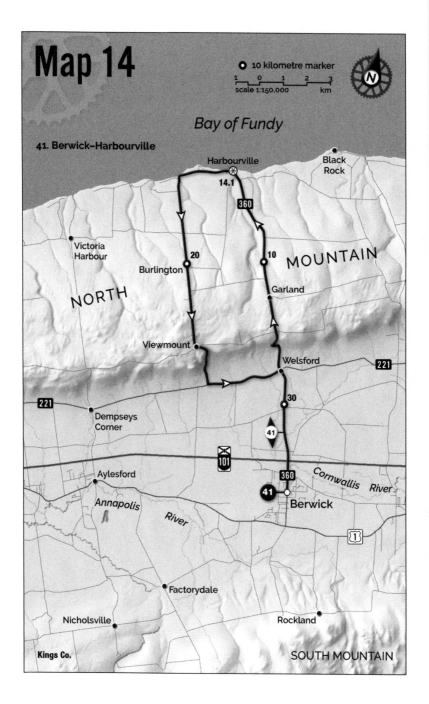

○ 10 kilometre marker

scale 1:150,000

km

N

Bay of Fundy

41. Berwick–Harbourville

Harbourville

Black Rock

14.1

360

Victoria Harbour

20

10

MOUNTAIN

Burlington

Garland

NORTH

Viewmount

Welsford

221

221

30

Dempseys Corner

41

101

Aylesford

360

Cornwallis River

Annapolis

41

River

Berwick

1

Factorydale

Nicholsville

Rockland

Kings Co.

SOUTH MOUNTAIN

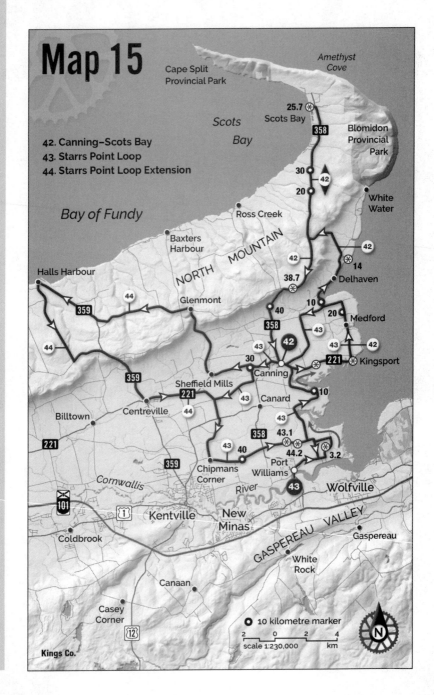

Map 15

Cape Split
Provincial Park

Amethyst
Cove

Scots
Bay

Blomidon
Provincial
Park

25.7 ⊛
Scots Bay

358

42. **Canning–Scots Bay**
43. **Starrs Point Loop**
44. **Starrs Point Loop Extension**

30 ◐ 42
20 ◐

White
Water

Bay of Fundy

Ross Creek

Baxters
Harbour

NORTH MOUNTAIN

42
⊛ 14

Halls Harbour

359

44

Glenmont

38.7
⊛

Delhaven

40
358

10

20 ◐ Medford

42

44

359

43

43

42

43
30

42

⊛ 221 ⊛ Kingsport

43

Canning

Sheffield Mills

221

Canard

10

Billtown

Centreville

44

43

43.1

221

359

358

⊛ ⊛

⊛

43 40

Chipmans
Corner

44.2

3.2

Port
Williams

43

Wolfville

Cornwallis

River

GASPEREAU VALLEY

101

1

Kentville

New
Minas

Gaspereau

Coldbrook

White
Rock

Canaan

Casey
Corner

12

○ **10 kilometre marker**

2 0   2   4

N

scale 1:230,000   km

Kings Co.

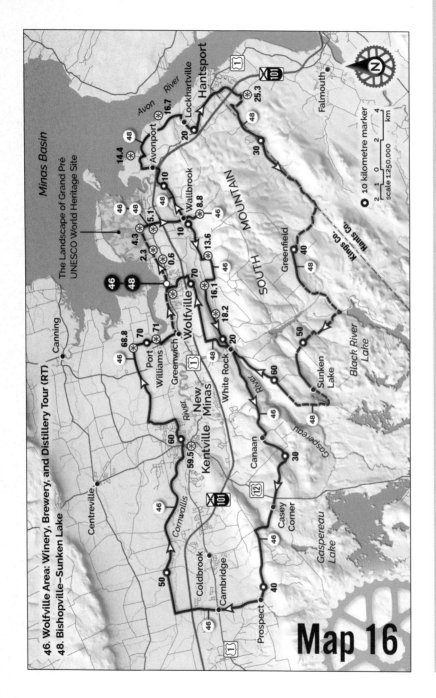

46. Wolfville Area: Winery, Brewery, and Distillery Tour (RT)
48. Bishopville–Sunken Lake

Minas Basin

The Landscape of Grand Pré
UNESCO World Heritage Site

Hantsport

Avon River

Lockhartville

16.7

Avonport

20

14.4

48

48

Wallbrook

10

48

8.8

5.1

4.3

2.3

0.6

10

13.6

46

70

16.1

18.2

20

Wolfville

White Rock

New Minas

Greenwich

Port Williams

68.8

70

71

46

59.5

60

Kentville

50

Centreville

Coldbrook

Cambridge

46

46

Cornwallis River

Canaan

48

46

30

12

Casey Corner

46

46

Prospect

40

SOUTH MOUNTAIN

Greenfield

40

48

Sunken Lake

50

60

48

Black River Lake

Gaspereau River

Gaspereau Lake

25.3

48

30

Falmouth

Kings Co.

Hants Co.

N

10 kilometre marker

scale 1:250,000

km

Map 16

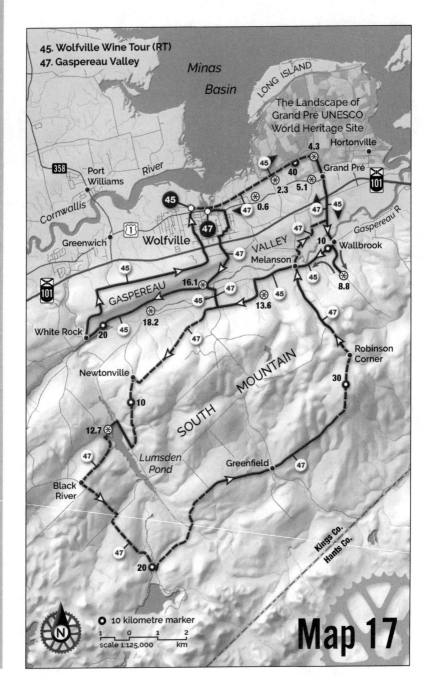

45. Wolfville Wine Tour (RT)
47. Gaspereau Valley

Minas Basin

LONG ISLAND

The Landscape of Grand Pré UNESCO World Heritage Site

Hortonville
4.3
Grand Pré
40
2.3   5.1
0.6
10   Wallbrook
8.8
Gaspereau R

358   Port Williams
River
Cornwallis
1   Wolfville
Greenwich
101
VALLEY
Melanson
GASPEREAU
16.1
13.6
18.2
45
White Rock
20

Robinson Corner
47
30

Newtonville
10

12.7
47
Black River

SOUTH MOUNTAIN

Lumsden Pond

Greenfield
47

Kings Co.
Hants Co.

47
20

N

○ 10 kilometre marker

1   0   1   2
scale 1:125,000   km

Map 17

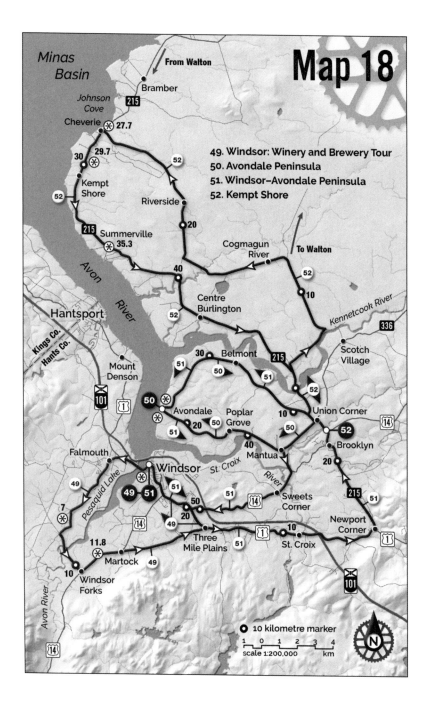

Minas
Basin

From Walton

Map 18

Bramber

Johnson
Cove
215

Cheverie ⊛ 27.7

30 29.7
⊛

Kempt
Shore

52

215 Summerville
⊛ 35.3

Riverside

52

20

49. Windsor: Winery and Brewery Tour
50. Avondale Peninsula
51. Windsor–Avondale Peninsula
52. Kempt Shore

Cogmagun
River

To Walton

52

40

Centre
Burlington

10

52

Kennetcook River

Avon River

Hantsport

Kings Co.
Hants Co.

Mount
Denson

30
51

Belmont
50

51

215

Scotch
Village

336

101

1

50 ⊛
⊛

52

Avondale

20 50

51

Poplar
Grove

10

50

Union Corner

14

52

Brooklyn

Falmouth

40

Mantua

20

Windsor St. Croix

49
51

49 51

51

50
20

49

51

14

Sweets
Corner

River

215

51

Newport
Corner

1

7
⊛

Pesaquid Lake

11.8
⊛

14

Martock 49

Three
Mile Plains

51

1

St. Croix

10

101

10
Windsor
Forks

Avon River

14

◉ 10 kilometre marker

1 0 1 2 3 4
scale 1:200,000   km

N

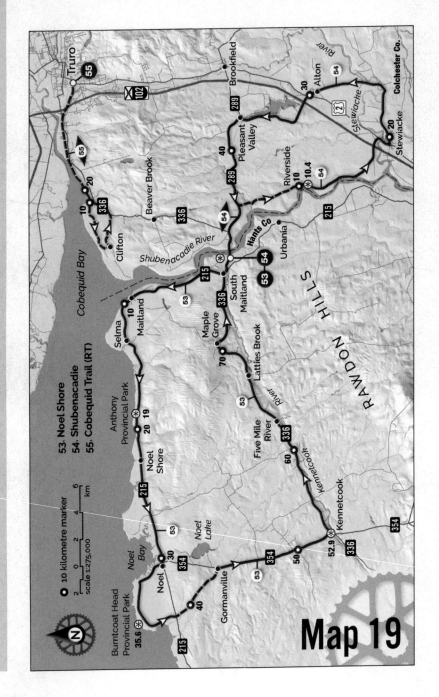

53. Noel Shore
54. Shubenacadie
55. Cobequid Trail (RT)

● 10 kilometre marker

km

scale 1:275,000

Map 19

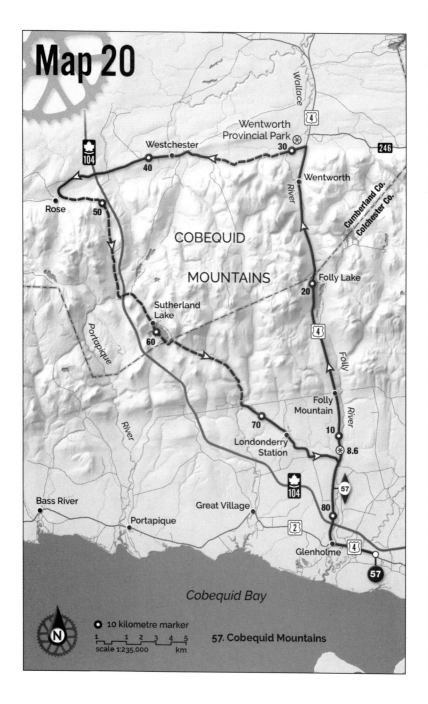

Map 20

Wallace

4

104

Westchester

Wentworth
Provincial Park ⊛
30

246

40

Wentworth

Rose

50

River

Cumberland Co.
Colchester Co.

COBEQUID

MOUNTAINS

Sutherland
Lake

Folly Lake
20

60

4

Portapique

Folly

River

Folly
Mountain
10

70

⊛ 8.6

Londonderry
Station

River

57

104

80

2

57

Bass River

Great Village

Portapique

Glenholme

4

57

Cobequid Bay

N

○ 10 kilometre marker

1 1 2 3 4 5
scale 1:235.000   km

57. Cobequid Mountains

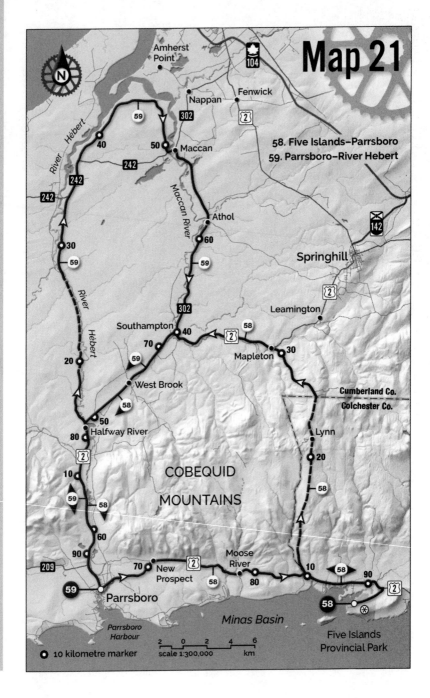

Map 21

58. Five Islands–Parrsboro
59. Parrsboro–River Hebert

10 kilometre marker

scale 1:300,000

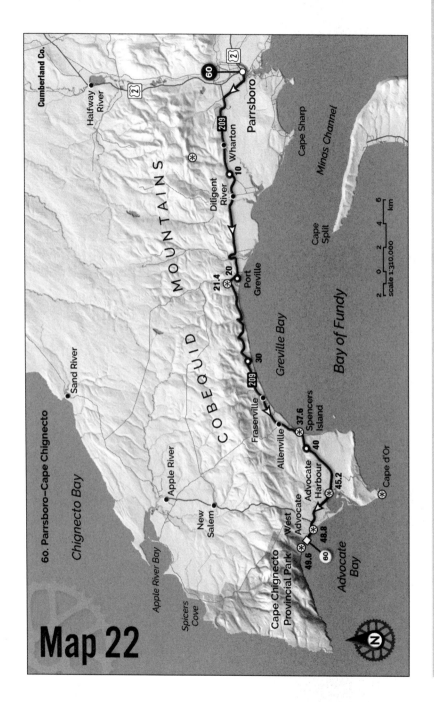

Map 22

60. Parrsboro–Cape Chignecto

Cumberland Co.

Halfway
River

②

②

60

Parrsboro

② 209

Wharton

10

Diligent
River

M O U N T A I N S

Port
Greville

20

21.4

C O B E Q U I D

Sand River

30

209

Fraserville

Greville Bay

37.6
Spencers
Island

Allenville

40

Advocate
Harbour

45.2

Cape d'Or

West
Advocate

48.8

49.6

60

Cape Chignecto
Provincial Park

Apple River

New
Salem

Apple River Bay

Chignecto Bay

Spicers
Cove

*Advocate
Bay*

Bay of Fundy

Cape Sharp

Minas Channel

Cape
Split

km
6
4
2
0
2
scale 1:330,000
2

N

Map 23

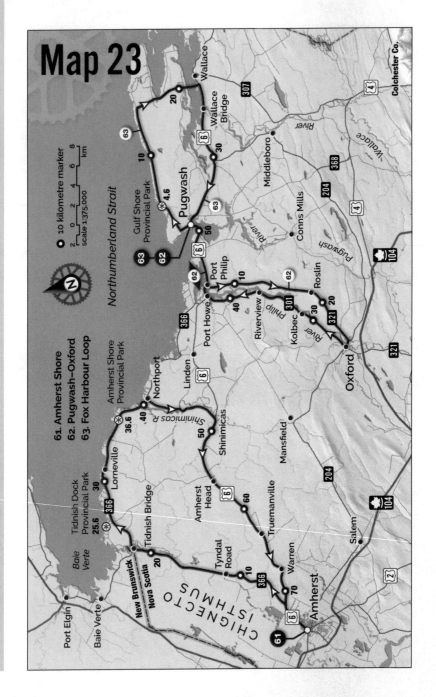

Northumberland Strait

61. Amherst Shore
62. Pugwash–Oxford
63. Fox Harbour Loop

10 kilometre marker

scale 1:375,000

CHIGNECTO ISTHMUS

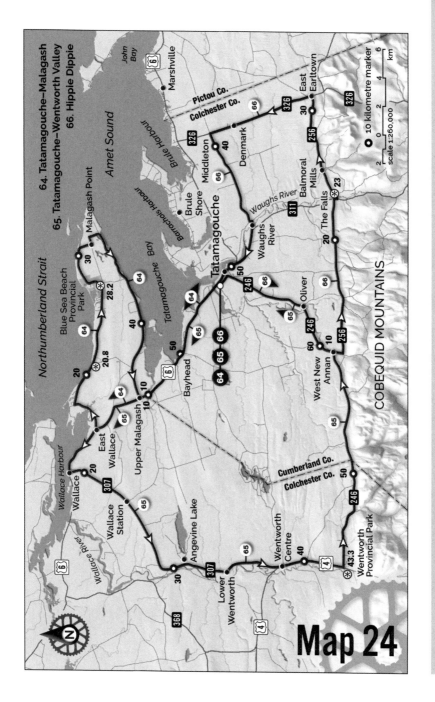

ROUTE MAPS

64. Tatamagouche–Malagash
65. Tatamagouche–Wentworth Valley
66. Hippie Dippie

10 kilometre marker

scale 1:260,000

Northumberland Strait

Amet Sound

John Bay

Marshville

Pictou Co.
Colchester Co.

East Earltown

Denmark

Middleton

Brule Shore

Brule Harbour

Barrachois Harbour

Malagash Point

Blue Sea Beach Provincial Park

Tatamagouche Bay

Waughs River

Balmoral Mills

The Falls

Tatamagouche

Oliver

West New Annan

COBEQUID MOUNTAINS

Bayhead

Upper Malagash

East Wallace

Wallace Harbour

Wallace

Wallace Station

Wallace River

Angevine Lake

Cumberland Co.
Colchester Co.

Wentworth Centre

Lower Wentworth

Wentworth Provincial Park

Map 24

N

Where to Cycle in Nova Scotia **241**

Map 25

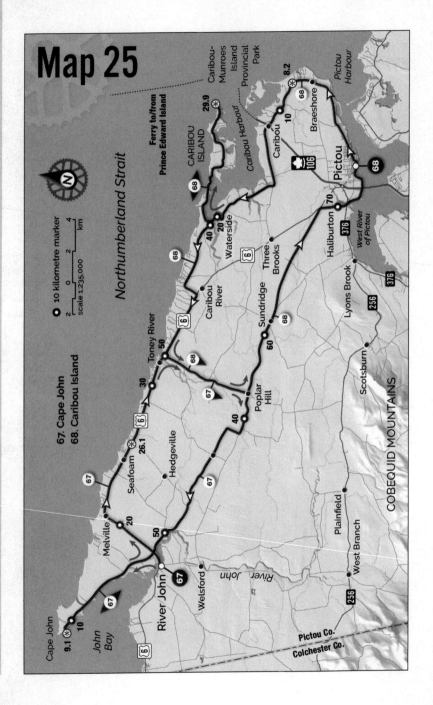

Caribou-Munroes Island Provincial Park

8.2

Pictou Harbour

68

Braeshore

Ferry to/from
Prince Edward Island

29.9

CARIBOU
ISLAND

Caribou Harbour

10

Caribou

68

Pictou

68

106

Northumberland Strait

68

70

376

Hatliburton

*West River
of Pictou*

20

40

Waterside

6

Three
Brooks

Lyons Brook

256

376

N

10 kilometre marker

scale 1:235,000

km

Caribou
River

6

Sundridge

60

68

Scotsburn

Toney River

50

30

68

67

Poplar
Hill

COBEQUID MOUNTAINS

67. Cape John
68. Caribou Island

6

40

26.1

Seafoam

Hedgeville

67

67

Plainfield

67

20

Melville

50

West Branch

67

River John

67

Welsford

River John

256

Cape John
9.1

10

*John
Bay*

6

Pictou Co.
Colchester Co.

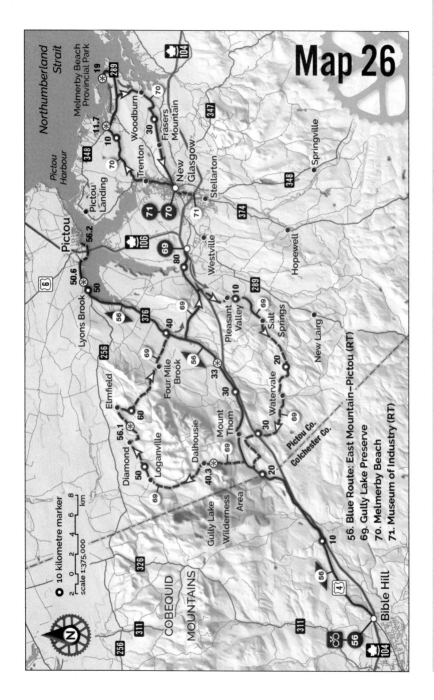

Map 26

ROUTE MAPS

Northumberland Strait

Melmerby Beach Provincial Park

Woodburn

Frasers Mountain

Trenton

New Glasgow

Pictou Harbour

Pictou Landing

Stellarton

Springville

Pictou

Westville

Hopewell

Lyons Brook

Pleasant Valley

Salt Springs

New Lairg

Elmfield

Four Mile Brook

Watervale

Picton Co.
Colchester Co.

Diamond

Loganville

Dalhousie

Mount Thom

Gully Lake Wilderness Area

COBEQUID MOUNTAINS

Bible Hill

56. Blue Route: East Mountain–Pictou (RT)
69. Gully Lake Preserve
70. Melmerby Beach
71. Museum of Industry (RT)

○ 10 kilometre marker

km

scale 1:375,000

N

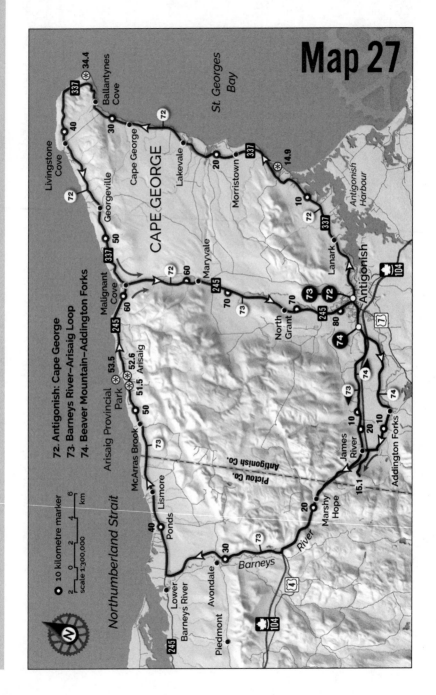

Map 27

St. Georges Bay

Antigonish Harbour

CAPE GEORGE

Northumberland Strait

72. Antigonish: Cape George
73. Barneys River–Arisaig Loop
74. Beaver Mountain–Addington Forks

Arisaig Provincial Park

10 kilometre marker
scale 1:300,000
km

Balantynes Cove
34.4
337
40
72
Livingstone Cove
72
Georgeville
50
337
Malignant Cove
60
245
53.5
52.6 Arisaig
51.5
50
McArras Brook
73
Lismore
Ponds
40
245
Lower Barneys River
Piedmont
Avondale
30
73
Barneys
104
4
Marshy Hope
20
River
James River
15.1
10
20
10
Addington Forks
74
74
74
73
74
80
245
73
72
North Grant
70
73
70
245
60
72
Maryvale
20
Lakevale
Morristown
337
14.9
10
Lanark
337
72
Antigonish
104
Cape George
30
72

Pictou Co.
Antigonish Co.

244   Adam Barnett

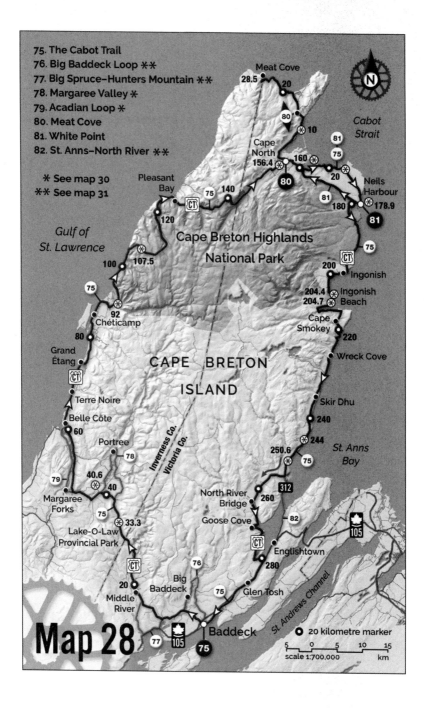

75. The Cabot Trail
76. Big Baddeck Loop ✳✳
77. Big Spruce–Hunters Mountain ✳✳
78. Margaree Valley ✳
79. Acadian Loop ✳
80. Meat Cove
81. White Point
82. St. Anns–North River ✳✳

✳ See map 30
✳✳ See map 31

Meat Cove
28.5   20

80

❋ 10

Cabot
Strait

Cape
North
156.4   160 ❋

81
75

80   20   Neils
Harbour
❋ 178.9

Pleasant
Bay
75   140   81   180

81

120   75

Gulf of
St. Lawrence

Cape Breton Highlands
National Park

100   ❋ 107.5

200   [CT]
Ingonish

75   204.4 ❋ Ingonish
204.7   Beach

❋
92
Chéticamp   Cape
Smokey   220

80   Wreck Cove

Grand
Étang
[CT]   Skir Dhu

Terre Noire   240

Belle Côte   244
❋ 60   250.6 ❋ 75   St. Anns
Bay

Portree   78

79   40.6
❋ 40   [312]
Margaree   North River   260
Forks   Bridge
❋ 75   82
33.3   Goose Cove
Lake-O-Law
Provincial Park   [CT]   Englishtown
                        280
[CT]   76
20   Big   Glen Tosh
Middle   Baddeck   75
River
105
CAPE BRETON
ISLAND

Inverness Co.
Victoria Co.

St. Andrews Channel

Map 28   ❍ 20 kilometre marker

77   105   Baddeck   scale 1:700,000
75   5 0   5   10   15
                        km

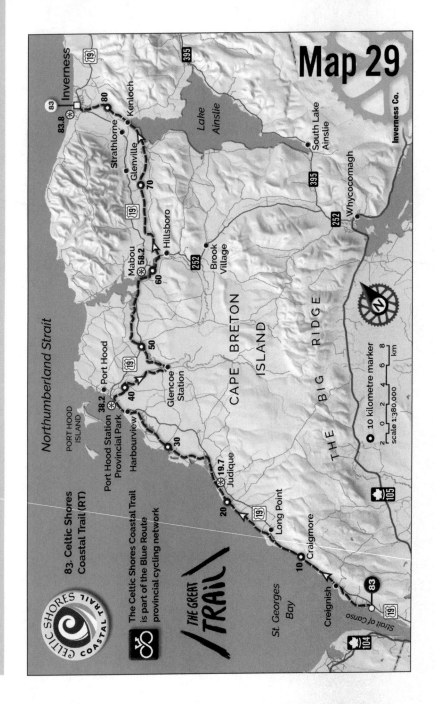

Map 29

ROUTE MAPS

Inverness

Inverness Co.

Lake Ainslie

South Lake Ainslie

Whycocomagh

19

395

83

83.8

80 Kenloch

Strathlorne

Glenville

70

19

Hillsboro

Brook Village

252

252

Mabou
58.2

60

Northumberland Strait

50

CAPE BRETON ISLAND

THE BIG RIDGE

Port Hood

PORT HOOD ISLAND

Port Hood Station Provincial Park

38.2

40

Glencoe Station

Harbourview

30

19.7

Judique

20

19

Long Point

Craigmore

10

Creignish

St. Georges Bay

Strait of Canso

83

19

105

104

83. Celtic Shores Coastal Trail (RT)

The Celtic Shores Coastal Trail is part of the Blue Route provincial cycling network

THE GREAT TRAIL

CELTIC SHORES COASTAL TRAIL

10 kilometre marker

km
2 0 2 4 6 8

scale 1:380,000

N

246   Adam Barnett

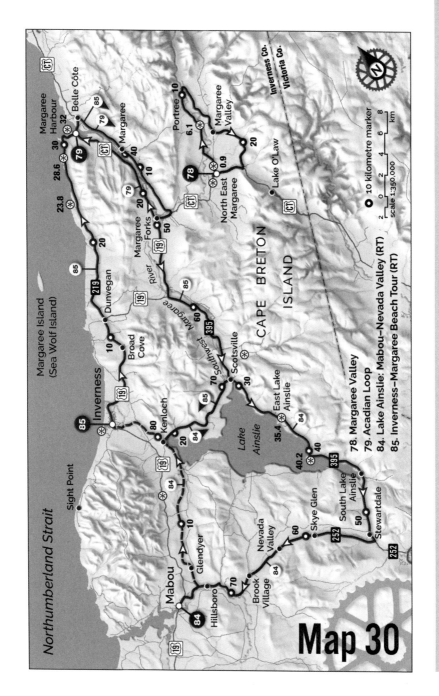

Map 30

Northumberland Strait

Margaree Island
(Sea Wolf Island)

Sight Point

Inverness

Dunvegan

Broad Cove

Kenloch

Mabou

Glendyer

Hillsboro

Brook Village

Nevada Valley

Skye Glen

South Lake Ainslie

Stewartdale

Lake Ainslie

East Lake Ainslie

Scotsville

Margaree Forks

Margaree River

Belle Côte

Margaree Harbour

Margaree

North East Margaree

Portree

Margaree Valley

Lake O'Law

Lake Law

CAPE BRETON ISLAND

Inverness Co.
Victoria Co.

78. Margaree Valley
79. Acadian Loop
84. Lake Ainslie: Mabou–Nevada Valley (RT)
85. Inverness–Margaree Beach Tour (RT)

O 10 kilometre marker

scale 1:350,000

km

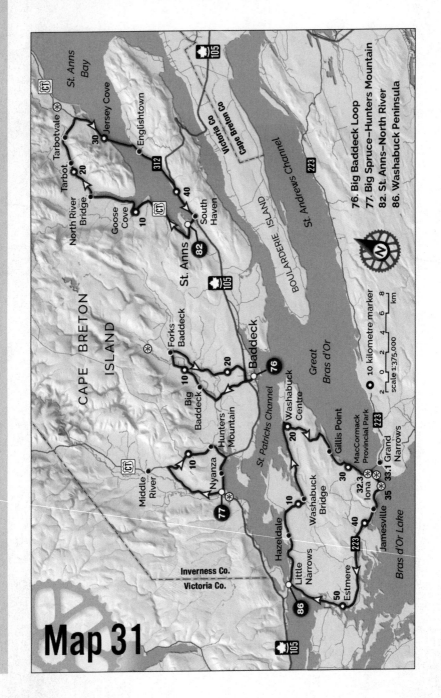

St. Anns Bay

Jersey Cove

Englishtown

Tarbotvale

30

20

Tarbot

North River Bridge

Goose Cove

10

South Haven

40

St. Anns

82

Forks Baddeck

Big Baddeck

10

20

Baddeck

76

Washabuck Centre

Hunters Mountain

Middle River

10

Nyanza

77

20

30

Gillis Point

MacCormack Provincial Park

223

Iona

32.3

33.1 Grand Narrows

35

Washabuck Bridge

10

Hazeldale

40

Jamesville

223

Little Narrows

Estmere

50

86

Inverness Co.

Victoria Co.

CAPE BRETON ISLAND

105

Victoria Co

Cape Breton Co

312

St. Andrews Channel

BOULARDERIE ISLAND

223

Great Bras d'Or

St Patricks Channel

Bras d'Or Lake

76. Big Baddeck Loop
77. Big Spruce–Hunters Mountain
82. St. Anns–North River
86. Washabuck Peninsula

N

10 kilometre marker

km

0 2 4 6 8

scale 1:375,000

105

105

Map 31

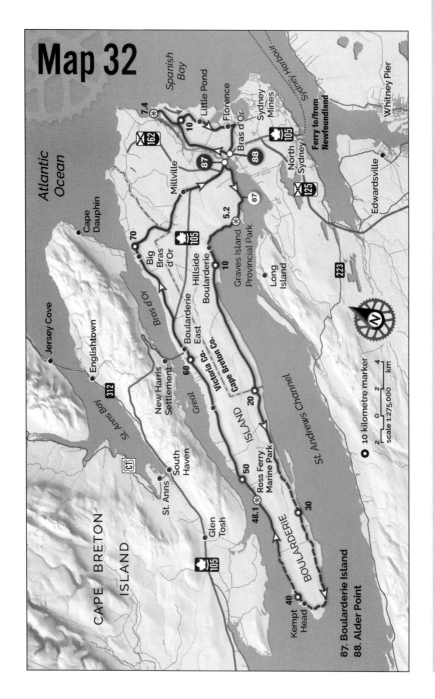

Map 32

Atlantic Ocean

Spanish Bay

Little Pond

Florence

Sydney Mines

Bras d'Or

Sydney Harbour

Whitney Pier

7.4

162

10

87

88

105

North Sydney

Ferry to/from Newfoundland

Millville

5.2

87

125

Edwardsville

Cape Dauphin

70

Big Bras d'Or

105

Hillside Boularderie

10

Graves Island Provincial Park

Long Island

223

Jersey Cove

Bras d'Or

Boularderie East

Victoria Co.

Cape Breton Co.

St. Andrews Channel

N

Englishtown

312

New Harris Settlement

Great

60

ISLAND

20

St. Anns Bay

South Haven

50

Ross Ferry Marine Park

10 kilometre marker

2 0 2 4 km
scale 1:275,000

St. Anns

CT

48.1

30

CAPE BRETON ISLAND

Glen Tosh

105

BOULARDERIE

40
Kempt Head

Boularderie Island

87. Boularderie Island
88. Alder Point

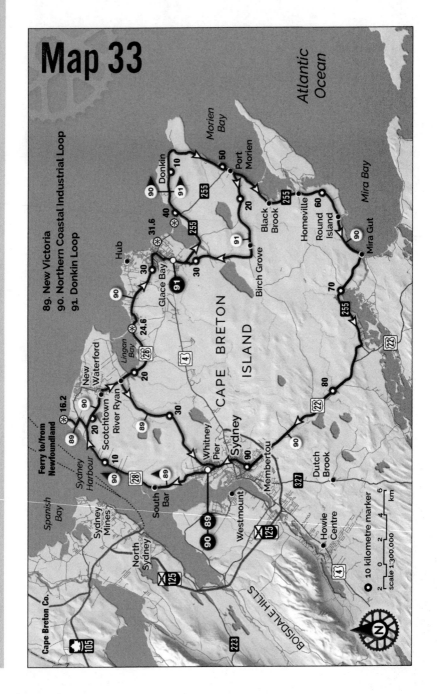

Map 33

Atlantic Ocean

89. New Victoria
90. Northern Coastal Industrial Loop
91. Donkin Loop

Morien Bay

Donkin 10
50
90 91 Port Morien
255
40 20
255 Black Brook 255
91 Homeville 60
Birch Grove Round Island *Mira Bay*
90 Mira Gut
31.6
Hub 30
30 70
Glace Bay 91 255
24.6 22
28
4
New Waterford 20
Lingan Bay 80
90 22
16.2 River Ryan 89
Scotchtown 30 22
20 Whitney Pier 90
10 Sydney 90
28 89 90 Membertou 327 Dutch Brook
South Bar 89 125 Westmount Howie Centre
North Sydney 90 223 4

Spanish Bay
Sydney Harbour
Sydney Mines
Ferry to/from Newfoundland

CAPE BRETON ISLAND

BOISDALE HILLS

Cape Breton Co. 105

125

● = 10 kilometre marker
km
6
4
2
0
2
scale 1:300,000

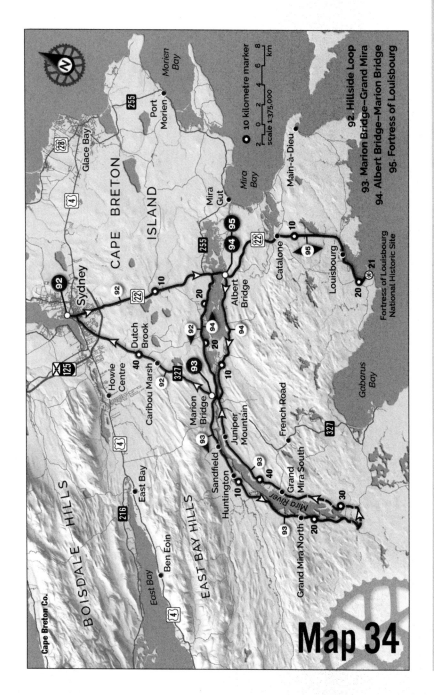

Cape Breton Co.

BOISDALE HILLS

EAST BAY HILLS

East Bay

Ben Eoin

East Bay

216

4

4

125

Howie Centre

Dutch Brook

Sydney

40

327

93

92

92

CAPE BRETON

ISLAND

4

28

Glace Bay

255

Port Morien

Morien Bay

92

92

10

22

255

Mira Gut

Mira Bay

Main-à-Dieu

20

94

94

94

95

Albert Bridge

22

10

Catalone

95

Louisbourg

20

21

Fortress of Louisbourg National Historic Site

Gabarus Bay

327

French Road

20

94

92

20

10

Marion Bridge

93

93

Sandfield

Juniper Mountain

Huntington

10

40

93

Grand Mira South

Mira River

30

20

93

Grand Mira North

10 kilometre marker

scale 1:375,000

km

92. Hillside Loop
93. Marion Bridge–Grand Mira
94. Albert Bridge–Marion Bridge
95. Fortress of Louisbourg

Map 34

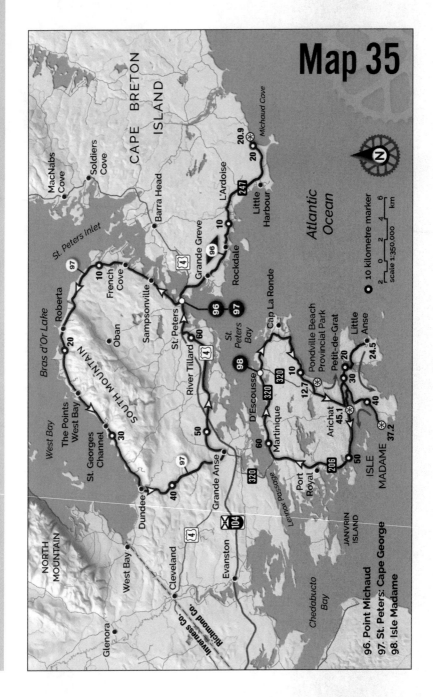

Map 35

CAPE BRETON ISLAND

Atlantic Ocean

● = 10 kilometre marker

scale 1:350,000

96. Point Michaud
97. St. Peters: Cape George
98. Isle Madame

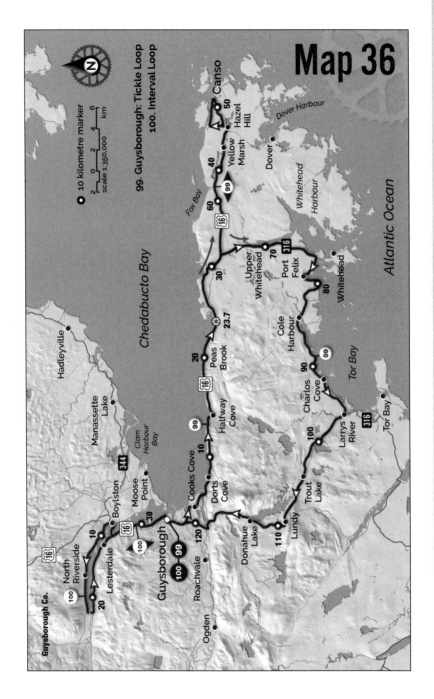

Map 36

10 kilometre marker

scale 1:350,000

99. Guysborough: Tickle Loop
100. Interval Loop

Canso

50

Hazel
Hill

Dover Harbour

40

Yellow
Marsh

Dover

99

Whitehead
Harbour

60

16

Fox Bay

Chedabucto Bay

Atlantic Ocean

316

70

Upper
Whitehead

Port
Felix

30

80

Whitehead

Hadleyville

23.7

Cole
Harbour

Manassette
Lake

20

Peas
Brook

99

Tor Bay

Clam
Harbour
Bay

16

90

Charlos
Cove

344

Halfway
Cove

99

Tor Bay

Boylston

10

316

Moose
Point

Cooks Cove

100

Larrys
River

North
Riverside

16

Dorts
Cove

Trout
Lake

Lesterdale

30

16

Guysborough

120

Donahue
Lake

Lundy

110

10

100 99

Roachvale

100

Guysborough Co.

100

20

Ogden

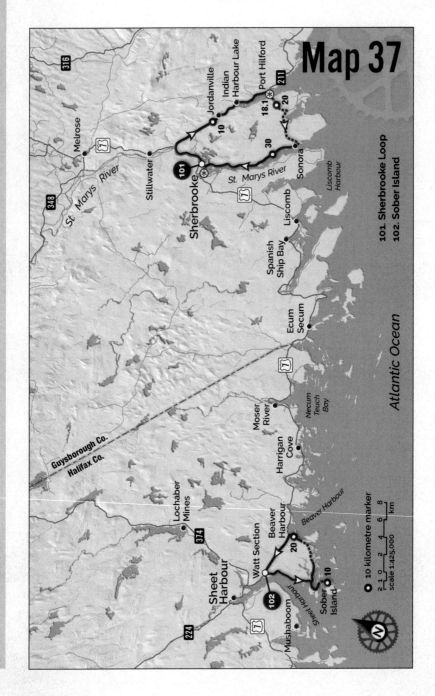

Map 37

101. Sherbrooke Loop
102. Sober Island

Atlantic Ocean

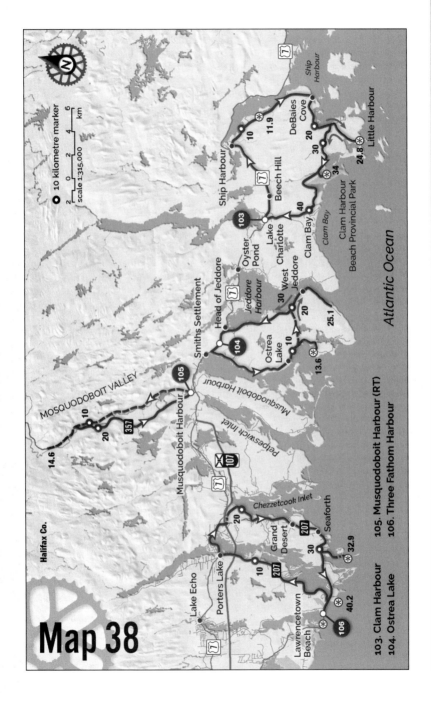

Map 38

Halifax Co.

● 10 kilometre marker

scale 1:315,000

km

Atlantic Ocean

Ship Harbour

DeBaies Cove

Little Harbour

10

11.9

20

30

34

24.8

Beech Hill

Clam Harbour
Beach Provincial Park

Clam Bay

Ship Harbour

Lake
Charlotte

Oyster
Pond

West
Jeddore

Clam Bay

40

103

30

Jeddore
Harbour

20

25.1

Head of Jeddore

Smiths Settlement

Ostrea
Lake

10

13.6

104

105

MOSQUODOBOIT VALLEY

Musquodoboit Harbour

10

20

357

14.6

Musquodoboit Harbour

Petpeswick Inlet

Chezzetcook Inlet

Seaforth

20

207

30

32.9

Grand
Desert

10

207

Lake Echo

Porters Lake

Lawrencetown
Beach

40.2

106

103. Clam Harbour
104. Ostrea Lake

105. Musquodoboit Harbour (RT)
106. Three Fathom Harbour

Where to Cycle in Nova Scotia   **255**

Go to **bicyclenovascotia.com** to find these routes online, and to

- View the elevation profiles
- Explore the routes interactively
- Download the route onto your device
- Comment on the route or read comments from others.

Route	Route Name	Distance (km)	Duration (22/15kmh)	Max Grade +	Elevation Gain (m)	Unpaved	Map	Page
Halifax Metro								
1	Halifax Peninsula	15.0	0:40/1:00	5.4	149	—	1	40
2	Shearwater Flyer and Salt Marsh Trail (RT)	37.3	1:41/2:29	1.9	146	100% (37 km)	1	43
3	Cow Bay	31.7	1:26/2:06	4.6	230	—	1	45
4	Sambro Loop and City Swim Spots	48.9	2:13/3:16	7.0	521	—	1	46
South Shore								
5	Peggys Cove	81.9	3:43/5:28	6.6	722	—	1	51
6	Rum Runners Trail (RT)	118.3	5:23/7:54	4.3	755	94% (111 km)	2	52
7	Aspotogan Peninsula	50.1	2:16/3:20	6.5	425	—	3	56
8	Seaside and Rail Trail (RT)	28.7	1:18/1:54	5.8	231	35% (10 km)	4	57
9	Second Peninsula	18.9	0:52/1:16	7.5	211	—	3	59
10	Blue Rocks (RT)	19.2	0:53/1:18	4.3	136	20% (4 km)	3	60
11	Hirtles Beach	47.5	2:09/3:10	7.1	386	—	4	62
12	Mahone Bay–Bridgewater–Lunenburg (RT)	64.4	2:55/4:17	5.2	455	22% (14 km)	3	64
13	Bridgewater–Petit Rivière–LaHave	50.8	2:18/3:23	6.7	391	—	5	66
14	Rissers–Liverpool	54.7	2:29/3:38	8.2	382	—	5	68
15	Liverpool–Carters Beach	46.7	2:07/3:06	6.7	388	—	5	69
16	Western Head	15.4	0:42/1:01	4.6	99	—	5	70
17	Molega Lake	78.8	3:36/5:17	4.6	543	—	6	71
18	Caledonia–Westfield	20.9	0:57/1:24	3.4	153	48% (10 km)	6	72
19	Brookfield Mines Trail (RT)	36.5	1:39/2:26	1.4	153	100% (36.5 km)	6	73
20	Jordan Bay	35.7	1:39/2:25	4.3	254	—	7	74
21	Crow Neck (RT)	51.5	2:18/3:23	2.3	212	20% (10 km)	7	75
22	Cape Sable Island	40.7	1:51/2:42	2.9	181	—	7	76
Yarmouth and Acadian Shores								
23	Pinkneys Point–Morris Island	87.0	3:57/5:48	4.8	484	—	8	80
24	Cape Forchu	24.6	1:07/1:38	6.0	193	—	8	81
25	Port Maitland	52.4	2:23/3:30	5.1	303	—	8	82
26	Mavillette Beach	27.2	1:14/1:48	5.3	119	—	9	84
27	Church Point–Meteghan	50.8	2:18/3:23	3.4	165	—	9	85
28	Weymouth–New Tusket	66.4	3:03/4:28	3.8	421	—	9	86

Route	Route Name	Distance (km)	Duration (22/15kmh)	Max Grade +	Elevation Gain (m)	Unpaved	Map	Page
Bay of Fundy: Annapolis Valley								
29	Digby Neck	72.4	3:17/4:49	8.1	586	—	10	90
30	Digby Lighthouse	18.0	0:49/1:12	5.3	258	—	10	92
31	Kejimkujik: Fire Tower Trail	35.8	1:37/2:23	6.0	326	100% (36 km)	6	92
32	Kejimkujik: Jakes Landing–New Grafton	17.6	0:48/1:10	3.8	117	55% (9.7km)	6	93
33	Bear River	21.0	0:57/1:24	6.6	247	—	11	94
34	Annapolis Royal–Milford	58.8	2:40/3:55	8.1	635	—	11	95
35	Annapolis Royal: Fort-to-Fort	52.1	2:22/3:28	3.4	347	—	11	97
36	Annapolis Royal–Bridgetown Loop	47.2	2:08/3:08	5.2	423	—	12	98
37	Annapolis Royal: North Mountain	62.0	2:49/4:08	10.1	824	—	12	99
38	Bridgetown: North Mountain	49.2	2:14/3:16	7.3	576	—	12	101
39	Middleton: North Mountain	50.8	2:18/3:23	8.2	610	—	12	102
40	Harvest Moon Trailway (RT)	110.0	5:00/7:20	2.7	395	98% (108 km)	13	104
41	Berwick–Harbourville	33.6	1:31/2:14	9.6	456	—	14	108
42	Canning–Scots Bay	49.1	1:59/2:55	11.5	555	6% (3 km)	15	109
43	Starrs Point Loop	48.0	2:10/3:12	5.5	326	—	15	111
44	Variation: Starrs Point Loop Extension	79.9	3:38/5:20	8.6	749	—	15	113
45	Wolfville Wine Tour (RT)	29.4	1:20/1:57	9.5	362	17% (5 km)	17	114
46	Wolfville Area: Winery, Brewery, and Distillery Tour (RT)	76.0	3:27/5:04	10.1	755	11% (8 km)	16	116
47	Gaspereau Valley	43.5	1:58/2:54	8.8	629	62% (27 km)	17	118
48	Bishopville–Sunken Lake	73.0	3:19/4:52	6.8	777	38% (28 km)	16	120
Bay of Fundy: Minas Basin								
49	Windsor: Winery and Brewery Tour	23.9	1:04/1:35	4.8	148	—	18	124
50	Avondale Peninsula	21.7	0:59/1:26	3.5	208	—	18	125
51	Variation: Windsor–Avondale Peninsula	54.3	2:28/3:37	5.6	465	—	18	126
52	Kempt Shore	53.2	2:25/3:32	5.8	562	—	18	127
53	Noel Shore	78.3	3:33/5:13	6.8	699	7% (5 km)	19	128
54	Shubenacadie	48.9	2:13/3:15	4.9	459	12% (6 km)	19	130
55	Cobequid Trail (RT)	28.7	1:18/1:54	2.8	175	90% (26 km)	19	131
56	Blue Route: East Mountain–Pictou (RT)	112.4	5:06/7:29	5.3	846	6% (7 km)	26	132
57	Cobequid Mountains	84.8	3:51/5:39	5.4	855	33% (28 km)	20	133
58	Five Islands–Parrsboro	94.6	4:18/6:18	6.7	847	16% (15 km)	21	135
59	Parrsboro–River Hebert	93.3	4:14/6:13	6.4	562	10% (9 km)	21	136
60	Parrsboro–Cape Chignecto	49.6	2:15/3:18	12.0	649	—	22	137
Northumberland Shore								
61	Amherst Shore	75.1	3:24/5:00	4.5	527	—	23	141
62	Pugwash–Oxford	51.2	2:19/3:24	5.6	432	—	23	142
63	Fox Harbour Loop	37.6	1:42/2:30	2.8	207	—	23	143
64	Tatamagouche–Malagash	56.2	2:33/3:44	4.8	347	—	24	144
65	Tatamagouche–Wentworth Valley	69.9	3:10/4:39	5.7	503	—	24	145

Route	Route Name	Distance (km)	Duration (22/15kmh)	Max Grade +	Elevation Gain (m)	Unpaved	Map	Page
66	Hippie Dippie	51.9	2:21/3:27	3.8	331	—	24	146
67	Cape John	52.6	2:23/3:30	2.9	271	—	25	148
68	Caribou Island	74.0	3:21/4:56	4.4	537	—	25	149
69	Gully Lake Preserve	82.1	3:43/5:28	9.5	870	46% (38 km)	26	150
70	Melmerby Beach	37.6	1:42/2:30	7.3	389	—	26	152
71	Museum of Industry (RT)	6.0	0:16/0:24	5.3	39	100% (6 km)	26	153
72	Antigonish: Cape George	75.4	3:25/5:01	8.7	833	—	27	154
73	Barneys River–Arisaig	81.4	3:42/5:26	5.6	606	—	27	155
74	Beaver Mountain–Addington Forks	29.0	1:19/1:56	11.2	314	—	27	156
Cape Breton Island: The Cabot Trail								
75	The Cabot Trail	298.6	3-4 days	14.0	3578	—	28	164
76	Big Baddeck Loop	24.3	1:06/1:37	5.3	255	—	28/31	169
77	Big Spruce–Hunters Mountain	18.7	0:51/1:14	6.9	226	—	28/31	170
78	Margaree Valley	25.5	1:09/1:42	3.6	188	—	28/30	170
79	Acadian Loop	29.0	1:19/1:56	6.7	286	—	28/30	171
80	Meat Cove	56.9	2:35/3:47	7.3	825	25% (14 km)	28	172
81	White Point	31.6	1:26/2:06	5.4	458	—	28	174
82	St. Anns–North River	44.4	2:01/2:57	6.0	399	—	28/31	175
Cape Breton Island: Beyond the Cabot Trail								
83	Celtic Shores Coastal Trail (RT)	83.8	3:48/5:35	2.6	458	100% (84 km)	29	178
84	Lake Ainslie: Mabou–Nevada Valley (RT)	77.2	3:30/5:08	5.9	557	19% (15 km)	30	182
85	Inverness–Margaree Beach Tour (RT)	85.4	3:53/5:42	7.0	813	7% (6 km)	30	183
86	Washabuck Peninsula	56.5	2:34/3:46	8.1	593	—	31	185
87	Boularderie Island	80.6	3:39/5:22	5.1	677	20% (16 km)	32	186
88	Alder Point	17.1	0:46/1:08	3.7	116	—	32	188
89	New Victoria	37.0	1:40/2:28	3.8	241	—	33	189
90	Northern Coastal Industrial Loop	93.9	4:15/6:15	7.0	706	—	33	190
91	Variation: Donkin Loop	32.1	1:27/2:08	3.5	207	—	33	192
92	Hillside Loop	49.0	2:14/3:16	5.9	353	—	34	192
93	Variation: Marion Bridge–Grand Mira	50.4	2:17/3:21	3.6	318	23% (12 km)	34	193
94	Albert Bridge–Marion Bridge	29.3	1:19/1:57	3.2	203	—	34	193
95	Fortress of Louisbourg	42.9	1:57/2:51	8.0	377	—	34	194
96	Point Michaud	41.7	1:53/2:46	7.7	363	—	35	195
97	St. Peters: Cape George	64.6	2:56/4:18	8.0	663	—	35	196
98	Isle Madame	67.3	3:03/4:29	6.5	503	—	35	197
Eastern Shore								
99	Guysborough: Tickle Loop	123.3	5:35/8:12	6.3	1250	—	36	202
100	Interval Loop	33.3	1:30/2:13	4.0	229	3% (1 km)	36	204
101	Sherbrooke Loop	39.5	1:47/2:38	6.9	320	20% (8 km)	37	205
102	Sober Island	26.1	1:11/1:44	3.9	220	13% (3.5 km)	37	206
103	Clam Harbour	44.0	2:00/2:57	4.4	357	—	38	207
104	Ostrea Lake	38.1	1:48/2:38	4.5	322	8% (3 km)	38	209
105	Musquodoboit Harbour (RT)	30.0	1:21/2:00	3.5	218	50% (15 km)	38	210
106	Three Fathom Harbour	41.3	1:52/2:45	5.4	293	2% (1 km)	38	211

FOLD OUT MAP HERE

QUICK REFERENCE PRE-RIDE CHECKLIST

If leaving your car behind, be sure to lock your vehicle and hide or remove any valuables.

Before Heading Out

- ○ Check the Bicycle Nova Scotia website for any route updates.
- ○ Download map (Google Map of area) or route to your device.
- ○ Check wind and weather; plan and pack accordingly.
- ○ Print out cue sheets, notes, maps, important details.
- ○ Set up odometer if using cue sheets.
- ○ Check that your phone/GPS device is charged.
- ○ Check that your front and rear lights are charged.
- ○ Check over your bike to make sure it is running properly.
- ○ Fill water bottles and pack food.

Essentials

- ○ Helmet
- ○ Front/rear lights
- ○ Keys (house, car, bike lock)
- ○ Wallet (credit card, ID, cash)
- ○ Water (water bottles/water bladder)
- ○ Food (power snacks)
- ○ Phone/GPS device
- ○ Wrist watch (safety, emergencies; in case phone dies)
- ○ Small first-aid kit

Bike Tools and Accessories

- ○ Pump (with correct adapter and/or CO_2 cartridges)
- ○ Patch kit and/or spare tube
- ○ Multi-tool
- ○ Tire levers (3)

Optional

- ○ Extra clothing (different layers, depending on the day)
- ○ Maps and/or guidebook
- ○ Camera
- ○ Bike lock
- ○ Sunglasses
- ○ Wet wipes (with zipper-lock bag)
- ○ Sunscreen
- ○ Spare phone battery
- ○ Towel and bathing suit
- ○ Non-cycling shoes/sandals

...ovascotia.com to find these routes online, and to:
- ...tion profiles
- ...tes interactively
- ... route onto your device
- ... route or read comments from others

80
81
75
Cape Breton
Island
79
78
87
85
82
88
76
90
91
Inverness
89
77
Sydney
92
84
94
95
83
86
93
d Strait
67
68
73
72
69
96
70
97
71
New
Glasgow
74
Antigonish
98
100
56
Canso
99
Sherbrooke
101
Eastern
Shore
102
103
...6
104
Atlantic
Ocean

Halifax Metro ●

South Shore ●

Yarmouth and Acadian Shores ●

Bay of Fundy: Annapolis Valley ●

Bay of Fundy: Minas Basin ●

Northumberland Shore ●

Cape Breton Island: The Cabot Trail ●

Cape Breton Island: Beyond the Cabot Trail ●

Eastern Shore ●

Destination Trail ●

20 0 20 40
scale 1:2,300,000 km

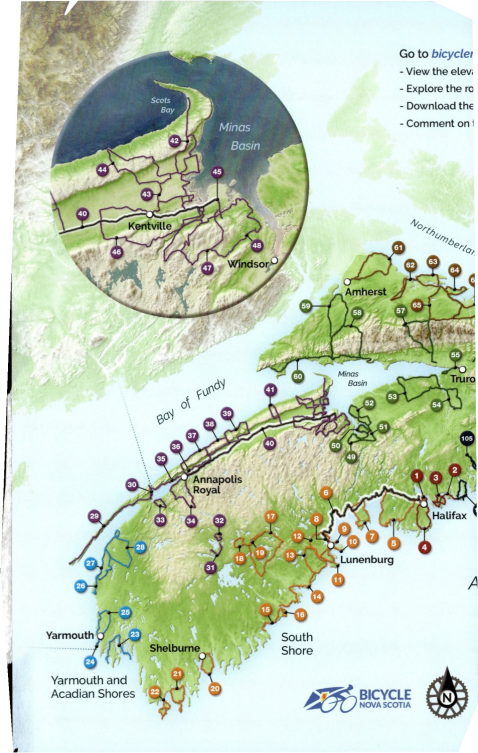

Scots
Bay

Minas
Basin

42

44

43

45

40

Kentville

46

48

47

Windsor

Go to *bicycle*
- View the eleva...
- Explore the ro...
- Download the...
- Comment on t...

Northumberlan...

61

62   63

64

59

Amherst

65

57

58

55

Truro

60

Minas
Basin

53

52   54

41

51

39

38

40   50

49

Bay of Fundy

37

36

35

105

30

Annapolis
Royal

1   3   2

6   **Halifax**

29

33   34   32

17

8   9   7

28   12   10   5

18   19   13   4

27   **Lunenburg**

31   11

26   14

25   15   16

Yarmouth   *South*
Shore

23

24   **Shelburne**

Yarmouth and   21
Acadian Shores   22   20

BICYCLE
NOVA SCOTIA

N